Patron

Her Majesty, Juliana, Queen of the Netherlands

Contents

INTRODUCTION

THIS VOLUME, and the exhibition in New York of all of the works illustrated and discussed here (12 December 1979 – 16 March 1980, The Pierpont Morgan Library), is a guide to some of the collections of the House of Orange. The focus is on the lives and the artistic interests of William III (1650–1702, Stadholder of the Netherlands, King of England) and Queen Mary (1662–1695); however, we include representative works of art, and some books, collected by the other members of the House: from a richly carved knife of the founder, Prince Willem I (William the Silent, 1533–1584), to a drawing by Queen Wilhelmina (1880–1962), who was a devoted landscape artist to the end of her long life.[1] William and Mary dominated the religious, political, and artistic life of northern Europe—and America—as no other members of the family have done, but many others were also patrons or collectors of outstanding merit, and some were or are artists; their stories and their collections remain largely unknown outside of the Netherlands, and even there much may have been forgotten.

William & Mary and Their House is the result of the close collaboration of two institutions, the Rijksmuseum Paleis Het Loo in Apeldoorn and The Pierpont Morgan Library in New York, and the wholehearted support of Dutch and American governmental agencies. Without the help of the Ministry of Cultural Affairs, Recreation, and Social Welfare and The Prins Bernhard Fonds in the Netherlands, and the National Endowment for the Arts and the Federal Arts and Artifacts Indemnification Act in the United States, this project would never have been possible. Dutch ministries in The Hague and the directors and curators of state collections, museums, libraries, palaces, and archives have assisted us in every way.

In the past there have been major exhibitions and catalogues concerning William and Mary (*De Stadhouder-Koning en zijn tijd*, Rijksmuseum, Amsterdam, 1950; *William & Mary and Their Time*, Arts Council of Great Britain, 1950) and about the three successive Stadholders who married English Princesses: Wil-

1. Dutch spelling is used for the names of all members of the House of Orange except for those of Stadholder-King William III and Queen Mary.

lem II, William III, and Willem IV, who wed the Princesses Mary, daughter of Charles I, Mary, daughter of James II, and Anne, daughter of George II (*The Orange and the Rose: Holland and Britain in the Age of Observation 1600–1750*, Victoria and Albert Museum, 1964); there is an excellent survey of the growth of the collections of the House of Orange from the sixteenth to the nineteenth century by Th. H. Lunsingh Scheurleer (*150 jaar Koninklijk Kabinet van Schilderijen, Koninklijke Bibliotheek, Koninklijk Penningkabinet*, The Hague, 1967) and a fine summary (in English) in H. W. Hoetink's Introduction to the General Catalogue of the Mauritshuis (The Hague, 1977); there is a catalogue with essays which re-creates the picture gallery of Stadholder Prince Willem V (1748–1806; *De schilderijenzaal Prins Willem V te 's-Gravenhage*, The Hague, 1977) and an article by H. E. van Gelder on the collections of King Willem II ("De kunstverzameling van Koning Willem II," *Maandblad voor beeldende kunsten*, 1948, pp. 137–148). S. W. A. Drossaers and Th. H. Lunsingh Scheurleer have compiled a three-volume inventory of the collections of the House of Orange, 1567–1795 (*Inventarissen van de inboedels . . .*, The Hague, 1974–1976).[2] Aside from these, and some more specialized articles, there is not much information on the Dutch royal collections; the world generally, including the Netherlands as well as the rest of Europe, and America, has remained uninformed concerning the achievements of the House of Orange in art collecting. The present book and the exhibition in New York are attempts to remedy this. We could not have made these without the gracious permission and help of Her Majesty the Queen of the Netherlands. More than one-third of the objects shown here are from the collection of Queen Juliana; many of them have not been illustrated before, and the loan from the royal collections on such a scale is unprecedented.

Seventeenth-century Dutch paintings constitute the most conspicuous part of the collections in the past, just as they are the principal contribution of the Dutch to art. The number and the quality of the "little masters" as well as of the great masters of seventeenth-century Dutch painting remain unexcelled in the history of art. This extraordinary number of painters found a ready clientele right at home. The passion for collecting paintings in the Netherlands at that time was frequently commented on by travellers. Farmers, butchers, and bakers as well as the considerable well-to-do middle class bought pictures. "Blacksmithes, Cob-

2. These works are frequently cited in our text. We have usually mentioned only the most important catalogues, books, and articles in the literature concerning the various objects.

lers, etts., will have some picture or other by their Forge and in their stalle," wrote Peter Mundy in 1640. John Evelyn reported (in the following year) that " 'tis an ordinary thing to find, a common Farmor lay out two, or 3000 pounds in this Commodity, their houses are full of them, and they vend them at their Kermas'es to very great gaines." The Stadholders and Kings were no exception to the custom of the land in collecting pictures.

Portraits predominate in the selection of paintings shown here: there are about twenty, from Holbein, Miereveld, Moreelse, and Honthorst, to Van Dyck, Rembrandt, Tischbein, and Toorop. Many of these artists, as might be expected, are Dutch. There are even more miniatures (some of the small portraits are not painted, but done in mother-of-pearl or are medallion portraits in marble, silver, and gold). Nonetheless almost every aspect of Dutch seventeenth-century painting is illustrated: genre, historical, allegorical, interiors and exteriors, and animal paintings. There are, however, no pure landscapes nor seascapes, and no flower paintings, although these were also collected, primarily by Stadholder Willem V. In addition to the paintings there are more than a dozen drawings and a number of etchings, including two by Rembrandt.

A few sculptures are shown, including a bust of Willem I by (or after) Hendrick de Keyser, who is recognized as the most important native sculptor in the Netherlands in the seventeenth century. One of the most notable works here is the only known gold object done by one of the two greatest masters of Dutch silver and gold work, Paulus van Vianen. The peak of the accomplishment in Dutch silver is early in the seventeenth century; it was then that a wholly new form of decoration was created by Paulus van Vianen, born in Utrecht about 1570, member of the leading family of silversmiths in the Netherlands, who was from 1603 until his death in 1613 *Kammergoldschmied* to the Emperor Rudolf II in Prague. After his death, Paulus' elder brother Adam, and Adam's son Christiaen, who worked for Charles I in England, developed the "auricular" style (shaped like the ear) to its fullest form—in which various motifs flow into one another to produce designs of amazing freedom and one continuous sculptural ornament. Dutch silver of the time was also highly pictorial, and the Van Vianen family excelled in creating embossed pictures. Paulus' favorite scenes appear to have been ones telling the story of Diana and Actaeon; they are the principal pictures on this gold cup and cover commissioned in 1610 by Heinrich Julius, Duke of Brunswick Wolfenbüttel Lüneburg, whose second daughter, Sophia Hedwig, inherited it and brought it into the possession of the House of Dietz, whence it came into the House of Orange Nassau, and subsequently into the collection of the House of Wied. This unique gold object has never before been fully illustrated and has not been exhibited for many decades.

The silver objects shown here are not, of course, of such singular importance, but there is a beautiful baby-linen basket made by the Nuremberg silversmith Hans Coenraadt Brechtel who worked at The Hague from 1640 to 1675. Some of the most splendid silver objects—a chandelier and two sets of sconces—were made in London and used by William III in England and at his palace Het Loo at Apeldoorn. There are smaller silver objects: beakers, snuffboxes, knives, spoons, and forks. Some of the flatware is made of ivory or horn. The medals cover three hundred years (1637–1938) and are made of gold and silver. It should be obvious from the objects illustrated here that the standard of craftsmanship and design in Dutch metalwork of the Golden Age was extraordinarily high, as it was in furniture, earthenware, glass, needlework, and bookbindings. We also see that outstanding work was done in the later periods as well.

Some of the furniture is breathtaking: Her Majesty the Queen has permitted us to show the set of silver furniture made about 1700 by the Augsburg artist Johann I Bartermann who also made the set of silver furniture owned by the Danish Crown. Such sets of silver furniture are today very rare and the table top in the set belonging to the Queen of the Netherlands is the only engraved one known on an Augsburg silver table; the other pieces have embossed table tops. From an earlier period there are chairs and cabinets, including a silver-mounted ebony cabinet on stand made in Antwerp about 1630 set with thirteen panels painted by Frans Francken II. There is a superb long-case clock made about 1699 in London by Thomas Tompion, probably for the bedchamber of William III at Hampton Court. There are some pieces of furniture from the sets ordered from the Paris maker François Honoré Georges Jacob-Desmalter for the various Dutch palaces of Louis Napoleon, younger brother of Napoleon, when he was King of Holland, 1806–1810.

The blue-and-white Delftware, made especially popular by William and Mary, is of unusual distinction, and the Meissen and other china are also exceptional. There are many kinds of small *objets d'art*, as well as sabers and pistols, a hunting horn, a whip, and fans. The jewelry shown is very personal, not the grand jewels of state occasions. All of the objects have, in fact, been chosen to be representative of their time and of the taste of the Stadholders, Kings, and Queens for whom they were made or by whom they were acquired.

The history of Dutch binding from the middle of the sixteenth century to the middle of the eighteenth century is illustrated in ten examples from the Royal

Library, The Hague, a state institution founded in 1816. Such a range and quality can be found in only one or two libraries outside of those in the Netherlands. A few letters, documents, and pamphlets have been included to point up some of the most important moments in Dutch history.[3]

One letter is a milestone in the artistic heritage of the country; it marks the watershed between the most baroque Dutch painting and a style of more inward emotion and balance. This is a letter of Rembrandt, one of only seven known today. All of his surviving letters were written between 1636 and 1639 to Constantijn Huygens (1596–1687), a man of great culture—poet, painter, and musician—and secretary to Stadholder Frederik Hendrik (1584–1647) who already owned several works by Rembrandt and had now commissioned him to paint a series of five paintings on the Passion. Later (1646) Frederik Hendrik had Rembrandt add a *Nativity* and the *Circumcision* (now lost; the six others are all in Munich) to this group. Rembrandt's letter of 12 January 1639, owned by Her Majesty the Queen, is perhaps the most celebrated of the seven surviving letters because one word, *beweechgelickheijt*, has caused as much discussion as some of the often-vexed passages in Shakespeare. Does it mean "the greatest and most natural movement" or "most innate emotion"? "The inference is that in the Passion sequence, especially in the *Entombment* and in the *Resurrection*, Rembrandt had wished to express the greatest inward emotion. . . . It is not accidental that problems of interpretation arise at the very point where Rembrandt's conception breaks away from baroque pathos and develops towards a balanced style of painting, where the emotions no longer escape to the surface" (H. Gerson, *Seven Letters by Rembrandt*, The Hague, 1961, page 10).

Thus it is that a short letter becomes one of the most significant items—as well as one of the rarest—in this volume. And it is altogether fitting that the greatest of Dutch artists received one of his most important commissions from the Stadholder.

Before the catalogue begins there are three essays. The first, by Professor J. W. Schulte Nordholt of the University of Leiden, deals with America and the House of Orange. He reminds us that the name of the House of Orange, especially that of King William III, is "inseparably linked with the history of America." To the names of the early American educational institutions established because of the Glorious Revolution, which resulted in the accession of the Prince and Princess of Orange to the English throne as King William III and

3. For the most part these have not been reproduced among the illustrations at the end of the book; otherwise, all objects described in the catalogue are also illustrated.

Queen Mary, should be added that of Princeton University. The events of 1688 were still close to the Governor of New Jersey in 1755 when he asked the Trustees of the College of New Jersey to name the first building "Nassau Hall" as expressive of "the honour we retain, in this remote part of the globe, to the immortal memory of the glorious King William III, who was a branch of the illustrious House of Nassau." In the name of its main street as well as of its first building, and in its colors, Princeton still honors that immortal memory. The House of Orange Nassau rightly stands for freedom from tyranny, for tolerance and bravery, for the defense of Protestantism. In the catalogue letters and documents of Stadholder Willem I, Stadholder-King William III, King Willem II, and Queen Wilhelmina are chosen to illustrate that heroic, unending fight against tyranny.

This is the stirring background against which we must see the members of the House of Orange as collectors and patrons, and even, on occasion, as artists. As Princes of Orange they were the richest citizens of the Northern Netherlands and traditionally held the chief offices of the Dutch republic: the federation of seven of the seventeen provinces of the Netherlands, each of which had its own assembly or states and sent a delegation to the States-General which represented the United Provinces in foreign affairs. (The name of the province of Holland, by far the richest of the seven, chiefly through trade, often stood—as it still does —for the union of all seven.) It is just four hundred years ago, in 1579 in the Union of Utrecht, that a defensive bond against the Spanish King formed the basis of this republic.

No Prince of Orange until Willem IV in the eighteenth century was ever Stadholder of all seven of the provinces, and his powers were limited for the most part to law and order and to the command of the army and navy of the United Provinces. These offices were not, however, hereditary. "The princes of Orange thus exercised quasi-royal power but without the title of King . . . power was to be used for a constructive purpose, it was not an end in itself" (John Miller, *The Life and Times of William and Mary*, London, 1974, page 19). The founder of the House, Willem I, eldest son of Willem the Rich of Nassau, in 1544 inherited the tiny principality of Orange on the Rhône near Avignon, with properties in the Netherlands, from his cousin, René of Chalon. René had inherited from his uncle Philibert, brother of his mother, Claudia of Chalon, the name of Chalon and the principality of Orange.[4]

4. The male descendants of Willem I had the title Prince of Orange, Count of Nassau. The descendants of one of the younger sons of Willem I's brother Jan the Elder, Count of Nassau,

With their lands in France, Germany, and the Netherlands, and through their marriages, the Princes of Orange were international in background; they were brilliant militarists and political leaders, sovereign princes but also citizens of a republic. By the time we reach Stadholder Prince Willem III of the Netherlands, King William III of England, the most important man in Europe beside Louis XIV of France, we find a Prince who was the great-grandson of a French king, a Scottish king, a Medici princess, and a German count; the grandson of an English king and a Dutch Stadholder; and he himself was married to the daughter of an English king.

Although Willem I had formed an excellent collection of paintings, silver, tapestries, coins, and jewels, part of it was taken by the Spaniards (including Bosch's *Garden of Delights* now in the Prado), and most of it had to be sold to help pay for the war against Spain. In a period of such fierce warfare there was not much time for the Stadholders to create a court which was also a center of culture.

His three sons were all collectors: Maurits (1567–1625) and Frederik Hendrik (1584–1647), the two younger ones, were particularly notable because of their close association with Dutch artists. Maurits commissioned Jan van Ravesteyn to paint a number of portraits, and Jacques de Gheyn's celebrated *Exercise of Armes* (1607) was done according to Prince Maurits' order. Prince Maurits was a hero, both as soldier and patron of arts, to Henry, Prince of Wales, the first of England's royal art collectors. Maurits was the great hope of those responsible for the new, truly scientific spirit and of the entire Protestant world.

Frederik Hendrik was even more influential in encouraging the arts. His important commissions to Rembrandt have already been mentioned; he also collected outstanding sculpture. Maurits had begun to extend the Stadholder's Quarter in The Hague, and Frederik Hendrik continued this building program.

---

were Counts of Nassau Dietz until 1652 when Willem Frederik (1613–1664), married to Albertine, daughter of Stadholder Frederik Hendrik, became Prince of Nassau Dietz. Johan Willem Friso, Willem Frederik's grandson, was the heir of Stadholder-King William III, and inherited his title of Prince of Orange. Johan Willem Friso and his male descendants bore the title of Prince of Orange Nassau until the foundation of the monarchy in 1815. Thereafter the Crown Princes bore the title Prince of Orange and the other sons of the King, Prince of the Netherlands.

Willem I was Stadholder of the provinces of Holland, Zeeland, and Utrecht. His sons Maurits and Frederik Hendrik and his grandson Willem II were Stadholders of Holland, Zeeland, Utrecht, Gelderland, Overijssel, Groningen, and Drente. His great-grandson, the Stadholder-King William III, was Stadholder of Holland, Zeeland, Utrecht, Gelderland, and Overijssel. Johan Willem Friso, like his father, grandfather, and great-grandfather, was Stadholder of Friesland, Groningen, and Drente. Willem IV and Willem V were Stadholders of all the provinces.

He and his wife, Amalia van Solms, established a sophisticated and cultured court; they also created an art gallery in The Hague with about fifty paintings by contemporary Dutch artists such as Honthorst, Lievens, Moreelse, and Poelenburgh, together with older masters like Jan Brueghel, Paulus Bril, and Cornelis van Haarlem. He and Amalia favored Flemish artists, including Rubens and Jordaens, and she continued this patronage after his death, especially in the decoration of the Oranjezaal in the Huis ten Bosch near The Hague. Amalia had the splendid main room in the villa decorated after 1647 as a memorial to her husband. It has the only Dutch seventeenth-century interior which still contains its original large-scale painted wall decorations. Jordaens had the principal commission for this work. Three other Flemish artists and eight Dutch painters also received commissions. The architect of the villa (begun in 1645) was Pieter Post. It was only one of a number of houses and palaces built by Frederik Hendrik and Amalia. He was responsible for the real break with traditional Dutch architecture and the introduction of new, radically different French ideas. These could be seen in his palaces of Honselaersdijk (begun 1621) and Rijswijk (begun 1630), neither of which survives.

Amalia still dominated the court at The Hague when William III was born in 1650 and she overpowered his mother, Princess Mary, the daughter of Charles I of England, who died when he was ten. Amalia lived for another fifteen years; at her death her art collections (considerably expanded beyond those of Frederik Hendrik) were divided among her four daughters, three of whom had married German princes. A large part of the collections of the House of Orange therefore left the Netherlands, and it was up to William III to rebuild them. He shared his grandfather Frederik Hendrik's love of architecture, and far excelled him in his interest in paintings. He encouraged the use of paintings as permanent parts of interiors at the new palaces of Soestdijk and Het Loo, as well as in those he remodelled at Breda, Honselaersdijk, and The Hague. With his wife, Mary, he rebuilt Kensington Palace and Hampton Court, she working very closely with Sir Christopher Wren. He purchased many paintings for these palaces and was personally involved in the re-hanging of the pictures at Windsor Castle. At Het Loo he hung some of the paintings from the English royal collection, among them the two marvellous portraits by Piero di Cosimo and a remarkable group of portraits by Holbein. It is extraordinary how much the joint rulers accomplished in the arts as well as in government although Mary lived to be only thirty-two and reigned in England for just five years, and William III was fifty-two when he died. He had been King for thirteen years, a great part of which time, as in the years in the Netherlands, had to be spent in the field with his armies.

Their influence in the Netherlands and England was considerable in every aspect of taste—not only in architecture and in paintings. They were both keenly interested in interior design; Mary did much to popularize blue-and-white Delftware and china, particularly in the creation (through designs by Daniel Marot) of the tiled room and tableware for the dairy at Hampton Court, and the use of ornamental objects for the palaces, like the tall tulip vases shown here (no. 56). William and Mary spent much time in the planning and enjoyment of gardens and in laying out parks and woodlands. William seems to have had a special concern in the waterworks and fountains; Mary in the trees and shrubs (always including orange trees, of course) and flowers. Together they furthered a passion for gardening in both England and the Netherlands, and their taste in garden design became the fashion in those countries and elsewhere.

Although King William inspired little love in England, unlike Queen Mary who was not only deeply respected by all but truly loved there, he played a significant rôle in the development of the arts in that country. He as well as she encouraged the taste for Dutch pictures which had been strong in England for many generations, and for Dutch furniture design, veneering, marquetry-work, and metal inlaying (above all for the work of such a distinguished craftsman as Gerreit Jensen who had already come to work in London for Charles II). The city churches of Sir Christopher Wren frequently show a Dutch influence, and William's reign witnessed much of the building of St. Paul's Cathedral (the choir, with Tijou's ironwork and Dutch-born Grinling Gibbons' carving, was completed in 1697). Hawksmoor became Clerk of the Works at Greenwich in 1698. We can see, therefore, that it is not only for William's heroic deeds and statesmanship, and for Mary's piety and the love she inspired, that the Painted Hall at Greenwich is such a fitting tribute to them. Thornhill's vast painted ceiling of the apotheosis of William and Mary and the superb buildings at Greenwich are also the apotheosis of their taste.

The Stadholder-King William III as a collector and a "man of taste" is so important in surveying the history of the collections and the artistic interests of the House of Orange that we have asked Professor Emeritus J. G. van Gelder of the University of Utrecht to write an introductory essay concerning him. The ultimate source of new ideas in art and architecture for William and his time was to be found neither in the Netherlands nor in England, but in France. It was in the person of Daniel Marot. He was a Huguenot who went to the Netherlands in 1685 or 1686, after the revocation of the Edict of Nantes. He became interior architect and finally chief architect in the Netherlands to William III, and it is Marot, as much as the Stadholder-King himself, who is the focus of this volume.

Marot's ideas became all-pervading in the two countries. French-Dutch design in architecture, decorative painting, furniture, ceramics, textiles, and gardens flows from him. He did some work for William III in England, but it was mainly in the Dutch republic, in royal palaces, the audience chamber of the States-General (the Trêveszaal in the Binnenhof at The Hague), country houses, and town houses (notably the Hôtel Huguetan, now the Royal Library, in The Hague)—in architecture and in interior design—that his accomplishment and influence may be seen. This is especially true of Het Loo, the summer palace at Apeldoorn, for which he executed or supervised the interiors and the gardens. During the Napoleonic period the palace was ransacked, and when Louis Napoleon was King of Holland, the sober but beautiful red brick work was plastered white, and much of Marot's work was destroyed. But Het Loo is now being lovingly and thoroughly restored. In a few years' time we shall again find it one of the handsomest and most important palaces in Europe.

Marot's work at Het Loo is so vital to our history that it also has an introductory essay devoted to it and a special section of drawings and prints of it at the end of the catalogue.

William III's heir in 1702 was his second cousin Stadholder Johan Willem Friso (1687–1711). The will was contested, various claims were made, and in 1713 Johan Willem Friso's widow auctioned sixty-one of the paintings, some of them masterpieces of Dutch, Flemish, or Italian art. Gradually during the first half of the eighteenth century most of the wonderful collections of art built up by William and Mary were dispersed. Fortunately, about 1732, Stadholder Willem IV (1711–1751), aged twenty-one, began to build the collections again. Some of the paintings which had belonged to Frederik Willem and Amalia, William and Mary, and Johan Willem Friso had come to him. In the year before he married Anne, the Princess Royal of England, 1733, Willem IV bought Rembrandt's *Simeon's Song of Praise*. Therefore, once again, there was a painting by Rembrandt in the collections of the Stadholders. Fifteen years later he bought the famous huge painting of a young bull by Paulus Potter (also in the Mauritshuis today), and in the meantime he had acquired a number of documentary and historical paintings, as well as works by Schalcken, Van Mieris, Dou, Wouwermans, Poelenburgh, and other Dutch masters of the seventeenth century.

When Willem IV died at the age of forty, Anne acted as Princess-Regent for her three-year-old son, who became Willem V (1748–1806). The son must have inherited his parents' collecting instincts (Anne was a distinguished collector in several fields). His first acquisition was made in 1760 when he was only twelve years old, the year after his mother had died; his last when he was twenty-three years of age. By that time he had about two hundred paintings, including those from the collections of William III and Willem IV, and a fine library, extensive ethnographical and natural history collections, and medals, coins, engraved gems, and curiosities. Many of the leading artists of his day (for example, Houdon, Perronneau, Tischbein, and Liotard) came to visit the Stadholder and his collections.

During 1773–1774 Willem V transferred his collection to a gallery specially built for it on the Buitenhof in The Hague. The gallery has recently been restored and hung as an eighteenth-century collection would have been arranged—in symmetrical groupings, one wall mirroring the other insofar as it was possible.

Willem V opened it to the public on set days each week; it was the first one officially open to the public in the Netherlands. Precedents had already been set by other rulers; for example, Louis XV had put part of his collection on show in the Palais de Luxembourg in Paris in 1750.

Willem V's collection contained major works by Holbein, Rubens, Van Dyck, Rembrandt, Steen, Terborch, Metsu, Ostade, Teniers, Houckgeest, the Van de Veldes, and Vernet—in addition to some of the masterpieces like Holbein's *Robert Cheseman* and the two Piero di Cosimo portraits which he had inherited. It was clearly for the most part a collection of Dutch seventeenth-century paintings (only twenty from the eighteenth and two from the sixteenth century), with forty Flemish, twelve Italian, five French, and seven German and Swiss paintings. There were about sixty genre pieces, at least fifty landscapes, forty history paintings, twenty portraits, and fifteen still lifes. Altogether they constituted a somewhat old-fashioned private cabinet, unlike the grander royal collections in London, Paris, Berlin, or Dresden.

In 1795 Prince Willem V had to flee before the invading French armies and the best part of the art collections was removed to Paris as "property of the French nation won by force of arms" and displayed in the Louvre. Other parts of the Stadholder's collections from the various palaces and country seats were auctioned.[5] With much trouble the most significant part was recovered in the

5. With the secularization of German monasteries in 1802, the abbey of Weingarten, with its magnificent treasures, became the property of the Prince of Orange Nassau. He sent some

autumn of 1815. Approximately 125 of the pictures came back to the Netherlands, where 109 of these form the nucleus of the Royal Cabinet of Paintings in the Mauritshuis; 30 or 31 are in French museums; 38 or 39 of them remain untraced.

Upon the collapse of the Napoleonic empire, the House of Orange was restored in the person of Willem, son of the last Stadholder Willem V. He was inaugurated as King Willem I (1772–1843) of the Netherlands in 1815. He returned the pictures to his father's gallery in The Hague, and then in 1821 the paintings were transferred to the Mauritshuis which became a national museum open to the public. There they remain a charming, intimate collection in a most beautiful building—for many persons one of their favorite museums anywhere in the world. The house itself—a masterpiece of Dutch Classicism—was built ca. 1633–1644 by Pieter Post to plans by Jacob van Campen (architect of the handsome Royal Palace in Amsterdam, formerly the city hall). It was a little palace for Count, later Prince, Maurits of Nassau Siegen (1604–1679), a grandson of Willem I's brother, Jan the Elder, who became Governor of the Dutch colony in Brazil (1637–1644). Among the six artists in his retinue in Brazil was Frans Post, the brother of Pieter.

King Willem I continued to have a keen interest in the museum. In 1822 he made certain that the Mauritshuis acquired Vermeer's *View of Delft;* five years later he bought Rogier van der Weyden's *Lamentation of Christ;* in 1828 he ordered the purchase of Rembrandt's *Anatomy Lesson* from special funds under his control. He insured that important works of Rubens, Terborch, Cuyp, and Van der Helst were purchased. And the Mauritshuis flourished, until the Belgian uprising of 1830. After that there were no purchases until 1874.

The Dutch nation, therefore, did not acquire any of the paintings and drawings from the greatest collection formed by a member of the House of Orange— that of King Willem II (1792–1849; King 1840–1849), the eldest son of Willem I. King Willem II was also passionately fond of architecture and built a large neo-gothic palace in The Hague with galleries for his paintings and drawings. After his death his personal collections had to be sold in order to settle his

of the finest manuscripts, including the masterpiece of the Weingarten school (late twelfth and early thirteenth centuries), the Berthold Missal, to his palace in Fulda. In 1806, during the Napoleonic wars, Fulda was taken by the French, and many of the manuscripts were sent to Paris. In 1818, four of the most outstanding of them, including the Berthold Missal and the Gradual and Sacramentary of Hainricus Sacrista with their original jeweled bindings, were acquired by Thomas William Coke of Norfolk. In 1926 they were purchased from his heir, the third Earl of Leicester, by J. P. Morgan and presented to The Pierpont Morgan Library.

complicated and troubled estate: the 1850–1851 catalogues had 192 paintings by old masters, 162 works by modern artists, and 370 lots of drawings. Among the early Netherlandish pictures were three paintings ascribed to Jan van Eyck, and others to Dirk Bouts, Memling, Quinten Metsys, Van Orley, Mabuse, and Lucas van Leyden. Then Rubens (8), Van Dyck (4), Jordaens (3), Rembrandt (8), Ruysdael (2), Hobbema, Steen, and other Dutch seventeenth-century artists; works by or attributed to Dürer, Holbein, Cranach; Clouet, Claude, Poussin; Murillo (4), Velásquez (4), Ribera (13); Bellini, Leonardo, Giorgione, Titian, Raphael, Del Sarto, the Carraccis, Domenichino, Guercino, Reni—and many, many more. The drawings included large numbers by Michelangelo and Raphael.

Only a few paintings and drawings from the collection of King Willem II remain in the royal collection today (three of the drawings are shown here, nos. 118–120). After the creation of a public museum for the Royal Cabinet of Paintings by King Willem I, and the sales of vast collections of King Willem II, the present royal collections of art consist chiefly of works acquired in the nineteenth century and objects of a personal and intimate character. Among them are pieces of furniture and many table ornaments, boxes, etc., made out of malachite and gold or other metals, in addition to objects of gold (such as the chalice, no. 117), which came as part of the dowry of Queen Anna Pavlovna (1795–1865), wife of King Willem II, and daughter of the Russian Emperor Paul I.

Subsequent Kings and Queens have only occasionally added earlier works of art. Notable are the silver baby-linen basket by Brechtel presented by Queen Wilhelmina to Queen Emma (1858–1934) (no. 37) and the cabinet on stand with painted panels by Frans Francken II presented to Queen Wilhelmina in 1902 (no. 32). Some, like King Willem III (1817–1890), were very much interested in contemporary art. He built a gallery for this collection at Het Loo, the palace which he loved deeply, and where he invited a number of artists to stay. Music was an even greater interest of the King. His second wife, Queen Emma, was an avid collector of lace, and of Rembrandt's etchings. Her collections remain in the possession of the Royal Family.

Their daughter, Queen Wilhelmina, shared in her father's love for Het Loo, and lived there from 1948, when she resigned from the throne after a reign of fifty years, until her death at the palace in 1962. She was most knowledgeable about the history of its buildings and grounds and she restored some of its interiors. Queen Wilhelmina was not a collector of art, but a most devoted artist. She drew and painted landscapes from early youth to the very end of her life.

She drove around the parks and woods of Het Loo in a special wagon for painting which can still be seen at the palace.

The interests in collecting and in creating art goes on to this day. There is, for example, the collection of contemporary Dutch painting and sculpture by H. R. H. Princess Beatrix, herself a sculptor. She, like her mother, Queen Juliana, has been concerned in the plans for this exhibition. H. R. H. Princess Christina and her husband, Mr. Jorge Guillermo, have been involved in every detail of the exhibition and this volume. Their great discrimination as collectors is reflected in the choice of so many of the objects illustrated here.

ACKNOWLEDGEMENTS

This book and the exhibition in New York have been made possible because of the strong support of many persons and institutions in the Netherlands and the United States. We are first of all indebted to Her Majesty the Queen of the Netherlands for her patronage and for her gracious permission to lend so many and such significant objects to the exhibition and to have them reproduced in this volume. H. R. H. Princess Christina of the Netherlands and Mr. Jorge Guillermo played vital rôles in initiating the exhibition and helped throughout in the planning of it and in the choice of the objects to be shown. Various divisions of the government and their officials in both countries have been of primary importance in this project. We are deeply grateful to the Minister of Cultural Affairs, Recreation, and Social Welfare, Mrs. M. H. M. F. Gardeniers-Berendsen, for the special grant to realize this exhibition; to the Minister of Foreign Affairs, Dr. C. A. van der Klaauw; and to The Prins Bernhard Fonds, for financial support in preparing the catalogue. The exhibition was also made possible by grants from the National Endowment for the Arts, the Federal Arts and Artifacts Indemnification Act, the New York State Council on the Arts, an anonymous foundation, and Mrs. Lily Auchincloss. A grant from The Charles Engelhard Foundation helped in the printing of this volume as it does with all publications of the Morgan Library. The corporate sponsor of advertising for the exhibition was International Flavors and Fragrances, Inc. Mr. Henry G. Walter, Jr., Chairman of that corporation, has taken a keen interest in the plans for the exhibition and its catalogue.

From the first moment when this exhibition and publication were proposed, the Consul General of the Netherlands in New York, Jonkheer Leopold Quarles van Ufford, has been of the greatest help. He and Mr. Th. J. M. van den Muysenberg, Consul for Press and Cultural Affairs, have assisted us at every turn. We are also most thankful to Mr. R. Hotke, Director-General of the Ministry of Cultural Affairs, Recreation, and Social Welfare, The Hague, for his help in the coordination of the activities in the United States and the Netherlands; to Mrs. R. J. C. Gosschalk, Central Directorate for International Relations of the Ministry of Cultural Affairs, Recreation, and Social Welfare. Others who have played critical rôles are the late Dr. A. F. Ian Schendel, retired General Director, Rijksmuseum, Amsterdam; Prof. Th. H. Lunsingh Scheurleer, University of Leiden; and Drs. R. R. de Haas, Director, State-Owned Art Collections Department, The Hague, who were especially helpful in the first stage of the elaboration of the exhibition program. Also, Prof. Dr. J. G. van Gelder, University of Utrecht, retired, and Mrs. Dr. I. van Gelder–Jost; and Prof. Dr. J. W. Schulte Nordholt, University of Leiden, who were active in planning and in writing the introductions. We are thankful to Colonel L. van Dorp, Extraordinary Aide-de-Camp of H. M. the Queen, Director of the Royal House Archives, for acting as a mediator for the loans of the Royal Collection and the Stichting Historische Verzamelingen van het Huis van Oranje-Nassau; Mr. A. F. Ubels Jr. and Mr. Martin Loonstra of the Royal House Archives; Drs. G. Kotting of the Rijksbureau voor Kunsthistorische Documentatie, The Hague; Jonkheer F. G. L. O. van Kretschmar, Director of the Iconografisch Bureau, The Hague, and Mrs. Drs. M. E. Tiethoff-Spliethoff; Prof. Dr. F. L. Bastet of the Rijksmuseum voor Oudheden, Leiden—all of whom helped in research during the preparation of the catalogue. His Excellency, Mr. A. R. Tammenoms Bakker, Ambassador from the Netherlands to the United States, was also most interested in our project.

We are grateful to the directors and curators of the museums and collections, who generously lent for this exhibition, especially to Mr. Frans Baudouin, Director, Museum Rubenshuis, Antwerp; J. J. C. Baron Taets van Amerongen, Curator of Castle Amerongen; Mr. J. G. C. van Dijk van 't Velde, Intendant, Royal Palace, Amsterdam; Dr. S. H. Levie, General Director, Mr. P. J. van Thiel, Director of the Department of Paintings, Drs. A. L. den Blaauwen, Director of the Department of Sculpture and Applied Arts, Drs. W. H. Vroom, Director of the Department of Dutch History of the Rijksmuseum, Amsterdam; Dr. J. W. Niemeijer, Director, and Mr. M. D. Haga of the Rijksprentenkabinet, Rijksmuseum, Amsterdam; Drs. R. A. Leeuw, Director of the Stedelijk Museum Het Prinsenhof, Delft; Drs. H. R. Hoetink, Director, Royal Cabinet of Paintings, Mauritshuis, The Hague; Dr. C. Reedijk, Director, Mrs. Dr. S. A. Korteweg, Dr. H. J. Storm van Leeuwen, curators of the Royal Library, The Hague; Drs. R. R. de Haas, Director, State-Owned Art Collections Department, The Hague; Mr. A. E. M. Ribberink, Director of the State Archives, The Hague; Miss Drs. M. E. Deelen, Curator of the Stichting Atlas van Stolk, Rotterdam; Dr. D. Hannema, Director, and A. C. A. W. Baron van der Feltz, Curator, the Stichting Hannema–De Stuers Fundatie, Heino; Dr. Richard H. Randall, Jr., Director, The Walters Art Gallery, Baltimore; Mr. Philippe de Montebello, Director, Miss Yvonne Hackenbroch, Consultative Curator of European Decorative Arts, and Miss Jessie McNab, Assistant Curator, European Sculpture and Decorative Arts, and Miss Marceline McKee, Senior Assistant for Loans, of The Metropolitan Museum, New York; Mr. Carlisle H. Humelsine, Chairman, and Mr. Graham Hood, Curator and Director of Collections, of The Colonial Williamsburg Foundation, Williamsburg. It is especially noteworthy that because of the generosity of The Colonial Williamsburg Foundation we are able to show so many extremely important objects associated with William and Mary, now in America, with comparable works from Holland. All of the lenders to the exhibition and for this catalogue are named in a separate list.

At The Pierpont Morgan Library the following have played important rôles in the realization of *William & Mary and Their House*: on the Board of Trustees, Mrs. Vincent Astor, Mrs. Charles W. Engelhard, and Jonkheer John H. Loudon; on the staff, Miss Priscilla C. Barker, Mrs. Ronnie Boriskin, Mr. Timothy Herstein, Mrs. Mary Mallon Hollanda, Miss Mary Ann Kelly, Mr. Francis S. Mason, Jr., Mrs. Patricia Reyes, Miss Felice Stampfle, Miss Deborah Winard, Mr. David W. Wright. We are thankful to Mr. Eugene V. Thaw and Mr. Armin Brand Allen for their special assistance. The staffs of The Stinehour Press and The Meriden Gravure Company worked valiantly and with great skill to produce this beautiful book by the time of the opening of the exhibition.

Dr. A. W. Vliegenthart, Director of the Rijksmuseum Paleis Het Loo, Apeldoorn, has been concerned in all aspects of this project. He collaborated with Miss Drs. A. M. L. E. Erkelens, Curator of the Rijksmuseum Paleis Het Loo, in writing the catalogue. They were assisted by Mrs. Drs. J. M. Vliegenthart–Van der Valk Bouman, Prof. Dr. J. G. van Gelder (who wrote in particular article no. 39 on the gold palette, etc., given to Daniel Seghers), Miss Felice Stampfle (who wrote sections 118–120 and 131 on the old master drawings), and Mrs. Drs. E van Heuven–van Nes. The staff of the Rijksbureau voor Kunsthistorische Documentie, The Hague, and Dr. Anne-Marie Logan also provided information. The technical part of the catalogue was made possible through the tireless efforts of the staff of the Rijksmuseum Paleis Het Loo: Mr. J. A. Borsboom, Mrs. G. J. Eggink–Siepermann, Mrs. A. E. Piekema–van den Berg, and Mr. W. R. M. van der Vegt. Translations were made by Mrs. Patricia Griffiths Wardle, Miss Francesca Mallard, Miss Henriette ten Harmel, Mrs. Johanna C. Prins, and Mrs. Ruta Butkus Vanderheide. Mrs. Prins also made many helpful suggestions concerning the catalogue entries.

CHARLES RYSKAMP
Director
The Pierpont Morgan Library

America and the House of Orange

J. W. SCHULTE NORDHOLT

ON FIRST VIEW the two words *America* and *Orange* have precious little in common. The House of Orange has been connected, for more than four centuries, not with the great nation in the West but with the small nation in the old world—the Netherlands or the Low Countries. Orange and Holland—to use the name of the most important province of the country for the whole nation, as is often done—belong together in an historical, almost sacred alliance. The nation of the Netherlands, at least the northern part of it, became an independent political unity in the rebellion against Spain at the end of the sixteenth century; the inspiring leader of this revolt was a German prince, a Count of Nassau, who inherited a French title, Prince of Orange, and who was educated in the international atmosphere of the court of the Emperor Charles V at Brussels. Willem of Orange, also known in history as William the Silent, became the Father of the Fatherland, the *Pater Patriae*, of the Dutch nation.

He and his descendants were, for more than two centuries, not really the sovereigns but only the stadholders of the Dutch Republic—a constitutional anomaly, since a stadholder was originally nothing but the representative of a king. In the Netherlands, however, the Stadholder kept his position after the King, Philip II of Spain, had been solemnly abjured in 1581. Thus the House of Orange became the symbol of the Dutch national consciousness, the guarantee of its civil and religious liberties, and the champion of Protestantism not only in the Netherlands itself but all over Europe.

There is something of a paradox in this development. William the Silent had, all his life, tried to form a state in which all the seventeen provinces—the present Netherlands, Belgium, and Luxembourg—were brought together, and in which both Christian religions, Catholicism and Protestantism, would tolerate each other. But the result of his endeavor was a republic consisting of only the seven northern provinces and dominated by the Calvinist Dutch Reformed Church. His successors had to contend with the powerful merchants of the cities, especially Amsterdam, to maintain their position. In that struggle they became more and more the exponents of a radical Protestantism, sustained by the established church and the common people, while the tolerance for which the Dutch Republic became rightly famous was due to the liberal attitude of the merchants, known as regents. William's greatest descendant, his great-grandson William III, became the defender of the Protestant religion against Louis XIV, the King of France, not only in his own country but also in all of Europe and in the European colonies in America.

For the Dutch, the House of Orange was the symbol of their national identity; the song of Willem of Orange, the "Wilhelmus van Nassouwe," became their national anthem; everywhere the color of Orange was displayed as the emblem of recognition. Wherever they went in the world to found their colonies—in Africa, Asia, or America—they carried that symbol with them. The first relationship between the House of Orange and America can be seen in the names given by the Dutch sailors to rivers, forts, and settlements: Fort Orange, Fort Nassau, the Mauritius river (after William's son and successor, Maurits). On the map of the present United States there are still many such names to be found, towns called Orange, Orangeburg, or Nassau—and, even more obviously, Williamsburg or Williamstown.

But that last name originated chiefly at a later time, dating from the years when Orange and America became much more closely connected, when a Dutch Prince was proclaimed the sovereign of the American colonies. He was the same William III as mentioned before. At the time that he became Stadholder in 1672, the Dutch had already lost their colony of New Netherland in 1664. Pieter Stuyvesant had been forced to surrender to the British. The Dutch had, however, left a strong imprint on the colony, to which many geographical names still bear witness. But the Dutch colony had never truly been ruled by a Prince of Orange, for, as indicated above, he never was the real sovereign of the country; moreover, in the Dutch system, the administration of the colonies was given to special trade companies, in the case of America to the "West-Indische Compagnie."

William III became the sovereign of the American colonies not through his Dutch stadholdership, but because in the year 1689 he and his wife, Mary, were crowned King and Queen of England. Invited by the English Protestants, he had crossed the Channel to oust his father-in-law, King James II, who was a Roman Catholic. Through his coronation, in the spring of 1689, he became the effective head not only of the United Kingdom but also of the American colonies. This Glorious Revolution, as it has been called ever since, restored the civil rights of the English and made possible a coalition of many European countries against the threat of a French hegemony. That was the great aim of William's policy, to unite all enemies of France and thus to preserve the Protestant religion. Protestants all over Europe and America considered him as the Defender of the True Faith against what they called the French-Popish conspiracy.

The rule of William and Mary lasted only a short time. The Queen died in 1694, the King himself in 1702. It is from these years that most of the names like Williamsburg and William and Mary date. But the reign of Dutch William, as he also was called, meant more than only names. For, as we have said, *Orange* was a symbol of more than only Dutch significance. *Orange* meant freedom against tyranny, whatever interpretation that word *freedom* might be given; and freedom is, after all, one of the most vague yet precious words we have. The name *Orange* stood also—and even more emphatically—for Protestantism against Catholicism. In America both of these meanings were gratefully accepted. Most of the colonists—transplanted Englishmen and in New York the Dutchmen— were strong Protestants who acclaimed the Glorious Revolution with great enthusiasm.

In the new world, as in the old, the same motives brought about the revolution against the Stuarts: resistance against centralization and arbitrary rule, and fear of a French-Catholic conspiracy. The Stuarts, especially the last King, James II, had worked hard to bring more unity and efficiency to colonial rule. In 1686 a Territory and Dominion of New England was formed, comprising under one governor all the colonies from Massachusetts to New Jersey. That Governor, Sir Edmund Andros, ruled, at least according to many of the citizens, as a dictator; he tried to do away with forms of local government like the New England town meetings; he irritated the Boston Puritans by giving special privileges to the Church of England; he arbitrarily raised the taxes; and so on. In all colonies discontent was growing, and it burst into the open when the news of the Glorious Revolution reached the American shores.

Especially in three of the most important colonies—Massachusetts, New York, and Maryland—the inhabitants started to revolt. The name of Orange was their first stimulant. An eyewitness wrote from Boston that as soon as "the Prince of Orange was Gone for England, ye Country Ros in Armes [and] Imprisoned ye whole crew." With that crew the writer meant Governor Andros and his henchmen, such as Edward Randolph and Joseph Dudley, who were arrested by the enraged people of Boston and put into prison. In New York, Andros' Lieutenant Governor, Francis Nicholson, escaped the same fate by fleeing to England.

In Maryland the Protestant part of the colonists rebelled against the Lord Proprietor of the colony, the Catholic Lord Baltimore, who was absent in London.

The simplest interpretation of the revolts in the colonies would be to see them all as part of the same struggle of liberty against tyranny. But we cannot explain the past with such a clearcut Whiggish pattern. In reality the conflicts that were fought were rather complicated. There were all kinds of parties and factions, but what is significant here is that most of them appealed in their contest to the name of the new King. William of Orange became the symbol of their aspirations.

Sometimes the revolt had rather conservative aspects, in spite of the use of the word *freedom*. In Massachusetts what the rebels really were after was the restoration of their old charter. On the day that they started their revolution (18 April 1689), they published a declaration—probably written by Cotton Mather, the youngest scion of the great family of puritan leaders—in which they professed their Protestant convictions and warned against the "great Scarlet Whore" or Rome. They praised God for the "noble Undertaking of the Prince of Orange, to preserve the three kingdoms from the horrible brinks of Popery and Slavery."

While Andros was still in power, one of the chief leaders of Massachusetts, Increase Mather—father of Cotton and President of Harvard—succeeded in escaping to England to lay the complaints of the colony before the proper authorities. He had just arrived and even had a first audience with King James when the revolution began; with eagerness he now addressed himself to the new King, as staunch a Protestant as he was himself. As a matter of fact, William did not have much sympathy for the rebellion, but he appreciated its Protestant aspect. Mather proved a skilled diplomat who convinced him to make some concessions. Mather wrote home: "I humbly prayed the Continuance of his Royal Favour to his Subjects in that Territory [i.e., New England]. The King was then pleased to ask me, what I would have to be done for New England? I humbly put his Majesty in mind to our Old Charter-Privileges. And that if they should, by his Royal Favour and Goodness be restored, that would make his Majesty's Name Great in those Ends of the Earth, as long as the World would stand; That none of his Subjects prayed more for his Royal Person, and for the Success of his Arms, than they did. That they were all of them Protestants." The King, cautious in his response, promised to discuss matters with the Lords of Trade, the administrators of the colonies.

In the end Massachusetts received a new charter, not the old one it had asked for—which, after all, had given freedom only to the elect. Now the colony had to accept a Governor, appointed by the King and with the power of veto over all the decisions of the Assembly. All Mather was able to obtain was that Andros would not be restored in his function and that the name of the new Governor might be suggested by the colonists themselves. For Massachusetts a new era began—an era in which it no longer could keep its pure puritan character but became more a part of the empire.

Yet the most essential question was not really solved. Were the English in the colonies, through the revolution, now the equals of those at home or did they remain more directly dependent upon the crown? Mather was dreaming of an "Empire of equal parts," but the new charter did not recognize this constitutional equality. On the contrary, the politics of centralization and "streamlining" of the empire were carried on. And so one of the deepest roots of another revolution, almost a century later, began to grow.

In New York things were different. There the Dutch element in the population was still in the majority, but the Dutch were strongly divided among themselves: between the settlers of New York City and those of Albany; and also, on the one hand, between the men of prominence, proprietors of the land, with resounding names like Van Rensselaer, Schuyler, Livingston, Van Cortlandt, Bayard, and the like; and, on the other hand, the burghers of the middle class, who during the revolution found a strong but impetuous leader in Jacob Leisler. Leisler was a German who in 1660, when New York was still under the Dutch rule, had arrived in the new world, who had done well in business, and married into the high society, but who had never yet been accepted by them as an equal. Just as in Boston, the revolution in New York began when the rumors of the crossing of the Prince of Orange began to spread. Leisler—captain of the militia—seized power, and Nicholson—Andros' deputy—barely managed to escape. But with his *coup d'état* Leisler collided with the powerful aristocracy and imprisoned several of their leaders, among them his strongest opponent, Nicholas Bayard. For almost two years Leisler was able to uphold his position, but when the King sent a new Governor, Colonel Henry Sloughter, he was arrested, and after a biased trial, in which his enemies requested his death, he was hanged and quartered in 1691.

Leisler's rebellion is a rather complicated event, liable to various interpretations. There are several aspects in it: a Dutch aspect, a Protestant aspect, a social aspect. The Dutch aspect does not mean that people were striving for a restoration of Dutch rule, although there may have been some who believed that this was implied by the accession of a Dutch prince to the English throne. But the Dutch in New York, from all parties, acclaimed with great approval a prince

· 23 ·

whose ancestors "had delivered our forefathers from the Spanish yoke." Bayard confessed, but a bit after the event, his great joy over the "Noble, though Hazardous Enterprise of the late Prince of Orange, our most dread Soveraign King of England, Scotland, France and Ireland, Defender of the Faith, etc., the Noble Heroe of his Age, for the Protestant Religion, and the preservation of the Laws and Liberties of the English Nation inviolated." And one of his henchmen asserted in another pamphlet that the gentlemen of the council like Bayard and Van Cortlandt were especially loyal to the new King, because they were Dutchmen, "Elders and Deacons of the Dutch Protestant Church in New York, and the most affectionate to the Royal House of Orange." This was not a "Dutch plot" but on the contrary old and truly tested loyalty.

But Leisler and his men declared as loudly their love for the House of Orange and proclaimed William and Mary solemnly to be their sovereigns (22 June 1690). The Protestant aspect was especially emphasized. Leisler himself was a strong Calvinist, "of fervent Seale for the Protestant Religion," and long angry about the Catholic tendencies of the Stuart administration. He liked to talk about a "Popish plot" and exchanged letters with the revolutionaries in Maryland and Massachusetts about the "papistical tricks" of the common enemy. The invasion of an army of French and Indians from Canada in the winter of 1690, in which Schenectady was burned and Albany threatened, seemed to prove Leisler's worst fears. But his expedition against the French turned into a fiasco, and this event contributed to his fall.

Perhaps the core of his rebellion must be found in its social aspects. He and his son-in-law Jacob Milborne, who was his chief adjutant, and who in the end would share his fate, loved to use rather radical language. In their opinion King William owed his power to the people: they gave the *droit divin* a new twist by explaining it as the *vox populi vox Dei*. It would be too modern an approach to see Leisler's as a democratic movement, for the conflict between the parties is very complicated. Yet there is this element of radicalism, of resistance against the aristocrats, the "Grandees" as Leisler loved to dub them, while they in their turn detested him and his movement as "plebeian." When the new Governor arrived in 1691, he was on the side of the old order. William III might have been the leader of a Whig revolution, yet he strongly tried to maintain the royal prerogative, and was opposed to popular rebellions. Leisler's downfall seemed inevitable; his enemies accused him of usurpation of power and rejoiced in his death.

It seems an irony of history that so Protestant a prince as William III abandoned his most fervent Protestant followers exactly because he wanted to strengthen his power on behalf of his fight for the Protestant cause. He allowed no more freedom than he had to. In New York the Glorious Revolution concluded with the introduction of a relative liberty. A form of representative government was established, even a "Charter of Libertyes" drafted, in which the rights of the citizens were guaranteed. But a governor with the right to veto maintained the royal sovereignty. The colonists were—again as in Massachusetts —not allowed the same rights as their countrymen at home. They remained second-class Englishmen.

Leisler had lost. Yet his influence was not completely wiped out. His supporters, led by his son, Jacob Leisler, Jr., even succeeded seven years later in receiving an official repeal of his sentence by the Parliament in London—a late rehabilitation for a man who had played a disputed role in history.

The third colony where the Glorious Revolution played an important role was Maryland, in the South. Circumstances there were quite different from those in the other colonies. Maryland had been governed, since the early seventeenth century (1632), by a family of proprietors, the Calverts, Lords Baltimore, who, in their admiration for the Stuarts, had named their colony after the wife of Charles I, Queen Henrietta Maria. The Calverts were Roman Catholics and they induced many of their co-religionists to emigrate to their colony. The actual proprietor in 1689 was Charles Calvert, third Lord Baltimore, but, since 1684, he had been absent from his lands, and so gave all the more opportunity to the strong Protestant element in the colony to start a rebellion once they received the news of the Glorious Revolution of William III. For a long time Protestants and Catholics of Maryland had clashed. Now rebellious citizens, led by Jacob Coode, who called themselves the Protestant Association, appealed to the new King to deprive the Baltimores of their powers and bring Maryland directly under the crown. At the same time an assembly was called together, which gave out a solemn declaration of warning against the Catholic conspiracy. The same words were used again: William III has been sent by God "to put a Check to the great Innundation of Slavery and Popery"; the Jesuits were behind it all, and already "solemn Masses and Prayers are used . . . in their Chappels and Oratories, for the prosperous Success of the Popish Forces in Ireland and the French Designs against England."

The same complaints as in Boston and New York were heard again. Arbitrary government, unlawful taxes, biased trials—all these grievances were formulated and another was added in Maryland: the discrimination against the Protestants.

Coode met less resistance than Leisler: he was a more careful man, and in general his revolution may be called a success. The colony was taken away from the proprietors, a governor was instituted, as in the other colonies, with a council in which several of the chief rebels were appointed, and people—at least the holders of property—were represented in an assembly. But here, too, the last essential aspect of freedom was lacking. The Marylanders beseeched the King to give them equal rights with all Englishmen at home, but their entreaties were all in vain: they remained directly dependent on the crown.

In general it must be said that the Glorious Revolution in America was only a partial reversing of the situation before. What the King needed were obedient subjects, who could give him full support in his defense of the Protestant cause. He was not willing to give them a real reform; he was an autocrat, not a democrat. As soon as possible all the colonial servants from before the revolution were reappointed in high positions. Sir Edmund Andros might not be allowed to return to Boston, but he was now installed as Governor of Virginia. Francis Nicholson again became his Lieutenant Governor and later on (1694) Governor of Maryland, of Virginia (1698), and of South Carolina (1721). Another faithful supporter of Andros, Edward Randolph, with him imprisoned in Boston, was appointed (in 1691) as Surveyor of Customs for all North America. Joseph Dudley, also one of the most hated henchmen of Andros, returned as Chief of the Council of New York, and later was re-assigned as Governor of Massachusetts (1702).

Men like these expressed their gratitude to the King by naming cities and institutions after him. Especially Francis Nicholson must be mentioned here: it was he who moved the capital of Virginia to a new settlement, which he gave the name Williamsburg. With James Blair, the Bishop of London's commissary in Virginia, he urged the establishment of a college for the education of Anglican clergymen. It received its charter in 1693 and was called William and Mary. After Harvard it is now the oldest university in the United States; among its alumni are such famous men as Thomas Jefferson, John Marshall, and James Monroe. Francis Nicholson was really indefatigable in his gratitude. As Governor of Maryland he again founded, in the new capital, Annapolis, a school named after King William (1696; now St. John's College). This example was followed in many other places; in this way the name of William of Orange is inseparably linked with the history of America.

But it is not in this way that the Dutch Stadholder exerted his deepest influence in the new world. Far more important, for Europe as well as for America, are the results of his stubborn struggle against King Louis XIV of France. William III was not a reformer, he was a fighter. He was the first of the great English leaders (William Pitt and Winston Churchill were to follow his example in later times) who dedicated himself to the maintenance of the balance of power against the hegemony of a Continental dictator. Neither in his own country, the Dutch Republic, nor in his English dominions, was he willing to start new experiments: he needed them all for his great political goals. Therefore he really continued the policy of centralization, of incorporation of the colonies into the structure of the British empire. By doing this he involved them in the great wars between England and France, the second Hundred Years' War, which was fought not only in Europe but also in America, and which has been so magnificently described in the many volumes by Francis Parkman. With the Glorious Revolution the first of these wars begins, and in the new world it is appropriately called King William's War.

Or to say it differently: it was King William's policy of great vision that for the first time drew the American colonies from their provincial isolation and involved them in global conflicts and responsibilities. He was the first one to understand that the old world and the new need each other, that they cannot exist separately when the freedom of mankind is at stake. That is the real significance of the House of Orange for America.

The Stadholder-King William III
as Collector and "Man of Taste"

J. G. VAN GELDER

THE STADHOLDER-KING William III's role as collector of works of art is not very clear to us today. The image we have of this brilliant opponent of Louis XIV is entirely formed by his political and military activities. His diplomacy and steadfastness are universally celebrated, and his passion for hunting is well known, but no mention is ever made of his artistic sensitivity.

It cannot be denied that the time of his reign, the last quarter of the seventeenth century, saw the appearance in the Northern Netherlands of a highly individual style, with characteristics that lend an unusual air to a number of art objects and in particular to interiors. At first sight it appears French in nature, but it basically remains Dutch. The impulse, which brought about a new stage in architecture as well, was stimulated in part by the building activities of William III. As a result the somewhat isolated Dutch character of the art of the Netherlands acquired a more internationally oriented flavor.

That international flavor had certainly not been lacking in the Northern Netherlands up to then, but it had not been the dominant feature, although it must be said that it had been precisely the members of the House of Orange, with Frederik Hendrik and Amalia van Solms in the forefront, who had had an eye for what was happening in the artistic field in France, England, and, above all, the Southern Netherlands. Frederik Hendrik's collection of paintings, which his widow kept intact until her death in 1675, contained more works by Rubens, Van Dyck, Jordaens, Van Thulden, Willeboirts Bosschaert, Gonzales Coques, Daniel Seghers, Jan Breughel, etc., than any other collection in the country. By contrast, there was scarcely any representation in it of French, Italian, or German art.[1] The Huis ten Bosch, where Amalia lived almost permanently after

---

1. The only Italian picture that Frederik Hendrik possessed was by Franciabigio, *Mars,* *Venus, and Cupid* with five life-size figures in all. A work of French origin was the *Group Por-*

1650 and where her grandson William III must regularly have stayed, was not only a "second mausoleum,"[2] in memory of her "incomparable" husband, but also a monument of Dutch classicist art and of Flemish seventeenth-century baroque, in complete contrast to what was to be found in the houses of most Dutch patricians. Nor was it just a question of the Huis ten Bosch, for a more internationally minded approach was already to be seen at an earlier date in the palaces at Honselaersdijk, with the staircase designed by a French architect, and in the Huis te Rijswijk, which also clearly evinces French inspiration. This was primarily due to the painter-architect Jacob van Campen, who in 1633–1634 designed the Mauritshuis in The Hague and in 1640 modernized Noordeinde Palace.

It was at Noordeinde that the young Prince (born in 1650) who would become King William III grew up. Whether he, like his father Willem II, was given drawing lessons, is not definitely established, but it can be taken for granted that he was, because, since Castiglione,[3] instruction in drawing had formed part of the education of a prince. The Prince's teacher was probably Abraham Raguineau (born in London in 1623), who also taught him to write and who became a citizen of The Hague in 1645. Raguineau became keeper of the Prince's pictures in 1666. Between 1660 and 1662 Raguineau made a number of portraits of the Prince, as well as a group portrait with the Prince's Frisian cousins. William III was, indeed, repeatedly portrayed, from the age of two onwards, by more than thirty different artists:[4] painters, sculptors, and engravers. It is

trait of Admiral Gaspard II de Coligny Chatillon (1526–1572) *with His Brothers Cardinal Odet* (1517–1571) *and General François, Comte d'Andelot* (1521–1599), formerly a chimney-piece painting in Noordeinde Palace (now in the Mauritshuis, no. 432). A *Venus and Cupid* by J. Rottenhammer was the only German painting.

2. The phrase a "second mausolea" (*sic*) was used in a letter of 23 April 1651 from Jacob Jordaens to Constantijn Huygens. The wife of Mausolos was Artemisia and in his dedication of the publication on the Huis ten Bosch (1655) Post calls Princess Amalia "une autre Artimise." A picture of *Artemisia* by G. Honthorst (Princeton, University Museum) hung in the Huis ten Bosch as a chimney-piece painting. For Artemisia, Honthorst, and Post see T. H. Lunsingh Scheurleer, "De woonvertrekken in Amalia's Huis in het Bosch," *Oud Holland*, 84, 1969, 57–58 and note 55. The ideas about the interpretation of the building and its decoration are further developed in a forthcoming study on Huis ten Bosch by Mrs. Beatrijs Brenninkmeyer–De Rooy.

3. Baldassare Castiglione, *Libro del Cortegiano*, first edition, Venice, 1527.

4. Among others may be mentioned G. Honthorst (1652, 1653), A. Hanneman (1654, 1658, 1664), W. Honthorst (1656), C. Jonson van Ceulen (1657), A. Raguineau (1660, 1661), J. de Baen (1667, 1673), C. Netscher (1670, 1674), G. Terborch (1672, 1673), J. F. van Douven (1676), Jan Blommendael (1676, 1699), Sir Peter Lely (1677, etc.), R. Verhulst (1683), W. Wissing (1685), G. Kneller (1690), G. Schalcken (1693, 1699), Jan Wijck, J. van Huchtenburgh (1690), and J. H. Brandon (1694, 1699). The number of portraits still in existence amounts to well over 200.

inconceivable that all those portraits were made without any contact with the artists themselves. We know that William III was not displeased with the first portrait that Caspar Netscher painted of him around 1670, which is now at Buckingham Palace. In 1672 he sat for hours for Gerard Terborch, both in Deventer and The Hague, and later legends were going the rounds about their conversations. He also sat, in March 1690, with his wife for Godfrey Kneller, as well as for the seal-engraver J. Cavalier. He knew by then what posing involved, for we also know that in 1664 the young Prince was totally uncooperative when required to sit still for Hanneman; and Terborch also intimated this in 1672.

In the years when William III could have been receiving lessons from Raguineau, his upbringing devolved entirely upon his grandmother, Amalia van Solms, after his mother's departure for England (20 September 1660) and her death from smallpox shortly afterwards (end of December 1660); but at the same time his "personal education" was left to the States of Holland. Preliminary drawings and a painted *Allegory* of 1661 by Theodoor van Thulden depict the young Prince committing himself to the armed goddess Minerva in the presence of the Muses, with the figure of his grandfather Frederik Hendrik visible in the sky.[5] The latter's art collection, formed at an early date and enormously enlarged, partly thanks to the advice of Constantijn Huygens the Elder, formed the artistic milieu in which the young Prince, now an orphan, grew up. The collection had been extended still further during the short period of Willem II's rule (1647–1650).[6] To Willem II, who was married to the eldest

5. Amsterdam, Rijksmuseum, inv. no. A4654, *Allegory of William III's Leavetaking from Amalia van Solms after the Transferral of the Regency to the States-General*, canvas: 115 x 95 cm; R-A. d'Hulst in *Album Amicorum J. G. van Gelder*, 1973, p. 188, fig. 7.

6. By, among other things, a *Peasants Dancing outside an Inn*, by D. Teniers, dated 1649, now in Buckingham Palace. A Saenredam of 1648 (now belonging to the Marquess of Bute, but in 1660 presented by the States of Holland and West Friesland to Charles II) was offered to Willem II in the year in which it was painted, but he did not buy it. J. Eysten, *Het leven van Prins Willem II*, Amsterdam, 1916, writes on pp. 82–83 about Willem II as patron of the arts: "Honthorst received F16,605 for paintings between 1648 and 1650. Adriaen Hanneman supplied the Princess Royal with paintings to the value of F700. By contrast, the painter C. Garnet received only F30 apiece for portraits of the Prince and Princess. In 1650 the Prince bought a 'nude Venus' from the painter Dirck Bleker for no less than F1,700. The painters Dirck van der Lisse, Frans Post, Jan van Goyen, and Johannes Boreman [=Brosterhuizen] supplied paintings; the last-mentioned, landscapes from Burgundy. In March 1649 the Jesuit painter D. Seghers received a curious gift from the Prince, namely, a palette and six brush-sticks, all of gold, for which His Highness had paid F1,495.10 to the silversmith H. C. Brechtel." See also H. Schneider, "Een prinselijke opdracht aan David Teniers D.J.," *Oudheidkundig Jaarboek*, II, 1933, 37, 38, pls. VII, VIII. For H. C. Brechtel see A. J. J. Delen, "Daniel Seghers en het Huis van Oranje," *Oude Kunst en graphiek*, Antwerp, 1943, 73–102, fig. 4.

daughter of Charles I, the fame of the latter's collection must have been all too well known. Yet later on the young William III, overburdened with military duties above all, was scarcely able to embark on art purchases before the death of his grandmother. After Amalia's death in 1675, however, a change took place. The larger part of her art collection was divided among her three surviving daughters and the two sons of her dead eldest daughter, Louise Henriette, who had married the Elector of Brandenburg. There was certainly something left over for Amalia's grandson William III, but nearly all the works by Rembrandt, Lievens, Rubens, and most of the Flemish masters disappeared from The Hague. Only the chimney-piece paintings, by Van Dyck and others, and anything else set into the walls remained.

If one compares the inventories of the Oranges of 1632–1675 with the first big inventories of 1696 and 1712, again a great many works appear to have been bought. In June 1676, during campaigns in the Southern Netherlands, William III stayed for eight days with the greatest Antwerp dealer and collector, Diego Duarte, eldest son of Gaspard Duarte (see also no. 34 of the present catalogue). The following year, in June 1677, William III acquired in Antwerp two works by Rubens,[7] visited dealers, and even paid a call on the eighty-six-year-old Jacob Jordaens, who was carried in on a chair but was no longer in full possession of his mental faculties. During pauses in the campaigns William III studied with approval the drawings of the towns and villages made by his secretary, Constantijn Huygens the Younger; and Jonkheer van der Does, Lord of Bergesteyn, one of the greatest collectors of drawings in Holland at that point, belonged among his friends. When William III later, as King, had his portrait painted with Queen Mary by Kneller in London in 1690, he requested both Huygens and Van Bergesteyn to be present. One of his artistic advisers, for furniture and in particular for the gardens, was his bosom friend Hans Willem Bentinck, soon to become first Earl of Portland. If Maurits Post (1645–1677) was initially William III's architect, for Soestdijk and elsewhere, after Post's

7. The inventories were published with annotations by S. W. A. Drossaers and T. H. Lunsingh Scheurleer, *Inventarissen van de inboedels in de verblijven van de Oranjes . . . 1567–1795*, The Hague, I and II, 1974; III, 1976. *Pomona and Virtumnus in a Landscape* "by the Velvet Breugel" was sold to Wittert van Valkenburg for F2,805 on 26 July 1713, no. 7; later with Valerius Röver (1733); in 1750 in Cassel; disappeared under King Jerôme Bonaparte, *Inventarissen, op. cit.*, I, 697, 28. The *Venus Anadyomene* now in Sanssouci; these two paintings were bought in succession in Antwerp for F1,400 and F900 respectively. See also J. G. van Gelder, "Rubens in Holland in de zeventiende eeuw," *Nederlands Kunsthistorisch Jaarboek*, III, 1950–1951, 102–150, fig. 29.

death Jacob Roman (1640–1715/16) as architect and Daniel Marot (1661–1752) as designer of interiors and gardens had their hands full with work for him, both on the country estate of Het Loo near Apeldoorn and in England, where Sir Christopher Wren was called in as well.

In England the re-installation of the galleries in Kensington Palace (1695) and later in Hampton Court received the constant attention of the King, who also continued to concern himself with the hanging and rehanging of the works of art in them. The Raphael cartoons were at last restored, and Mantegna's canvases with the *Triumph of Caesar* were also restored on the instigation of William III and placed on display, likewise for the public. The King must already have studied and admired the "four or 5 books with drawings" by Leonardo and Holbein, which came to light in Kensington Palace, in January 1690. A week later Huygens and Van Bergesteyn examined the rich store of "drawings in a chest . . . including many single figures by Parmigiano and various other good artists." On 1 September 1690, at the Queen's request, Huygens, at 9 o'clock in the morning!, again examined the books with drawings by Holbein and Leonardo, and also "other books of Italian drawings, from which it certainly appeared that some thefts had been made and it was said that Lilly, having borrowed the books from [William] Chiffins ['page of the backstairs'], had removed things from them and placed in them copies made by his people, etc. . . ."[8]

In Holland William III possessed, besides a comprehensive library which was to be sold later (in 1749), prints and drawings as well. In 1686 twenty-one "Art and Print books" were counted, but, alas, we no longer know their contents. This does, however, make it certain that William had an interest in this field of art.

While Walton, Norris, and Cooke furnished the technical aid for the Raphaels in England and the French restorer-painter Louis Laguerre was the restorer of the Mantegnas, William III had his "Keeper of the Cabinet and Art," the painter Robert Du Val (1644–1732), come over from Holland to England. His task was to refurnish the King's country houses, first and foremost in the Netherlands. Apart from purchases from and commissions to artists, G. de Lairesse, J. Glauber, M. d'Hondecoeter, J. Lotyn, and others, Du Val's activities also in-

8. The drawings undoubtedly came from the collection of the Earl of Arundel and were presumably presented or sold to Charles II through the offices of Sir Peter Lely. What concerns us here is that this was the first time this unique collection attracted royal attention. The sources are to be found in the *Journaal van Constantijn Huygens, den zoon, 1688–1696*, Utrecht, I, 1876, 227, 230, 326, and *passim*.

cluded the sending of over thirty works of art and seventeen tapestries from England, which must have arrived in the Gallery at Het Loo shortly before 1700. We shall return to these later in this essay.

For the rest, the prime mover and organizer of all the royal possessions was Daniel des Marets (1634–1714), originally a Walloon preacher, who rose in William III's favor from Comptroller of "His H[ighness'] country houses, estates, and Gardens" (1685) to librarian first of all and then to director of "the library and of the mathematical instruments, Maps, models, etc." (1689), until he was finally appointed "Comptroller-general of His Majesty's household in the Netherlands" (1692). In addition to this, in 1687 Des Marets' eldest daughter married the above-mentioned Robert Du Val, who had already been taken on by William III in 1682. In short, father Des Marets and son-in-law Du Val virtually pulled all the strings.

Before his appointment Du Val had spent two years in Rome and ten in Venice, where he had made friends with Godfrey Kneller among others. As cofounder, in 1682, of the Hague Academy, of which he was director for many years,[9] he had a certain authority in the world of artists. With the architect Jacob Roman and with Daniel Marot, Du Val as it were conjured up a monarchical setting for William III. The etcher Romeyn de Hooghe, the most productive illustrator of this period, fitted in with this to perfection. Du Val confined himself to ceiling paintings, over-door pieces, and a few allegories, but—more important —through him, and undoubtedly also through what William III bought in Holland and what he had had selected in England for this purpose, the paintings gallery and cabinets at Het Loo acquired an entirely new and more varied composition.

The collection of William III in the Northern Netherlands still contained at the end of the seventeenth century, alongside several masterpieces by Rubens and Van Dyck, a large number of other Flemish paintings. Besides these it numbered mainly Italian works, by Bassano, Carracci, Cerquozzi, Palma, Veronese, Parmigianino, Raphael, Titian, Turchi, and others: a combination which also occurred more than once in other Dutch collections alongside works by Dutch landscape and genre painters. What was unusual for the Northern Netherlands, however, was the purchase by William III of a major work by Valentin de Bou-

9. The *Portrait of R. Du Val* by G. Kneller, in the Hague Academy; reproduced in J. H. Plan-tenga, *De Academie van 's-Gravenhage . . . 1682–1937*, The Hague, 1938, fig. 15.

logne, whereby French Caravaggism was splendidly represented.[10] And last, but not least, these were joined by the Holbeins brought from England and two so-called Dürers or Cranachs, which, as it proved possible to establish in 1879, turned out in reality to be masterpieces by Piero di Cosimo (figs. 3 and 4). In short, William III possessed a surprising series of works of the first half of the sixteenth century.

If we now ask ourselves, first of all, where William III acquired the paintings that were not brought from England, then attention must be drawn to a hitherto unnoticed passage from the travel diary of Zacharias Conrad von Uffenbach, the burgomaster of Frankfurt, who visited Het Loo in 1711. This bibliophile mainly describes the garden and the menagerie, part of which had perished in the cold winter of 1708. But then, of all the pictures that hung at Het Loo at that time, he mentions only one, that of the *Portrait of Edward VI as a Child* of 1538 by Holbein, which was in those years wrongly regarded as a portrait of Henry VIII. Uffenbach noted down the complete inscription by Sir Richard Morison (fig. 5).[11] This painting, which is indeed superb, had come to the Netherlands with part of the Arundel Collection, including seventy paintings which were taken to Amersfoort in 1646 and, after the death of Lady Arundel in 1654, were valued by Jacob van Campen, Paulus Bor, and M. Withoos on 3 January 1655. Various paintings from the Arundel Collection were later sold privately in a sale at Utrecht;[12] exactly when has not been established to this day. Holbein's *Portrait of Edward VI* was sent to Friesland in 1713. How it reached Hanover in the eighteenth century is still an unsolved problem, but relations between the Frisian Stadholders and Brunswick and Hanover were so close (William IV later married Anne of Hanover), that a transferal in the eighteenth century must be counted among the real possibilities. The portrait left Hanover in 1937 and is now in the National Gallery in Washington (Mellon Collection). At Het Loo this Holbein hung in the cabinet of paintings next to the King's bedchamber. It remains pos-

10. This canvas, 190 x 265 cm, was shown in Paris at the exhibition *Valentin et les Caravagesques Français*, Grand Palais, 13 Feb. – 15 Apr. 1974, 182–184, no. 57 as *Réunion avec une diseuse de bonne aventure*. (Now in Toronto, Canada).

11. For this portrait see Paul Ganz in *The Burlington Magazine*, 1943, 272. See also A. Chamberlain, *Holbein*, II, 164; and, for the text and translation of the Latin verses by Sir Richard Morison, Roy Strong, *Holbein and Henry VIII*, London, 1967, 17–18, pl. 15. See also Z. C. von Uffenbach, *Merkwürdige Reisen durch ... Holland ...*, Frankfurt and Leipzig, 1753, 372–377.

12. F. H. C. Weytens, *The Arundel Collection*, Utrecht, 1971, 29–31. The print of 1650 by W. Hollar reproduced here (Parthey 1395) is in reverse after a drawing which Hollar made while still in London and which is preserved in Cambridge, Pepys Library, Magdalene College, 236 x 178 mm.

sible that William III owed his admiration for Holbein to this portrait, but that is only a guess. What is not a guess is that appreciation of Holbein's work is found only very sporadically in the Netherlands in the seventeenth century.

The purchase of the two paintings by Rubens in Antwerp in 1677, one of *Vertumnus and Pomona*, the other of a *Venus Anadyomene* (see note 7 above), has already been mentioned; another Rubens, *The Tribute Money* ("Render therefore unto Caesar the things which are Caesar's"), now in San Francisco (fig. 1), came from the collection of Joh. Philip Silvercroon in The Hague, where it was still admired by Nicolaes Tessin the Younger in 1687.[13] An exceptional painting, both in respect of its subject and the artists to whom it is attributed, is that of *Portraits of Two Women and a Man*, which according to tradition was painted by Giorgione, Sebastiano del Piombo, and Titian: the woman on the right, who is reminiscent of Giorgione's *Laura*, by Giorgione; the second woman by Titian; and the man by Sebastiano. It now bears the title *The Appeal* and is in The Detroit Institute of Arts (fig. 2). William III had acquired this canvas in The Hague in or after 1695; it originally came from the collection of the Amsterdam merchant Nicolaes Sohier (d. 1642), who presumably had acquired it in the 1620's in Venice.[14]

From what remained of Frederik Hendrik's collection a number of important chimney-piece paintings (acquired before 1632), a *Pastor Fido* scene, an *Achilles among the Daughters of Lycomedes* (both now in Pommersfelden), and the *Rest on the Flight into Egypt* bought in 1645 (now in the Hermitage), all by Van Dyck, were moved to Het Loo and hung in the large gallery. The same was true of a *Sophonisba* or *Artemisia* (Sanssouci, Potsdam) by Rubens. A *Caritas* by Rubens (now in Pommersfelden) hung on the same wall at Het Loo and

13. See J. G. van Gelder, *op. cit.*, 1951, 102–150, fig. 30 (p. 147). Since 1944 in the M. H. de Young Memorial Museum, San Francisco; panel: 142 x 189 cm. The painting was in the collection of King Willem II between 1840 and 1850 (cat. 1850, no. 65).

14. The painting appears in the estate of Nicolaes Sohier. After the death of his grandson, it passed into the possession of Marinus de Jeude, bailiff of the Court of Holland. Constantijn Huygens the Younger saw it there in The Hague on 13 October 1695 (*Journaal*, II, 1877, 542) and wrote: "a painting with two women and a man in it . . . being said to be by Giorgione, Titian,

and Sebastiaen del Pombo, but wrongly." For further literature see T. Pignatti, *Giorgione*, Venice [1969], 117–118, fig. 203 (J. Palma?).

Huygens also saw at De Jeude's an *Annunciation to the Shepherds* by Bassano. Both pieces from the N. Sohier (later Warmenhuizen) collection "are among his best things." William III presumably bought this painting as well at that time. "A Christmas night, full of figures, strongly and powerfully executed, 3 x 4 foot" was sold for F1,480 in 1713 (no. 24) to the young art dealer and copyist Robert Griffier (a son of Jan Griffier).

1. P. P. Rubens (1577–1640)
   The Tribute Money. Panel: 143.5 x 189 cm
   The Fine Arts Museums of San Francisco
   Purchased with funds from various donors. 44.11

2. Giorgione – Sebastiano del Piombo – Titian
   The Appeal. Canvas: 84 x 69 cm
   The Detroit Institute of Arts

3. Piero di Cosimo (1461/1462–1521)
   Portrait of Giuliano da San Gallo (1445–1516).
   Panel: 47.2 x 33.5 cm
   The Hague, Mauritshuis, on loan to
   the Rijksmuseum, Amsterdam

4. Piero di Cosimo (1461/1462–1521)
   Portrait of Francesco Giamberti (1405–1480).
   Panel: 47.5 x 33.7 cm
   The Hague, Mauritshuis, on loan to
   the Rijksmuseum, Amsterdam

6. Alessandro Turchi (1578/1580–1649)
   Allegory, Cupid Shooting (Omnia vincit Amor).
   Canvas: 100 x 123 cm
   The Hague, Mauritshuis, on loan to
   the Rijksmuseum, Amsterdam, and exhibited in
   The Hague, Gallery of Willem V

5. Wenzel Hollar after Hans Holbein
   Portrait of Edward VI, 1538,
   in reverse in the Arundel Collection.
   Etching, 1650 (Parthey 1395)
   Paris, Fondation Custodia (F. Lugt Collection)

7. Gerard Dou (1613–1675)
   Young Mother with Her Child, 1658.
   Panel: 73.5 x 55.5 cm
   The Hague, Mauritshuis

must have been a purchase of William III.[15] Also in the gallery were the twelve paintings by Otto van Veen with the *Revolt of the Batavians against the Romans*, which the States-General had acquired for 2,200 guilders in 1613, and which they presented to William III in 1699. His heirs gave these pictures back to the "High and Mighty Gentlemen" of the States-General in 1713 and they are now in the Rijksmuseum in Amsterdam.[16]

Finally, we should also like to focus special attention on three paintings. First of all on what was—so far as can be ascertained—the last purchase of William III, since it was made at the Philips de Flines sale in Amsterdam on 20 April 1700. It was a painting that had long been in the Netherlands, at all events since before 1670: "A shooting (Amor) Cupid," an *Allegory on the Power of Amor* (Omnia vincit Amor), by Alessandro Turchi. William III paid more than 2,000 guilders for it. It remained in the possession of the House of Orange and now hangs in the Gallery of William V on the Buitenhof in The Hague (fig. 6).[17]

The second painting we should like to draw attention to here is a panel of 1658 by Gerard Dou, *Young Mother with Her Child*, now in the Mauritshuis in The Hague (fig. 7). After the death of the Queen (1694/5) and the completion of the gallery and cabinet at Het Loo, it was sent from England to Holland along with the Holbeins[18] and other paintings and seventeen tapestries. It had in 1660 been added to the gift of twenty-four Italian paintings and twelve antique sculptures from the Amsterdam collection of Gerard Reynst to Charles II, William III's uncle. To this gift of the States of Holland and West Friesland—the famous "Dutch gift"—was added the *ameublement* that William II had bought for F67,000 in Paris in 1650 which was meant to adorn the lying-in room at the birth of William III. However, it was never used, since the court was plunged into mourning when William II died eight days before this happy event. In July 1660 it was bought back from Princess Mary for F100,000. It was the *pièce de résistance* of the States' gift to her brother Charles II, to which, in addition, the city of Amsterdam added a yacht, the *Mary*. From descriptions by eyewitnesses

15. Rubens, K.d.K. (4th impression), no. 64. This panel (195 x 127 cm) was also already in Holland before 1670 and was copied by Jan de Bisschop.

16. Inv. nos. A421 to A432, each panel 38 x 52 cm.

17. Property of the Mauritshuis, The Hague, cat. 1977, no. 342, canvas 100 x 123 cm. This painting was also copied by Jan de Bisschop

around 1665 (Rijksprentenkabinet, Amsterdam).

18. Seven Holbeins are mentioned in the inventories: (1) *Robert Cheseman*, (2) *Man with Falcon*, (3) *Henry VIII*, (4) *Edward VI*, (5) *A Man with a Ring*, (6) *A Person Having a Glove in His Hand*, (7) *A Portrait of a Gentleman*, "very fine" (1543). Nos. 2, 4, 7 (all withdrawn), and 3 (sold to Jan Smit for 405 guilders) were in the sale of 1713.

we know that Charles II very much admired Dou's *Mother and Child* panel and it must have been regarded as a prime masterpiece by William III as well. He did, indeed, possess three other works by Dou.[19] It was understandable that Queen Anne demanded that *Young Mother with Her Child* should be returned. The documents relating to this have not, or not yet, been discovered, so that we know nothing of the claims and counterclaims. From other documents, however, it appears that nothing went back to England, not even this Dou which—perhaps painted with a moral in mind—still retains its fascination today through its intimacy, tonality, spatial effects, and the cogent, extremely refined way in which the visible world is represented.

Finally, the third painting that merits attention is the *Double Portrait* of William III's parents painted by Sir Anthony van Dyck on the occasion of their wedding on 12 May 1641 (no. 34 of this volume). This too stands on the list of paintings that were sent from England to Holland. It appears along with the other works in the inventory of Het Loo of 1712/13, but a visitor already noted in 1705 that it had been placed in the center of the long wall of the gallery as a chimney-piece painting. That this painting is identical with that in the Rijksmuseum (and in this volume) is firmly established. Now in 1667 a painting of this subject is listed in the inventory of the possessions of Amalia van Solms in the Huis ten Bosch. Since the painting was not bequeathed to one of her daughters, it can be taken with a fairly high degree of certainty that this marriage portrait of his parents was allotted to William III on Amalia's death in 1675. It may be asked how it came to Holland. The Princess Royal came to Holland in March 1642, when she was not yet eleven years old, and it is not unlikely that the double portrait begun by Van Dyck in England in 1641 was not completely finished in his studio until 1642 (Van Dyck died on 9 December 1641) and was only then sent to Holland. William III must have had this portrait of his parents

19. *Young Mother with Her Child*, Maurits-huis, cat. 1977, no. 32. For the purchase and fortunes of the "Dutch gift" see Anne-Marie S. Logan, *The "Cabinet" of the Brothers Gerard and Jan Reynst*, Amsterdam/Oxford/New York, 1979, 75–82 and notes 82 and 96. See also P. J. J. van Thiel, exhib. cat., *Het Nederlandse Geschenk aan Koning Karel II van Engeland, 1660*, Rijksmuseum, Amsterdam, 12 May – 20 June 1965. In addition to the above-mentioned Dou, William III also owned two paintings with a "schoolmaster" and one night piece ("a shop by

night") by this artist.

We are no longer able to describe the bed in which William III was meant to have been born. Mrs. Logan does, however, write of "a bedstead complete with all the accessories," and "a richly embroidered bed." Van Thiel further mentions bed, chairs, and firescreens.

The yacht *Mary* was lost in 1675, but it is illustrated in the *Jaarboek Amstelodamum*, XIX, 1921, 1–13, after a drawing by Willem van de Velde the Younger.

brought over to England after his coronation in 1689. Less than ten years later it was, according to the list, sent with the other works to Het Loo. This explains why the painting is not mentioned at Honselaersdijk or elsewhere. So far as I know, it is not mentioned in the English royal collection either. Nor does it appear on the list drawn up by the painter Du Val of the pieces which Queen Anne asked to be returned (see below). As the property of William III it acquired a central place in the gallery at Het Loo, clearly evincing his secret sentimental attachment to a father he had never, and a mother he had scarcely, known.

William III had no children. His art collection went very different ways. First of all, after his death his sister-in-law Queen Anne requested the return of the works sent from England to the Netherlands and the jewels taken there. William III had named as the heir to his possessions Johan Willem Friso, a grandson of the second daughter of his grandfather Frederik Hendrik. But since Frederik Hendrik had laid it down in his will in 1647 that on the extinction of the male line, the children of his eldest daughter, the wife of the Elector of Brandenburg, should inherit, her son Frederick, who had meanwhile become King of Prussia, was able in 1702 to lay claim to all the old possessions that still stemmed from Frederik Hendrik. The contest over the inheritance that followed from this became even more complicated when Johan Willem Friso died in 1711 and his son was not born until shortly afterwards. The wife of Johan Willem Friso, Marie Louise of Hesse Kassel, who with her father, the Duke of Hesse Kassel, was guardian of the later Willem IV (1711–1751), got into financial difficulties and decided to sell some of the paintings from Het Loo in Amsterdam in 1713, after having them valued.[20] But not the works demanded by Queen Anne: they were temporarily moved to Friesland. Thus it must be taken that most of the paintings sold in 1713—certainly forty—including numerous Italian pictures, had been bought by William III.[21]

20. Gerard Hoet, *Catalogus of Naamlijst van schilderijen . . . in het openbaar verkocht*, I, The Hague, 1752, 149–154. In Hoet appears something that is not printed on the title page of the sale catalogue of 1713: ". . . paintings, coming from Het Loo." An annotated copy of the sale catalogue (Lugt no. 242) was presented to the Netherlands Institute for Art History in The Hague in 1933 from the collection of A. van der Willigen. This catalogue contains several pieces of information which do not appear again in Hoet. Van der Willigen's copy has, on the title page after "by a great Lord and Connoisseur," the addition in manuscript: "people say the King of England because the paintings come from Het Loo and belong to the Prince of Friesland."

21. As has already been said, the documents relating to Queen Anne's demand are not known, but it is not unlikely that part of Charles II's debts were settled by this.

A closer study of the collection of paintings of William III would undoubtedly produce further clarification. Nevertheless, it can be established on the information now available to us that among all the activities in which the Stadholder-King William III engaged, while his emotional fervor admittedly expended itself first of all on hunting (at Het Loo there hung more than three hundred antlers of stags he had hunted), he had certainly soundly developed an exceptional taste for special aspects of the visual arts. This was in addition to his activities in building and his concern for his gardens and parks. All of these things were true, however reticent he may have been as a person.

His taste in the visual arts received no special veneration in the various acts of homage paid him in Holland—and those of 1691 in The Hague, devised by Govert Bidloo and Romeyn de Hooghe, were undoubtedly the most extensive. It was just taken for granted that a prince would possess such taste. But in England, more than in the Netherlands, people continued to be impressed by it. And just how long that reputation held its own emerges, for example, from the speech made by John Wilkes in the House of Commons on 28 April 1777 to deplore the fact that the king then on the throne had had the Raphael cartoons moved from Hampton Court to Buckingham House, so that they were no longer accessible to the public. Elaborating on this protest Wilkes said: "King William, although a Dutchman, really loved and understood the polite arts. He had the fine feelings of a man of taste, as well as the sentiments of a hero. He built the princely suite of apartments at Hampton-Court, on purpose for the reception of those heavenly guests [*viz.*, the Raphael Cartoons]. The English nation were then admitted to the rapturous enjoyment of their beauties."[22]

William III "a man of taste"; it is no exaggeration to endorse this again today. For the rest, it is certainly remarkable that just after the gallery at Hampton Court had been closed in 1763, that of the later heir of William III, namely, the gallery of Willem V, was opened in The Hague in 1774. In this gallery on the Buitenhof part of the collection of the Stadholder-King, transferred from Het Loo, was still present. It had meanwhile been augmented by what Willem IV and Willem V had added to it. From the gallery at The Hague—the contents of which were carried off to Paris by the French in 1795, received back again in a

22. See *The Parliamentary History of England*, XIX, London, 1814, cols. 190ff. Quoted here after J. Shearman, *Raphael's Cartoons in the Collection of Her Majesty the Queen* . . . , London, 1972, 152 and note 106.

dilapidated state in 1815, and placed at the disposal of the Dutch nation by King William I on 1 July 1816—a number of paintings from the collection of William III are still to be found. They are the oldest nucleus of the Royal Cabinet of Paintings, which from 1822 to today has been housed in the Mauritshuis.[23]

23. "De schilderijengalerij van Prins Willem V op het Buitenhof te Den Haag" is discussed in detail, with an illustrated catalogue (202 nos.), by C. Willemijn Fock (I, 113–137) and Beatrijs Brenninkmeyer–De Rooy (II, 138–176) in *Antiek*, XI, 1976, no. 2. Additional material by Arnold Bréjon de Lavergnée and Jacques Foucart (pp. 273–281), F. J. Duparc (pp. 282–284), and J. G. van Gelder (pp. 285–290) is published in *Antiek*, XIII, 1978, no. 4. Of the 202 paintings which originally hung in the "Schilderijenzaal van Prins Willem V" from 1774 to 1795, 22 are to be found there today with 110 others. A summary catalogue, 16 pp. and 132 illus., has been published (1977).

Het Loo

A. W. VLIEGENTHART

AT THE END of the seventeenth century Het Loo was one of the most beautiful country estates in the Netherlands, and it attracted attention far beyond the borders of the country. Today the restoration of the palace and its gardens is considered to be one of the most important in Holland.

The Het Loo country estate was established in 1685 by William III, who had been since 1672 Stadholder of five of the seven United Provinces of the Netherlands, and his wife, Princess Mary Stuart. The mansion was erected in the midst of an extensive hunting ground in the park of the small mediaeval castle Het Loo, subsequently referred to as Het Oude Loo, which the Stadholder had bought in November 1684.

The country estate built by William III consisted of a mansion with a walled-in garden, together forming an indivisible architectural unity within the surrounding grounds. The building and the garden were laid out on a strongly marked axis and covered a nearly square area measuring 225 by 250 meters. The mansion stood in the southern half of this area, while the garden extended along the northern half. The main building, which was connected to low L-shaped wings by quarter-round colonnades, constituted the central point of the scheme. The walls were erected in brick and the only decorative features in the austere design were the stone surrounds of the entrance parts of the south front and north or garden front and the sculptured tympana. In the main building sash windows were put in, a very modern construction in those days. In addition to the rectangular garden behind the mansion, which was enclosed by three terraces and the old drive leading to Het Oude Loo, two small, more intimate gardens were created after the coronation of William and Mary, known as the Queen's Garden and the King's Garden respectively. These were added to the east and the west of the building. The gardens were laid out with beautiful parterres, in which elegant patterns were formed with the aid of box hedges, plants, grass, and colored stone chips. In addition, there were fountains, cascades, trimmed miniature trees, statues of marble and gilded lead, as well as a number of vases. The terraces afforded an excellent view of the garden.

After William III and Mary had been crowned King and Queen of England in 1689 it was deemed necessary to extend Het Loo. Already in 1691 plans were prepared to give the princely hunting lodge the character of a royal palace. The colonnades were replaced by two pavilions, and the garden was extended beyond the drive to Het Oude Loo to form a termination of the new upper garden where the colonnades were moved. The building and the walled-in garden were surrounded by a park with star-shaped woods, kitchen gardens, ponds, fish-ponds, and a maze. Previously, the surrounding areas had consisted of sandy moors overgrown with low shrubbery and heather.

Although drawings for Het Loo are known to have been made by the Académie d'Architecture in Paris between December 1684 and April 1685, these plans were very likely used only as a basis for the layout. Considering the Dutch character of the sober, brick building and of the garden, we must conclude that Jacob Roman (1640–1716), the architect responsible for the realization, must have had a substantial share in the ultimate design.

According to Ozinga's study published in 1938, it is evident that from 1692 on Daniel Marot (1661–1752), a French refugee, designed parts of the interior and at least made the designs for the main staircase (fig. 1), the drawing room, the new dining room (fig. 2), and the King's library with its ceiling composed of mirrors (fig. 3). It is certain that Marot had been charged with the supervision not only of the execution of his own designs but also of the interiors of the entire palace. Marot was also responsible for the garden, and it is probable that even before 1692 he had a substantial share in the layout and ornamentation of the rectangular garden which started in 1686.

After the death of William III in 1702, Het Loo remained in possession of the Stadholder's family until 1795. In the second half of the eighteenth century it was used intensively, but no drastic changes were made. It should be noted that the garden actually acquired a different appearance after 1784, when the part beyond the transverse avenue was laid out in "landscape" style. During the years 1795–1806 Het Loo was ransacked by the English, the French, and the Dutch, and the garden was totally destroyed. In 1806 Het Loo became the summer residence of Louis Napoleon (1778–1846), King of Holland from 1806 to 1810. The exterior walls were plastered white, the sash windows were replaced by empire-style windows, the palace was newly furnished, and the garden and the park were transformed into one large landscaped park.

After the founding of the Kingdom of the Netherlands, Het Loo became the summer residence of the reigning monarch. King Willem III (1817–1890) and

1. Daniel Marot (1661–1752)
   Main Staircase at Het Loo. Engraving.

2. Daniel Marot (1661–1752)
    New Dining Room at Het Loo. Engraving.
    Title page of his *Nouveaux Livre da Partements*

3. Daniel Marot (1661–1752)
    The King's Library at Het Loo. Engraving.

Queen Wilhelmina (1880–1962) especially liked to stay at Het Loo. King Willem III had an art gallery built behind the east wing. In the early days of her reign Queen Wilhelmina had a number of rooms, as well as the main staircase and the vestibule, restored and adapted in Louis XIV–style in accordance with the original decorations of the mansion. The building, which the government considered too small for receiving official visitors, was drastically altered in the period 1911–1914. The main building, two pavilions, and the wings were increased in height and on the east side the building was extended by a large ballroom and a new wing with kitchen and staff accommodation. These additions caused the proper proportions and the symmetry of the building to be altogether lost.

Queen Wilhelmina lived at Het Loo after her abdication in 1948 until she died in 1962. Princess Margriet, third daughter of Queen Juliana, was the last member of the House of Orange Nassau to live at the palace. She resided there from 1967 to 1975, when she moved with her family into their new house in the park. In 1969 Queen Juliana and the Government decided to turn Het Loo into a museum devoted to the House of Orange Nassau and the role it played in Dutch history. The inferior condition of the palace, partly due to the extensions made in 1911–1914, and its new function as a museum have made an overall restoration imperative.

From an architectural point of view the seventeenth-century country estate, with regard to both the garden and the buildings, is an example of distinguished, sober, Dutch baroque architecture. The seventeenth-century mansion was present under the plasterwork and under the later additions. So far as the garden is concerned, much historical data, such as maps, prints, and descriptions, are available, while excavations have revealed the exact locations of terraces, fountains, and basins. In regard to the interior, the rooms in the main buildings and in the pavilions will be decorated and furnished in such a way as to show how the various Stadholders and Kings lived there. The long gallery next to the King's library on the first floor will again be a picture gallery as in the time of William III. In his small cabinet of art next to his bedroom there will be part of the collection of contemporary art of King William III, as in the nineteenth century. The east wing will contain an exhibition of small objects, portraits, documents, etc., relating to the Stadholder and Royal Family. Changing exhibitions will be held in the west wing. The restoration work is in the hands of the architect J. B. Baron van Asbeck. The work, which will be carried out in two stages, was started in 1977 and is expected to be completed by 1983.

At the present time the stables, restored in 1972, accommodate a temporary museum. In this museum, opened to the public in 1972, are exhibited the most important pieces from the inventory of the palace which are on loan from Queen Juliana, together with loans from the foundation "Historical Collections of the House of Orange Nassau," the entire collection of the private society "Vereniging Oranje Nassau Museum," loans from private and state collections, gifts from the society of friends of the museum called "Stichting 't Konings Loo," and finally the purchases of the museum itself. Since 1972 more than one-and-a-half million people have visited this temporary museum.

LIT: M. D. Ozinga, *Daniel Marot: De schepper van den Hollandschen Lodewijk XIV–stijl*. Amsterdam, 1938, 49–77; C. W. Royaards, *De restauratie van het Koninklijk Paleis Het Loo*, The Hague, 1972; A. C. Kranenburg-Vos, *'t Konings Loo, bouwgeschiedenis en bewoning* (Nederlandse Kastelen XXV), 1975; J. B. van Asbeck and A. M. L. E. Erkelens, *De restauratie van Het Loo van paleis tot museum*, The Hague, 1976; J. B. van Asbeck and A. M. L. E. Erkelens, "De restauratie van de lusthof Het Loo," *Bulletin Koninklijke Nederlandse Oudheidkundige Bond*, 1976, 119–147; Jhr. H. W. M. van der Wyck, "Het Loo: De geschiedenis van een koninklijk domein," *Bulletin Koninklijke Nederlandse Oudheidkundige Bond*, 1976, 183–248; Jhr. H. W. M. van der Wyck, "De tuinsculpturen voorheen en thans op Het Loo aanwezig," *Bulletin Koninklijke Nederlandse Oudheidkundige Bond*, 1977, 165–177

ABBREVIATIONS

Anon.: Anonymous   Lit: Literature
Cat.: Catalogue   Pl.: Plate
Coll.: Collection   Prov: Provenance
Inv. no.: Inventory number   Vol(s).: Volume(s)

Cat. London 1950: *William & Mary and Their Time*, London (Arts Council of Great Britain), 1950

Cat. London 1964: *The Orange and the Rose: Holland and Britain in the Age of Observation 1600–1750*, London (Victoria and Albert Museum), 1964

Cat. Mauritshuis The Hague 1977: *Mauritshuis: The Royal Cabinet of Paintings, Illustrated General Catalogue*, The Hague, 1977

Cat. Rijksmuseum Amsterdam 1976: *Alle schilderijen van het Rijksmuseum te Amsterdam, Volledig geïllustreerde catalogus*, Amsterdam/Haarlem, 1976

Drossaers en Lunsingh Scheurleer: S. W. A. Drossaers en Th. H. Lunsingh Scheurleer, *Inventarissen van de inboedels in de verblijven van de Oranjes en daarmede gelijk te stellen stukken, 1567–1795*, 3 vols., The Hague, 1974–1976

Hofstede de Groot: C. Hofstede de Groot, *Catalogue Raisonné of the Works of the Most Eminent Painters of the Seventeenth Century*, 8 vols., London, 1908–1927

Van Loon: G. van Loon, *Beschrijving der Nederlandsche historipenningen*, 4 vols., The Hague, 1723–1731

F. Muller: F. Muller, *Beredeneerde beschrijving van Nederlandsche historieplaten, zinneprenten en historische kaarten*, 4 vols., Amsterdam, 1863–1870 [for historical prints]; and *Beschrijvende catalogus van 7000 portretten van Nederlanders*, Amsterdam, 1853 [for portraits]

Van Someren: J. F. van Someren, *Beschrijvende catalogus van gegraveerde portretten van Nederlanders*, 4 vols., Amsterdam, 1888

LENDERS

H. M. the Queen
H. R. H. Princess Margriet of the Netherlands
Friedrich Wilhelm, Fürst zu Wied, Neuwied, West Germany
Mrs. M. Wittop Koning, 's Hertogenbosch
Jonkheer Leopold Quarles van Ufford, New York

Castle Amerongen, Amerongen
The Colonial Williamsburg Foundation, Williamsburg
General State Archives, The Hague
The Metropolitan Museum, New York
Museum Rubenshuis, Antwerp
Rijksmuseum, Amsterdam
Rijksmuseum Paleis Het Loo, Apeldoorn
Rijksprentenkabinet, Rijksmuseum, Amsterdam
Royal Cabinet of Paintings, Mauritshuis, The Hague
Royal Library, The Hague
State-Owned Art Collections Department, The Hague
Stichting Atlas van Stolk, Rotterdam
Stichting Hannema–De Stuers Fundatie, Heino
Stichting Historische Verzamelingen van het Huis van Oranje Nassau
Vereniging Oranje Nassau Museum
The Walters Art Gallery, Baltimore

Family Tree of
The House of Orange Nassau

CHRONOLOGY OF SUCCESSION

1559–1584   Stadholder Willem I

1584–1625   Stadholder Maurits

1625–1647   Stadholder Frederik Hendrik

1647–1650   Stadholder Willem II

1650–1672   *Country governed by States-General*

1672–1702   Stadholder Willem III
             (King William III of England, 1689–1702)

1702–1747   *Country governed by States-General*

1747–1751   Stadholder Willem IV

1751–1795   Stadholder Willem V

1795–1813   *Country governed by France*

1813–1840   King Willem I

1840–1849   King Willem II

1849–1890   King Willem III

1890–1948   Queen Wilhelmina

1948–   Queen Juliana

Catalogue

STADHOLDER HENDRIK III

Count of Nassau

HENDRIK III (1483–1538) was the son of Jan, Count of Nassau Dillenburg (1455–1516), and Elisabeth, Countess of Hesse (1466–1523). He was the heir of his uncle Englebert II, Count of Nassau (1451–1504), who held Breda and other properties in the Netherlands. In 1505 Hendrik III became Knight of the Golden Fleece. He was one of the governors and a friend of Emperor Charles V (1500–1558), who appointed him in 1515 his Stadholder of the provinces of Holland, Zeeland, and Franche Comté.

He married: (1) Francisca Louise of Savoye (1486–1511) in 1503; (2) Claudia of Chalon (1498–1521) in 1515; and (3) Mencia of Mendoza, Marchioness of Zenette (1508–1554), in 1524. His only son was René of Chalon (1519–1544), who inherited from his uncle Philibert (1502–1530), brother of his mother, the name of Chalon and the principality of Orange in France. René also became Stadholder of Holland, Zeeland, Utrecht, and Franche Comté.

Hendrik III was an art-lover, and with his wife, Mencia of Mendoza, he embellished the castle of Breda, where he gathered a splendid collection of gold and silver objects and numerous tapestries. Manuscripts from his collection are now in the Royal Library in The Hague.

1 ST. THOMAS AQUINAS, INFORMACION DES PRINCES

French translation by JEAN GOLEIN. Manuscript made in France in 1453 for
JEAN ARNOULPHIN
Parchment: 33.9 x 21.9 cm
182 pages, 2 columns of 31 lines, Gothic bastarda
2 full-page miniatures, 3 small miniatures, gilt and colored initials, and ornamental borders
First page: coat of arms of Philip of Kleve, Lord of Ravenstein (1456–1528)
BINDING: brown leather, coat of arms of Prince Willem IV of Orange, tooled in gold, 18th century
SHOWN HERE: folio 6ʳ: Saint Thomas Aquinas (1225–1274) teaching an emperor, a king, a chancellor, and three other persons

Manuscripts inherited from the famous library of Philip of Kleve formed the main part of the collection of Hendrik III. In addition to the "Informacion des princes" by St. Thomas Aquinas, sixteen of these manuscripts are still in the Royal Library in The Hague.

LIT: *Supellectilem librariam sub sereniss.is de stirpe Nassauia Arausii Principibus in ordines digessit Constantinus Hugenius*, 1686, 143, no. 424 (catalogue of the library of Prince Willem III, made by Constantijn Huygens and Antoni Smets; manuscript, Royal Library, The Hague, 78D14); *Catalogue des livres de la bibliothèque de S.A.S. Frédéric-Henri, Prince d'Orange* . . . , The Hague, 1749, 218, no. 69; *De Oranje Nassau boekerij en de Oranjepenningen in de Koninklijke Bibliotheek en in het Koninklijk Penningkabinet te 's Gravenhage*, Haarlem, 1898, 13, no. 26; A. W. Bijvanck, *Les principaux manuscrits à peinture de la Bibliothèque Royale des Pays-Bas et du Musée Meermanno-Westreenianum à La Haye*, Paris, 1924, 53, 54; ill. 22, 23; *150 jaar Koninklijk Kabinet van Schilderijen, Koninklijke Bibliotheek, Koninklijk Penningkabinet, Herdenkingstentoonstelling in het Mauritshuis*, The Hague, 1966, no. 37
PROV: Libraries of Philip of Kleve, Hendrik III, and the Princes of Orange
ROYAL LIBRARY, THE HAGUE, INV. NO. 76E20

STADHOLDER WILLEM I

Prince of Orange, Count of Nassau

PRINCE WILLEM (1533–1584) was the eldest son of Willem, Count of Nassau Dillenburg (1487–1559), and his second wife, Juliana, Countess of Stolberg Wernigerode (1506–1580). In 1544 he inherited from his cousin René of Chalon (1519–1544) the principality of Orange and properties in the Netherlands. From 1544 onwards he was brought up at the court of the Emperor Charles V. He married four times: (1) Anna of Egmond, Countess of Buren (1533–1558), an heiress to large properties in the Netherlands; (2) Anna, Princess of Saxony (1544–1577); (3) Charlotte, Princess of Bourbon (1546–1582); and (4) Louise, Countess of Coligny (1555–1620). He had three sons: Philips Willem (1554–1618), son of Anna of Buren; Maurits (1567–1625), son of Anna of Saxony; and Frederik Hendrik (1584–1647), son of Louise of Coligny; there were as well several daughters.

Prince Willem became a Knight of the Golden Fleece in 1555. In 1559 Philip II (1527–1598), King of Spain, appointed him Stadholder in the provinces of Holland, Zeeland, and Utrecht. After 1567 he became the leader of the opposition and rebellion against Philip II in the Dutch provinces. He tried to unite the Southern (Roman Catholic) and the Northern (Protestant) provinces, but the differences between the two parts grew and on 6 January 1579 the southern provinces of Hainaut and Artois concluded the Union of Atrecht. On 23 January the Northern provinces in turn concluded the Union of Utrecht, which established the core of the later Dutch Republic.

To avoid confiscation of his belongings by Spain, Willem I removed his goods from his houses in the Netherlands to his native castle of Dillenburg. He possessed large and rich collections of silver, tapestries, furniture, jewels, coins, and paintings. The picture *The Garden of Delights* by Hieronymus Bosch (ca. 1450–1516), now in Madrid (Prado), originally was part of the gallery in his palace in Brussels. In the course of the war the Prince pawned many of his belongings to pay for military expenses, and later he was forced to sell most of them for the same reason.

In 1580 Philip II outlawed him, offering 25,000 ducats and a title of nobility to anyone who would kill him. Willem I answered with a defense and a justification presented to the States-General. An attempt on his life in 1582 by Jean Jaureguy failed, but in 1584 he was shot in Delft by Balthazar Gerards.

LIT: Drossaers en Lunsingh Scheurleer, I, 1–65

2 KNIFE AND SHEATH OF STADHOLDER WILLEM I

DATED: 1574
INSCRIBED: Prins van O. (below his coat of arms); DRIE DINGEN IS EEN GROOT BEHAGEN LIEFDE DES NAESTEN, EENDRACHT DER BROEDERS EN DAT MAN EN WIJF WEL OVER EEN DRAGHEN
Silver and boxwood: length 21.5 cm

The richly carved and decorated knife and sheath bears the coat of arms of the Prince and the insignia of the Order of the Golden Fleece. The maxim engraved on the border of the sheath reads: Three things are very pleasant, love of neighbor, harmony between brothers, and a good relationship between man and wife. The third part of the maxim seems rather strange if one realizes that the Prince had been divorced in 1571 and had not yet remarried.

STICHTING HISTORISCHE VERZAMELINGEN VAN HET HUIS VAN ORANJE NASSAU

3 BINDING WITH COLORED COAT OF ARMS OF STADHOLDER WILLEM I

Second half of the 16th century
INSCRIBED: LHeptameron
BINDING: brown calf, gold tooled and colored in red, gold, and blue; back renewed: 23.5 x 15.7 cm
CONTENTS: Marguerite de Valois, Royne de Navarre, *L'Heptaméron des nouvelles remis en son vray ordre* . . . , par Claude Gruget, Paris: B. Prevost, 1559

Both covers are decorated with the crowned and colored coat of arms of the Prince, with the insignia of the Order of the Golden Fleece. Very little can be learned about the library of the Prince because there is no inventory known. This volume, the hymnal (no. 4), and an armorial made for the Prince in 1556 (Royal Library, inv. no. 76F4) are the only books now known to have belonged to his library.

LIT: D. F. Scheurleer, "Twee boeken uit de bibliotheek van Prins Willem I," *Je Maintiendrai, een boek over Nassau en Oranje*, Leiden, 1905, I, 177
PROV: Ant. W. M. Mensing, Amsterdam
ROYAL LIBRARY, THE HAGUE, INV. NO. 341A23

4 HYMNAL DEDICATED TO STADHOLDER WILLEM I AND CHARLOTTE OF BOURBON

By CHARLES DE NAVIÈRES (1544–1616)
Printed by CHRISTOFLE PLANTIN, Antwerp
DATED: 1579
BINDING: calf, gold tooled: 17.1 x 11.2 cm

CONTENTS: *Les Cantiqves Saints, mis en vers François, partie sus chants nouueaux, & partie sus ceux d'aucuns Psalmes*, par Ch. De Navieres, S. G., Anvers, De l'Imprimerie de Christofle Plantin, Inprimeur de sa Majesté. MDLXXIX.

Both covers are tooled with the crowned coat of arms of the Prince and the insignia of the Order of the Golden Fleece. The dedication by the author, Charles de Navières, fills the first six pages of the volume. The book contains 22 hymns, the Lord's Prayer, the Creed, the Decalogue, and a Communion hymn. Music is added to the first stanza of each of the hymns. The privilege, printed on the last page but one, was granted on 7 November 1578.

LIT: D. F. Scheurleer, "Twee boeken uit de bibliotheek van Prins Willem I," *Je Maintiendrai, een boek over Nassau en Oranje*, Leiden, 1905, I, 173–177

H. M. THE QUEEN

5 LETTER FROM STADHOLDER WILLEM I TO JULIANA OF STOLBERG

SIGNED: Wilhelm, Printz zu Uranien

TEXT:

Mein gantz underthenigen dienst und was ich mehr liebs und guts vermag zuvor.

Wolgeborne freuntliche hertz alle liebste Frau Mutter,

Ich kan E.L. niet verhalten, wie mich das feber vor etliche dagen hat angestossen, dermassen, das ich ein dach sieben odder acht zu bett gelegen bin, aber, Got hab lob, bin widerumb frisch und gesundt. Dieselbige kranckeit hat der massen regniert, das von meinen kindren und haussgesinne über die fufzich dieselbige kranckeit haben gehabt, aber alle widerumb in gutter gesunthait, darum das Gott zu dancken ist, das niemants gestorben ist.

Was die sachen in dissen landen angehet, sein mihr [wir *throughout*] noch in ainem wesen, so dieff im krieg als mihr je gewesen sein; heut gewinnen mir, morgen verlieren mihr, dermassen das der feint noch wenich fortell auf uns hat. Es were wol zu wunschen, das es Gott die genad wolt thun, und uns ainen gutten friden wolt geben, sehe aber noch wenich hoffenung, dan alle die mittel, die man uns anbeut, das ist das mir Gottes wort sollen verlassen, welges dan, Gott hab lob, niemants gern thun wil, sonder liber das eusterste daran zu wagen dan den schatz zu verlieren.

Ich bitt E.L. gantz dienstlich, Sie wollen mir nit vor ubel auff nemen, das ich E.L. in so lang niett geschriben hab, dan hab befolen meiner dochter Maria, das sie E.L. alweg von unserem zustandt sol verwittigen. Ich wais, E.L. sollen ein mitlaiden mit mihr haben, wan Sie solte sehn, wie ich mit grossen sachen alle dach bemuht bin; nuhn Got, der wert es einmal besseren und mihr die genad thun, das ich balt E.L. einmal widerumb mach sehen, warzu ich dan ein sonderlich verlangen hab.

Hiemit wil ich E.L. in den schirm und schutz des Almechtigen bevolen haben und bin derselben die zeit meins lebens underthenigen dienst zu leisten allezeit willich und bereit.

Datum Antroff den 8ten Juny aº 1580.

E.L. underthenichster gantz gehorsamer sohn die zeit meins lebens

Wilhelm, Printz zu Uranien

MEASUREMENTS: 30.5 x 21 cm

The Prince tells his mother he has recovered from an illness which kept him in bed for seven or eight days. The Provinces are still at war and the Prince does not expect that there will be peace quickly. He wishes God will grant him the opportunity to see his mother soon. (Unfortunately this hope was not realized because Juliana van Stolberg died on 18 June of the same year.)

LIT: *Prins Willem van Oranje, Brieven,* uitgekozen en toegelicht door M. W. Jurriaanse, Middelburg, 1933, 164–168
H. M. THE QUEEN

6 EDICT PROCLAIMED BY KING PHILIP II

DATED: 11 September 1580
Printed by IAN SCHOEFFER, 's Hertogenbosch
Pamphlet, 16 pages: 20.5 x 15 cm
TITLE: *Ban / ende edict . . . ,* M.D.LXXX. Tot Tshertogenbossche by Ian Schoeffer.
Front cover printed with the coat of arms of King Philip II

In this proclamation of outlawry Philip II accuses Willem I of high treason and authorizes anyone to "injure, offend, and send him to eternity," offering a reward of 25,000 ducats and a title of nobility.

LIT: W. P. C. Knuttel, *Catalogus van de pamfletten-verzameling berustende in de Koninklijke Bibliotheek,* 1889–1910, no. 527
RIJKSMUSEUM PALEIS HET LOO, APELDOORN, INV. NO. A303
On loan from the Vereniging Oranje Nassau Museum

7 DEFENSE AND JUSTIFICATION OF STADHOLDER WILLEM I

DATED: 1581
Printed by CHARLES SILVIUS
TITLE: *Apologie / ofte Verantwoordinghe . . . Heeren Wilhelms van Godes ghenade Prince van Orangien . . .* By Charles Silvius / ghesworen Drucker der Statenslandts van Hollandt.
M.D.LXXXI.
Bound with a letter of the Prince to the Kings and Potentates of Christianity, dated 4 February 1581; a letter to the States-General, dated 13 December 1580; the answer of the States-General, dated 17 December 1580; a letter of the Prince to the States-General, dated 25 January 1581; a letter of King Philip II to the Prince, dated 1 August 1566; and the edict
BINDING: brown marbled paper, calf back, 18th century, 208 pages: 19 x 13.5 cm
SHOWN HERE: pages 16 and 17, the coat of arms of the Prince, and the first page of the Defense.

This Defense is the answer of the Prince to the edict issued by King Philip II. He presented it to the States-General on 13 December 1580.

RIJKSMUSEUM PALEIS HET LOO, APELDOORN, INV. NO. B282
On loan from the Vereniging Oranje Nassau Museum

8 MOTHER-OF-PEARL PORTRAIT MEDALLION OF STADHOLDER WILLEM I

By JEAN DE MONTFORT (Brussels, active 1595 – 1649)
SIGNED: I.M.F.
DATED: 1611
INSCRIBED: GVILEL. D.G. PR. AVRICAE CO. NASSAV. 1579. AET. 46.
Mother-of-pearl in gold frame: diameter 4 cm

The Prince wears armor and a sash. The portrait is copied from a medal made by Coenraad Bloc (Gent? 1550– ?) in 1577 with the portraits of the Prince and Charlotte of Bourbon (Van Loon, I, 240).

PROV: Prince Alexander of the Netherlands (1851–1884)
STICHTING HISTORISCHE VERZAMELINGEN VAN HET HUIS VAN ORANJE NASSAU

9 BUST OF STADHOLDER WILLEM I

By or after HENDRICK DE KEYSER (Utrecht 1565 – 1621 Amsterdam)
First quarter of the 17th century
Gilded wood, foot renewed: 58 x 48 x 30 cm

The bust is very similar to the bronze statue on the tomb of Willem I in the New Church in Delft. The commission to design a tomb for the Prince was given by the States-General of the Republic to Hendrick de Keyser in 1614. It was not completed until 1621. The members of the family of Orange Nassau have been buried in the crypt under the tomb from that time on.

There are two statues of the Prince on the tomb. One is made of bronze, of the Prince in armor, seated. The other one shows the Prince lying in state. Part of the tomb can be seen on the painting by Hendrick Cornelisz van Vliet (no. 98).

According to an eighteenth-century inventory (The Hague, Algemeen Rijksarchief, Nassause Domeinraad, inv. no. 1796), the gilded wooden bust, described as a "buste de bois bronzé sur un pied de marbre," stood in "la grande salle" of Huis ten Bosch, the palace built by Frederik Hendrik and Amalia van Solms. Queen Wilhelmina kept it in her study in the palace Het Loo.

There are two similar busts in gilded terra cotta, one in Delft in the Museum Het Prinsenhof (on loan from the Mauritshuis, The Hague, inv. no. 362); the other one in Amsterdam, Rijksmuseum (inv. no. NM5757). Also in the Rijksmuseum is a terra cotta model of the head only (inv. no. 1432a,b).

LIT: E. Neurdenburg, *Hendrick de Keyser, beeldhouwer en bouwmeester van Amsterdam*, Amsterdam, [1930]; E. Neurdenburg, *De zeventiende eeuwse beeldhouwkunst in de Noordelijke Nederlanden*, Amsterdam, 1948, 49, 52, 54, pls. 16–28; cat. *Herdenkingstentoonstelling Unie van Utrecht, 1579–1979*, Utrecht (Centraal Museum), 1979, no. VIII, 14a
STICHTING HISTORISCHE VERZAMELINGEN VAN HET HUIS VAN ORANJE NASSAU

10 THE SONS OF STADHOLDER WILLEM I, PRINCE OF ORANGE, AND THEIR COUSINS THE COUNTS OF NASSAU, ON HORSEBACK

Studio of ADRIAEN PIETERSZ VAN DE VENNE (Delft 1589 – 1662 The Hague)
Panel: 76.5 x 134 cm

In the first row, left to right, Prince Maurits (1567–1625), Stadholder of the central provinces of Holland, Zeeland, Utrecht, Gelderland, and Overijssel; Prince Philips Willem (1554–1618); and the future Stadholder, Prince Frederik Hendrik (1584–1647). In the second row between Maurits and Philips Willem: Willem Lodewijk, Count of Nassau (1560–1620), Stadholder of the northern provinces of Friesland, Groningen, and Drente; and on the extreme left his younger brother and successor, Count Ernst Casimir (1573–1632). The other five figures of their suite are painted too sketchily to be identified.

The style of painting is close to that of Van de Venne. The composition is related to the engraving *Nassovij Proceres* (The Prominent Nassaus) of 1621 by Willem Jacobsz Delff (1589–1662) after Van de Venne, with ten figures on horseback (Van Someren, I, no. 118), of which many copies were painted—cf. also the version with eleven figures on horseback including Frederick V, Elector of the Palatinate and King of Bohemia (1596–1632), nephew of the Princes of Orange; Amsterdam, Rijksmuseum, inv. no. A445. It is evident that the painting, which may be dated ca. 1620, does not represent a real cavalcade, but rather a group composed by the painter, based on portraits of the different persons, most of them by Michiel Jansz van Miereveld (1567–1641).

LIT: A. Staring, "De prinsen van Oranje. Toegeschreven aan Paulus van Hillegaert," *Jaarverslag Vereeniging "Oranje Nassau Museum,"* 1928, The Hague, 1929, 37–38
RIJKSMUSEUM PALEIS HET LOO, APELDOORN, INV. NO. A866
On loan from the Vereniging Oranje Nassau Museum

PHILIPS WILLEM

Prince of Orange, Count of Nassau

PHILIPS WILLEM was born in 1554, the eldest son of Willem I, Prince of Orange (1533–1584), and Anna of Egmond, Countess of Buren (1533–1558). At the age of thirteen, during his studies at the University of Leuven, he was arrested by his father's opponent, the Duke of Alva (1507–1582), Spanish Governor of the Netherlands (1567–1572). He was brought as a hostage to Spain, where he was educated as a Roman Catholic prince at the court of Philip II. Eighteen years later in 1595 he was permitted to return to the Southern Netherlands, where he lived in the family palace in Brussels. In 1608 he married Eleonora, Princess of Bourbon-Condé (1587–1619). In the same year he made efforts towards an armistice between the Dutch Republic and Spain, which was achieved during 1609–1612. In 1609 he also took possession of his ancestral castle in Breda in the Northern Netherlands. At his death in 1618 he left extensive properties and many art treasures both in Brussels and Breda.

LIT: Drossaers en Lunsingh Scheurleer, I, 91–166

11 PHILIPS WILLEM, PRINCE OF ORANGE, COUNT OF NASSAU

Studio of MICHIEL JANSZ VAN MIEREVELD (Delft 1567 – 1641 Delft)
Copper: 21.3 x 15.9 cm

A version, probably from the Van Miereveld studio, of which a signed original exists in The Hague, Mauritshuis (inv. no. 98, copper 28×23 cm), and another much enlarged and also signed version with the Prince in three-quarter length in Amsterdam, Rijksmuseum (inv. no. A256, canvas 122×106 cm). Philips Willem wears the Order of the Golden Fleece, conferred upon him by Philip III, King of Spain, in 1599. The portrait may be dated in the first years of the seventeenth century, probably before the Prince's marriage in 1608.

PROV: S. Nystad Oude Kunst, The Hague, 1962; Vereniging Oranje Nassau Museum, 1962
RIJKSMUSEUM PALEIS HET LOO, INV. NO. A3605
On loan from the Vereniging Oranje Nassau Museum

STADHOLDER MAURITS

Prince of Orange, Count of Nassau

BORN IN 1567, the second son of Willem I, Prince of Orange (1533–1584), and Anna, Princess of Saxony (1544–1577). He studied classics and mathematics at the University of Leiden, 1583–1584, before he succeeded his father as Stadholder of the provinces of Holland and Zeeland. In 1590 he also became Stadholder of Utrecht, Gelderland, and Overijssel, and after 1620 of Groningen and Drente as well. As Captain-General of the United Provinces, Maurits developed into an important strategist. He reformed the army, introduced the engineers into it, and founded a military school under the direction of Simon Stevin (1548–1620), his teacher and adviser in the art of fortification. Many foreign officers came to the Netherlands to receive their training in his army. His best-known feats of arms were the conquests of Breda in 1590 and Groningen in 1594, and the battles of Turnhout (1597) and Nieuwpoort (1600) against Albrecht, Archduke of Austria (1559–1621), Spanish Governor of the Netherlands after 1595. The Prince died in 1625, shortly after the end of the hard-won "Twelve Years' Armistice" (1609–1621) and was succeeded by his younger brother Frederik Hendrik.

12   BINDING FOR STADHOLDER MAURITS

Parchment, gold tooled, gilt edges: 20.8 x 14.5 x 4.4 cm
CONTENTS: Iohan Sems en Jan Pietersz. Dou., *Practijck des lantmetens* . . . Van nieus ghecomponeert ende in druck uyt ghegheven door –. Ghedruckt tot Leyden by Jan Bouwentsz. 1600; Iohan Sems ende Ian Pietersz. Dou. *Van het gebruyck der geometrijsche instrumenten*. Van nieuws ghecomponeert ende in druck uyt ghegheven door –. Ghedruckt tot Leyden by Jan Bouwentsz. 1600 [Iohan Sems and Jan Pietersz. Dou., *Practice of Land Surveying* . . . , printed by Jan Bouwentsz., Leiden, 1600; and Iohan Sems and Ian Pietersz. Dou., *The Use of Geometrical Instruments*, printed by Jan Bouwentsz., Leiden, 1600]
Printed dedication in first book: Mauritz geboren Prince van Orangien
Printed dedication in second book: VVilhelm Ludvvich Grave tot Nassauww

Both covers are tooled with the coat of arms of Prince Maurits, with lines, bands of oakleaves, and ornaments in the corners. In 1608 Abraham, Viscount of Dohna, made a catalogue of the library of the Prince, which then contained 403 books. About seventy-five books concerned military science, fortification, architecture, mathematics, and surveying. Willem Lodewijk, Count of Nassau (1560–1620), to whom

the second book is dedicated, was a cousin of Prince Maurits and Stadholder of
Friesland and Groningen and Drente.

LIT: *Supellectilem librariam sub sereness.is de stirpe Nassauia Arausii Principibus in ordines
digessit Constantinus Hugenius*, 1686, 195, no. 1944 (manuscript, Royal Library, The Hague,
78D14); *Catalogue des livres de la bibliothèque de S.A.S. Frédéric Henri, Prince d'Orange . . .*,
The Hague, 95, no. 503; *De Oranje Nassau boekerij en de Oranje-penningen in de Koninklijke
bibliotheek en in het Koninklijk Penningkabinet te 's Gravenhage*, Haarlem, 1898, 25, no. 91;
71, no. 225
PROV: Libraries of Prince Maurits and the Princes of Orange
ROYAL LIBRARY, THE HAGUE, 145D19 (1,2)

13 BEAKER WITH THE COAT OF ARMS OF STADHOLDER MAURITS

DATED: 1594
INSCRIBED: TANDEM FIT SVRCVLVS ARBOR / JE MAINTIENDRAY NASSAV
Glass, diamond-point engraved: height 15 cm

The beaker is engraved with the coat of arms of the Prince with a marquis' crown
and a cut oak of which the trunk is putting forth a shoot, symbolizing the personal
device of Prince Maurits, *tandem fit surculus arbor*, "the twig at length becomes a
tree." The same motif is noted on a "flute" glass in the Wilfred Buckley Collection
(Wilfred Buckley, *European Glass*, London, 1926, no. 57A) and on a roemer in Amsterdam, Rijksmuseum, dated 1606.

The device *Je Maintiendrai Nassau* ("I will maintain, Nassau") was borne by the
Stadholders Willem I and Maurits. It had been derived from the device of the family
of Chalon (*Je Maintiendrai Chalon*), of which Willem I became the heir after the
death of his cousin René of Chalon (1519–1544). The device *Je Maintiendrai* without
Nassau was used by Stadholder Fredrik Hendrik and by the members of the family
of Orange Nassau from that time on.

PROV: presented to King Willem III in 1861 by J. Nederveen Pieterse (1810–1869),
Chief Constable, Delfshaven
H. M. THE QUEEN

14 STADHOLDER MAURITS

By MICHIEL JANSZ VAN MIEREVELD (Delft 1567 – 1641 Delft)
SIGNED: M. Miereveld
Panel: 41 x 54 cm

This painting by Miereveld, who executed many portraits for the Princes Maurits
and Frederik Hendrik and their court, can be dated on the basis of a smaller version

of it, signed and dated "Ætatis 49 1617" (The Hague, Mauritshuis, inv. no. 99, 28×23 cm). Another version, enlarged as a full-length state portrait, is signed but not dated (Amsterdam, Rijksmuseum, inv. no. A255, 221.5×146 cm). The portrait of Prince Maurits is well known through many copies.

STICHTING HISTORISCHE VERZAMELINGEN VAN HET HUIS VAN ORANJE NASSAU

15   HUNTING HORN PRESENTED TO STADHOLDER MAURITS

DATED: 1618
Silver-mounted horn: length 52 cm; diameter 13 cm

The horn is engraved with the coat of arms of the Prince and the insignia of the Order of the Garter granted to him in 1613, and with armorial trophies and canons.

PROV: C. M. de Jong van Rodenburgh, Haarlem
H. M. THE QUEEN

16   SILVER PORTRAIT PLAQUE OF STADHOLDER MAURITS

By SIMON DE PASSE (Cologne ca. 1595 – 1647 Copenhagen)
SIGNED: (reverse) Simon Passaeus sculpsit Lo[ndon]
INSCRIBED: (obverse) ILL: ET: EXC: MAURITIUS PRI: AUR: CO: NAS: CAT: MU: L: B: BR: DI: GR: etc. MARC: VE: VL: BUR: ANT: etc. AU. PER: EQ: IMP: et CAP: G: EXE: POS: D:D: OR: FOE: BEL: GUB: GEL: HOLL: ZEL: WE: ULT: TRAN: (reverse, on banderoles) JE MAINTIENDRAI NASSAU, tandem fit surculus arbor, HONI: SOIT: QVI: MAL. Y: PENSE
Silver, oval: 6.1 x 4.9 cm

The obverse is engraved with a portrait of Prince Maurits wearing armor and a sash. The engraving is similar to the portrait by Michiel Jansz van Miereveld (compare no. 14), which was frequently copied in prints. The reverse is engraved with the crowned coat of arms of the Prince, with the insignia of the Order of the Garter, his personal device, and the device of the Princes of Orange.

The inscription indicates that the plaque may be dated between 1618 and 1620. Maurits is described as Prince of Orange and Count of Buren, titles he inherited from his elder brother in 1618, and not yet as Stadholder of the provinces of Groningen and Drente, which he became in 1620. This date agrees also with the signature, since Simon de Passe lived in London from 1615 until 1622.

Similar plaques are in London, British Museum, and The Hague, Royal Cabinet of Coins.

LIT: J. W. Frederiks, *Dutch Silver*, The Hague, II, 1958, no. 82, pl. 19
H. M. THE QUEEN

17 STADHOLDER MAURITS LYING IN STATE

By ADRIAEN PIETERSZ VAN DE VENNE (Delft 1589 – 1662 The Hague)
SIGNED AND DATED: ADr: v: Venne, fecit 1625
Copper: 7.8 x 11.8 cm

The fifty-eight-year-old Stadholder is lying in a state bed wearing a gold-embroidered robe and a lace-trimmed bonnet of the same red color as the hangings and the counterpane. The fur collar is wrapped around the white ruff of his suit.

A preparatory drawing exists in Amsterdam, Rijksmuseum (Prentenkabinet, inv. no. A1259, 8.1 × 11.8 cm). The composition was used for an enlarged representation of the complete death chamber with mourners, the princely coat of arms, and the floating figure of Fame, which was engraved by Jan Hendriksz Verstraelen, active in Amsterdam 1614–1634 (F. Muller, I, 1533; 17.1 × 28.3 cm, signed: "Adr. vande Venne Invent. et excud. Hagae; J. Verstraelen sculpt. 1625"), with a complaint of ninety-two lines by the painter-poet Van de Venne himself.

Two copies, not signed or dated, are in Amsterdam, Rijksmuseum (inv. no. A446), and Cracow, Poland, Wawel Museum.

LIT: cat., *Tentoonstelling ter gelegenheid van de Inhuldiging van Hare Majesteit Koningin Wilhelmina*, Amsterdam (Rijksmuseum), 1898, no. 263
PROV: coll. M. Maulde de la Clavière, Paris; auction, Paris, Couturier & Nicolay, 6 April 1978, no. 25; Stichting 't Konings Loo
RIJKSMUSEUM PALEIS HET LOO, APELDOORN, INV. NO. KL45

STADHOLDER FREDERIK HENDRIK

Prince of Orange, Count of Nassau

FREDERIK HENDRIK was born in 1584 as the third and youngest son of Prince Willem I and of his fourth consort, Louise (1555–1620), daughter of the French Admiral Gaspard of Coligny (1519–1572), one of the leaders of the Huguenots. His godfathers were Frederick II, King of Denmark (1534–1588), and Henry of Navarre, the future King Henry IV of France (1553–1610). Frederik Hendrik was only six months old when his father was assassinated. He was educated by his French mother and stayed at the court of Henry IV during the year 1597. At the age of fifteen he joined the army of the Dutch Republic, trained by his brother Stadholder Prince Maurits. In 1625 he married the German Countess Amalia of Solms-Braunfels (1602–1675) and in the same year he succeeded Maurits as Prince of Orange and Stadholder of the provinces of Holland, Zeeland, Utrecht, Gelderland, and Overijssel; in 1640 he was also appointed Stadholder of Groningen and Drente. In 1637 he received the title of Highness from Louis XIV of France. As Captain-General of the United Provinces he captured many important cities from the Spaniards between 1627 and 1645. Stadholder Frederik Hendrik and Princess Amalia lived in a regal manner and built several palaces, of which Huis ten Bosch near The Hague still stands and is in use as a royal residence. Their court was a center of artistic life in the Northern Netherlands.

In addition to the building of palaces, Frederik Hendrik and his wife made a vast collection of paintings and art objects of which we can get an impression from the detailed inventories of 1632 and 1654/68. Most of the paintings in the collection were by contemporary painters from the Northern as well as the Southern Netherlands. The presence of paintings by Rembrandt, Jan Lievens, and Rubens must be ascribed to the influence of Constantijn Huygens (1596–1687), the secretary of Frederik Hendrik, who admired these artists and sometimes acted, as we know from the letters by Rembrandt (see no. 24), as an intermediary. According to the Dutch laws of inheritance, by which maternal possessions were inherited only by daughters, the collection was divided among the four daughters of Frederik Hendrik and Amalia after Amalia's death in 1675. Frederik Hendrik died in 1647 and was succeeded by his only son, Prince Willem II (1626–1650).

LIT: Th. H. Lunsingh Scheurleer, "De stadhouderlijke verzamelingen," *150 jaar Koninklijk Kabinet van Schilderijen, Koninklijke Bibliotheek, Koninklijk Penningkabinet,* The Hague, 1967, 14–16; Drossaers en Lunsingh Scheurleer, I, 179–296

18 BINDING WITH WRITTEN CHRONOGRAM

Dutch, 1629
INSCRIBED: (written on lower cover): Anns[?] VIVat FreDerICVs AraVsIonensIVM
BINDING: white vellum, gold-tooled; smooth spine, with outlined panels: 34.7 x 22.4 x 0.9 cm
CONTENTS: Caspar Barlaeus, Sylvae, *Ducis obsidio, perfecta . . . cura et ductu Illustriss. Principis Frederici Henrici . . . Praecedit ad eundem Principem Panegyricus . . .* Lugduni Batavorum. G. Basson, 1629

The large capitals in the device ViVat FreDerICVs AraVsIonensIVM ("Long live Frederik of Orange") form the year 1629 (MDCVVVVVIIII). The garland of leaves is used on other bindings in the library of Stadholder Frederik Hendrik. It is very similar to the wreath on a binding made for Marguerite de Valois, now in The Pierpont Morgan Library (H. M. Nixon, *Sixteenth-Century Gold-Tooled Bookbindings in The Pierpont Morgan Library*, New York, 1971, no. 52a) and is perhaps originally a French motif.

LIT: *Supellectilem librariam sub sereness.is de stirpe Nassauia Arausii Principibus in ordines digessit Constantinus Hugenius,* 1686, 107, nos. 694–695 (manuscript, Royal Library, The Hague, 78D14); *150 jaar Koninklijk Kabinet van Schilderijen, Koninklijke Bibliotheek, Koninklijk Penningkabinet, Herdenkingstentoonstelling in het Mauritshuis,* The Hague, 1966, no. 47
PROV: Library of Prince Frederik Hendrik
ROYAL LIBRARY, THE HAGUE, INV. NO. 764A18

19 PORTRAIT OF STADHOLDER FREDERIK HENDRIK ENGRAVED ON MOTHER-OF-PEARL

Dutch, ca. 1630
Mother-of-pearl inlay in ebony: 49 x 36.5 cm, eight-sided frame

The Prince is represented as the defender of the Republic, holding in his left hand the coats of arms of the provinces and a bundle of arrows representing the seven United Provinces. The portrait is copied from a print designed by Adriaen van de Venne and engraved by Willem Outgersz Akersloot (active after 1624), issued in 1628. In the background of the print, the court of the government buildings of Het Binnenhof at The Hague is visible with groups of people (Van Someren, no. 241). In another version of the print, dated 1629, Het Binnenhof is replaced by the siege of 's Hertogenbosch, and the coats of arms of the provinces by those of the towns and villages captured in the same year (Van Someren, no. 242). The companion piece of these prints is a portrait of Amalia van Solms with Prince Willem II and Princess Louise Henriette. The small figures engraved on the mother-of-pearl are copied from these prints.

The inlay of engraved mother-of-pearl was used not only for decoration in Holland during the seventeenth century but also to make works of art like this portrait. The background consisted usually of a black material like ebony, black marble, or schist. Too few signed examples are known to make attribution to an artist possible.

LIT: *Jaarverslag Rijksmuseum Paleis Het Loo, 1973*, The Hague, 1975, 5; *Oude Kunst- en Antiekbeurs*, Delft (Stedelijk Museum Het Prinsenhof), 1973, 34
PROV: collection Lord Wharton (1941)
RIJKSMUSEUM PALEIS HET LOO, APELDOORN, INV. NO. RLI4

20 STADHOLDER FREDERIK HENDRIK

By GERARD VAN HONTHORST (Utrecht 1590 – 1656 Utrecht)
SIGNED AND DATED: GHonthorst. fe. 1631
Canvas: 73.4 x 60 cm

According to Tiethoff-Spliethoff, the first life-size profile-portrait was introduced into the Northern Netherlands by Honthorst after his stay in Italy and England. It followed the tradition of the classical portraits of Roman emperors on coins, which was revived in Italy during the Renaissance. After his first portrait Honthorst painted at least three other state portraits of Frederik Hendrik, all of them, like this one, with a matching portrait of Princess Amalia.

The painting is mentioned in the inventory of the palace Noordeinde, The Hague, of 1632 as: "A painting of His Excellency, painted in profile by Hondthorst, in a frame of ebony" (Drossaers en Lunsingh Scheurleer, I, 189, no. 186).

LIT: cat. London 1950, no. 14; H. Braun, *Gerard und Willem van Honthorst*, Göttingen, 1966, 236, no. 89; M. E. Tiethoff-Spliethoff, "De portretten van stadhouder Frederik Hendrik," *Jaarboek Centraal Bureau voor Genealogie, 1978*, The Hague, 1978, 107–110
STICHTING HISTORISCHE VERZAMELINGEN VAN HET HUIS VAN ORANJE NASSAU

21 STADHOLDER FREDERIK HENDRIK LEADING THE SIEGE OF 'S HERTOGENBOSCH IN 1629

By PAULUS VAN HILLEGAERT (Amsterdam 1595/6 – 1640 Amsterdam)
SIGNED AND DATED: Pouwels van Hilligaert Ao.1631
Panel: 57.5 x 104 cm

The siege beginning on 30 April and ending with the capitulation on 14 September was one of the most important feats of arms of Frederik Hendrik, through which he held off the advance of the Spanish army into the Northern Netherlands. The success of the siege shifted the balance of power in the war of independence and gave rise to expectations of an armistice, which, however, did not materialize at this time. 's Hertogenbosch was forced to surrender by draining the moats and the marshy surroundings of the city through a method invented by the hydraulic engineer Jan Adriaansz Leeghwater (1575-1650). By means of twenty-three watermills, the watercourses of the river Dommel (visible in the middle ground behind the clumps of trees) and the river Aa (it may be seen at the right of the city beneath the horizon) were joined in one wide stream outside the fortifications built by Frederik Hendrik (shown on the extreme right). The total length of his fortifications around the city, consisting of an inner offensive line and an outer line of defence, was forty kilometers. The enormous expense of this siege was covered through the capture of the Spanish Plate Fleet the previous year by the Dutch Admiral Piet Heyn (1577–1629).

In the first row of the cavalcade in the left-hand corner, from right to left: Frederik Hendrik as Captain-General: Crown Prince Frederick of Denmark, the future King Frederick III (1609–1670), who arrived at the end of July and assisted at the surrender of the city; and Ernst Casimir, Count of Nassau (1573–1632), Stadholder of Friesland, cousin of Frederik Hendrik and his Second-in-Command.

The view of the city is taken from the south. In the foreground is the church of the village Vught.

Another version, not signed or dated, exists in Amsterdam, Rijksmuseum (inv. no. A848, canvas, 107×178 cm).

LIT: A. Staring, "Het beleg van Den Bosch in 1629. Door P. van Hilligaert," *Jaarverslag 1926 Vereniging "Oranje Nassau Museum,"* The Hague, 1927, 21; cat. *Het Beleg van 's Hertogenbosch in 1629*, 's Hertogenbosch (Noordbrabants Museum), 1979

RIJKSMUSEUM PALEIS HET LOO, APELDOORN, INV. NO. A5
On loan from the Vereniging Oranje Nassau Museum

22 MEDAL COMMEMORATING THE CAPTURE OF BREDA IN 1637

By JOHANNES LOOFF (master in Middelburg 1627 – 1651 Middelburg)
SIGNED: (obverse) I.LOOFF.FE.MIDDEL.B.
DATED: (reverse) X. Octob An. M.DC.XXXVII.
INSCRIBED: (obverse) ANTE FAME. AVT ASTU. VI MODO FACTA VIA EST.; (reverse) D.O.M.E. Bredam primo Belgar. in Tyrann. Regem foedere nobilem; mox Mauritianae navis faelicib. insidiis nobiliorem; dein famelica March. Spin. obsidione nobilissimam; tandem ausp. Potentiss. Concord. Belgij Patrum, omnes bellandi gradus transcendens, aperto Marte, gladiata Fr. Henrici, Celsiss. Auria. Pr. dextera Faederatae Patriae, Familiaeque suae restituit; X. Octob An. M.DC.XXXVII. S.P.Q.F.B.
Silver gilt: diameter 6.9 cm

The medal symbolizes the three times Breda had been captured. In 1590 Breda had been taken by Stadholder Maurits, who smuggled soldiers inside the town by hiding them in a peat boat. The Spanish General Ambrogio Spinola (1569–1630) forced the city to surrender by starvation in 1624. The medal ascribes the re-conquest of the city in 1637 to the armed hand of the Prince and the force of arms.

Breda was very important to Stadholder Frederik Hendrik personally because the Barony of Breda was his principal property.

Among the works of Johannes Looff are several medals, three engravings, and an engraved silver dish.

LIT: Van Loon, II, 238, 239; J. W. Frederiks, *Dutch Silver*, The Hague, 1960, vol. III, no. 14
RIJKSMUSEUM PALEIS HET LOO, APELDOORN, INV. NO. AI517
On loan from the Vereniging Oranje Nassau Museum

23 MINIATURE OF STADHOLDER FREDERIK HENDRIK

Attributed to HENRI TOUTIN (Châteaudun 1614 – after 1683 Paris)
Enamel on gold, oval: 4.3 x 3.4 cm
On the back, the crowned monogram HAVOO in enamel

Frederik Hendrik is wearing the blue ribbon of the Order of the Garter, granted to him in 1627. The miniature was painted after the portrait of about 1637 by Gerard van Honthorst (The Hague, Mauritshuis, cat. 1977, no. 104). The monogram at the back signifies H[endrik] A[malia] V[an] [and twice the O for] O[range].

The attribution to the miniaturist, goldsmith, and enameller Toutin is generally accepted. He also made a watch case for Frederik Hendrik in 1641 with allegorical scenes concerning the marriage of his son, Willem II, and Mary Stuart in the same year (Amsterdam, Rijksmuseum, inv. no. NM638).

LIT: cat. Rijksmuseum Amsterdam 1976, 766
ROYAL CABINET OF PAINTINGS, MAURITSHUIS, THE HAGUE
On loan from the Rijksmuseum, Amsterdam, inv. no. A4371

24 LETTER FROM REMBRANDT TO SIR CONSTANTIJN HUYGENS

SIGNED: REMBRANDT
DATED: 12 Januwarij 1639
ADDRESS: Mijn Heer Mijn E Heer van Schuijlemburgh
TEXT: Mijn heer
           Door die grooten lust ende geneegenheijt die ick
           gepleecght hebbe int wel wtvoeren van die twe
           stuckens die sijn Hoocheijt mijn heeft doen maeken
           weesende het een daer dat doode lichaem Chrisstij
           in den graeve gelecht wert ende dat ander
           daer Chrisstus van den doode opstaet dat met
           grooten verschrickinge des wachters. Dees selvij
           twe stuckens sijn door stuijdiose vlijt nu meede
           afgedaen soodat ick nu oock geneegen ben om die
           selvijge te leeveren om sijn Hoocheijt daer meede
           te vermaeken want deesen twe sijnt daer die meeste

ende die naetuereelste beweechgelickheijt in
geopserveert is dat oock de grooste oorsaeck is dat
die selvijge soo lang onder handen sij geweest.
Derhalven soo versouck ick ofte mijn heer sijn Hoocheijt
daer van gelieft te seggen ende oft mijn heer soude
gelieven dat men die twe stuckens eerst tot uwent
ten huijsen bestellen sal gelijck als voormaels
is geschiet. Hiervan ick eerst een letterken tot
antwoort verwachten sal.
Ende om dat mijn heer in deesen saeken voor die 2de maels
bemoijt wert sal oock tot een eerkentenissen
een stuck bij gedaen weesende 10 voeten lanck
ende 8 voeten hooch dat sal mijn heer vereerweerden
in sijnen Huijsen ende met een wensschenden U allen
geluck ende heijl ter saelicheijt Amen.

U E mijns heeren d w enden
geneegen dienaer
Rembrandt

deessen 12 Januwarij
      1639.

[*in the margin*]
Mijn heer ick woon op die binnen emster / thuijs is genaemt die
suijkerbackerrij.

TRANSLATION:

My Lord,

Because of the great zeal and devotion which I exercised in executing well the two pictures which His Highness commissioned me to make—the one being where Christ's dead body is being laid in the tomb and the other where Christ arises from the dead to the great consternation of the guards —these same two pictures have now been finished through studious application, so that I am now also disposed to deliver the same and so to afford pleasure to His Highness, for in these two pictures the greatest and most natural movement [or: most innate emotion] has been expressed, which is also the main reason why they have taken so long to execute.

Therefore I request my lord to be so kind as to inform His Highness of this and whether it would please my lord that the two pictures should first be delivered at your house as was done on the previous occasion. I shall first await a note in answer to this.

And as my lord has been troubled in these matters for the second time, a piece 10 feet long and 8 feet high shall also be added as a token of appreciation, which will be worthy of my lord's house. And wishing you all happiness and heavenly blessings, Amen.

Your lordship, my lord's humble and
devoted servant
Rembrandt

This 12th January
      1639

[*in the margin*] My lord I live on the Binnen Amstel. The house is called the sugar bakery.

[*address*] My Lord
      My noble Lord van Schuylemburgh

MEASUREMENTS: 30 X 21 cm

Only seven letters written by Rembrandt Harmensz van Rijn (1606–1669) are known. They are addressed to Sir Constantijn Huygens (1596–1687), secretary of Prince Frederik Hendrik, who acted as an intermediary in commissioning a series of scenes of the Passion for the Prince. The letters were written between 1636 and 1639.

The paintings consisted of five Passion scenes, which were augmented in 1646 by a *Nativity* and a *Circumcision*. The paintings reached Germany in the eighteenth century either by sale or through inheritance. Except for the *Circumcision*, which is lost, all of the pictures are now in Munich, in the Alte Pinakothek.

The painting mentioned in the letter as a gift to Constantijn Huygens is probably the *Blinding of Samson*, dated 1636, now in the Städtliches Kunstinstitut, Frankfort.

The exact meaning of the word *beweechgelickheijt* (line 13) has caused considerable controversy among art historians.

LIT: H. Gerson, *Seven Letters by Rembrandt*, The Hague, 1961, 33–40; cat. London 1964, no. 355
PROV: anon. sale, Amsterdam, Jeronimo de Vries and others, 30 March – 2 April 1841, no. 67 (sold to Brondgeest, fl111.–); Queen Sophie (1818–1877) or Prince Alexander (1851–1884)
H. M. THE QUEEN

25 MEDAL IN HONOR OF STADHOLDER FREDERIK HENDRIK AND THE MARRIAGE OF THE FUTURE STADHOLDER WILLEM II AND PRINCESS MARY STUART

Dutch, ca. 1642
INSCRIBED: (obverse) LIBERTAS PATRIAE, ME DEFENSORE, TRIUMPHAT, INSIDIATA NIHIL VIS INIMICA NOCET.; (reverse) QUO TE MARS ET AMOR VOCAT INTRA. DIVA VIRETUM HIC LIBERTAS TE GENETRICE FERET.
Silver-gilt: diameter 7.1 cm

As in the portrait engraved on mother-of-pearl (no. 19), Prince Frederik Hendrik is represented as the defender of the Republic, holding the coats of arms of the provinces in his left hand and a sword in his right hand. He is sitting on a throne with his helmeted coat of arms on his right side and vanquished enemies at his feet. The background shows the Prince marching upon a town.

The reverse symbolizes the arrival of Princess Mary (1631–1660) in Holland. Prince Willem II (1626–1650) invites the Princess to enter the *Hortus conclusus* of Holland.

LIT: Van Loon, II, 264, 265
RIJKSMUSEUM PALEIS HET LOO, APELDOORN, INV. NO. A841
On loan from the Vereniging Oranje Nassau Museum

26 BINDING WITH THE COAT OF ARMS OF AMALIA VAN SOLMS

Northern Netherlands, ca. 1660

BINDING: gold-tooled brown morocco, back with five raised bands; the panel is decorated with a fleuron, traces of two clasps: 19.2 x 12.0 x 4.7 cm

CONTENTS: Q. Horatius Flaccus, *Cum commentariis variorum: et scholiis integris J. Bond. Accedunt indices locupletissimi . . . accurante C. Schrevelio.* Lugd. Batavorum, F. Hackius, 1658

Both covers are gold-tooled with the crowned coat of arms of Amalia van Solms as a widow. The coats of arms of the Prince of Orange and the Countess of Solms are impaled. From the ducal coronet hangs a knotted cord, the "cordelière" or "cordon des veuves," which signifies that the bearer of the arms is a widow. The escutcheon on the lower cover is placed upside down. The same tool appears on a cover sold in about 1905 (sale catalogue of English and foreign bindings, London, ca. 1905, no.98) on *Justinus cum notis selectissimis variorum*, editio accuratissima, 8vo, L. and D. Elzevier, Amsterdam, 1659. In the designs by Pieter Post (1608–1669) of the palace Huis ten Bosch, the same coat of arms is placed in the tympana of the façade and on the overmantel in the drawing room.

PROV: S. Bay, 1795 (written on the first pastedown)
LIT: *150 jaar Koninklijk Kabinet van Schilderijen, Koninklijke Bibliotheek, Koninklijk Penningkabinet, Herdenkingstentoonstelling in het Mauritshuis,* The Hague, 1966, no. 241
ROYAL LIBRARY, THE HAGUE, NO. 144C21

27 MARRIAGE LOTTERY OF LOUISE HENRIETTE, PRINCESS OF ORANGE, COUNTESS OF NASSAU

By ADRIAEN PIETERSZ VAN DE VENNE (Delft 1589 – 1662 The Hague)
Panel: 75.5 x 104 cm
SIGNED, vaguely: Adr.v.Venne

Princess Louise Henriette (1627–1677), eldest daughter of Stadholder Frederik Hendrik and Princess Amalia, was important to her family as a pawn on the chessboard of dynastic politics. Her own choice of husband, her cousin Henry Charles de la Tremoille, Prince of Tarente (1620–1672), was not acceptable to her ambitious parents. After negotiations for a marriage with the later Charles II of England (1630–1685) were broken off, she was married to Friederich Wilhelm, Elector of Brandenburg (1620–1688), and from this alliance would come the future Kings of Prussia and Emperors of Germany. It was probably these events which furnished the inspiration for this comic painting with the young Elector waiting for his lot in front of the lottery tent with Amor on top of it. There the lots were drawn from two urns with the inscriptions *siet* (look) and *niet* (not). His lot, the Princess Louise Henriette, is carried to him by two grooms. She is already wearing the diadem, his wedding present, which appears also in the painting of the marriage ceremony on 7 December

1646 by Jan Mijtens (ca. 1614–1670), at Rennes, Musée des Beaux Arts. On the right a less fortunate man tears his hair out in disgust over his fortune: an old crone.

As often in his allegorical scenes and depictions of proverbs in paintings (almost always grisaille) and prints, Van de Venne explains the meaning of this representation by inscriptions in the foreground and on two flags on the tent. In the foreground: Elck moet sijn deel hebben (Everyone gets his share); on the left-hand flag: Die gist, die mist (Guess twice, guess worse). On the right-hand flag the text is illegible.

In the background are the buildings of Het Binnenhof, the residence of the Stadholders and the center of government in The Hague.

There is another version of this painting (with two different principal personages) in The Hague, Gemeente Museum, and a third version with two brides and two candidates (probably Charles II and the future James II of England), dated 1660, in Heidelberg, Kurpfälzisches Museum.

LIT: A. W. J. Mulder, "De huwelijkslotery, Grisaille door Adriaan van de Venne," *Jaarverslag Vereeniging "Oranje Nassau Museum," 1937*, The Hague, 1938, 24, 25
RIJKSMUSEUM PALEIS HET LOO, APELDOORN, INV. NO. A1919
On loan from the Vereniging Oranje Nassau Museum

28 MINIATURE OF ALBERTINE AGNES, PRINCESS OF ORANGE, COUNTESS OF NASSAU

Attributed to DAVID DES GRANGES (London 1611 – 1675 London)
Board, oval: 4.7 x 3.7 cm

Albertine Agnes (1634–1696), fifth daughter of Stadholder Frederik Hendrik and Princess Amalia, married in 1652 her cousin Willem Frederik (1613–1664), Count (in 1652 Prince) of Nassau Dietz, Stadholder of the provinces of Friesland and Groningen and Drente. The direct descendants of this alliance between the branches of Orange Nassau and Nassau Dietz were the Stadholders in the eighteenth century and the Kings and Queens of the Netherlands from the nineteenth century to today. Albertine Agnes had a keen interest in paintings and enlarged the collection she inherited with many purchases of her own.

The miniature may be dated around 1650.

David des Granges, active in London, was probably the pupil of the London miniaturist Peter Oliver (ca. 1595–1647). He worked for Charles I and Charles II and their courts. Des Granges was also an engraver.

LIT: Drossaers en Lunsingh Scheurleer, II, 107–113, 222–224; cat. Rijksmuseum Amsterdam 1976, 755; cat. Mauritshuis The Hague 1977, 282
ROYAL CABINET OF PAINTINGS, MAURITSHUIS, THE HAGUE
On loan from the Rijksmuseum, Amsterdam, inv. no. A4315

29 MINIATURE OF WILLEM FREDERIK, COUNT (LATER PRINCE) OF NASSAU DIETZ

After ADRIAEN HANNEMAN (The Hague 1604 – 1671 The Hague)
Enamel, octagonal: 7 x 6.1 cm

Willem Frederik (1613–1664), son of Ernst Casimir, Count of Nassau Dietz, and Sophia Hedwig, Duchess of Brunswick Wolfenbüttel (cf. no. 31), married in 1652 Albertine Agnes, daughter of the late Stadholder Frederik Hendrik. In the same year Willem Frederik was created Prince. In 1640 he was nominated Stadholder of the province of Friesland and in 1650 of Groningen and Drente. Frederik Hendrik saw him as a rival and a barrier to his own ambition to be Stadholder of all seven provinces, and the two did not get along.

The miniature is painted by an unknown Dutch artist after the portrait made in 1661 by Hanneman (Weimar, Staatliche Kunstsammlungen, Schlossmuseum) and copied by Peter Nason (1612–1688/91) in 1662 (Apeldoorn, Rijksmuseum Paleis Het Loo; on loan from the Royal Cabinet of Paintings, Mauritshuis, The Hague).

The original enameled black frame bears a crowned monogram FWF with two hearts. The skull and bones indicate that the picture was painted after the Prince's death in 1664.

LIT: O. ter Kuile, *Adriaen Hanneman*, Alphen aan de Rijn, 1976, 106, no. 66; cat. Rijksmuseum Amsterdam 1976, 782; cat. Mauritshuis The Hague 1977, 280
ROYAL CABINET OF PAINTINGS, MAURITSHUIS, THE HAGUE
On loan from the Rijksmuseum, Amsterdam, inv. no. A4436

30 CUP AND COVER

By PAULUS VAN VIANEN (Utrecht ca. 1570 – 1613 Prague)
SIGNED AND DATED: S[uae].Caes[aris].M[aiesta]tis avr[ifex] Pavlvs de Viana. Vltraiectensis fe[cit] 1610.
Gold: 19 cm

This, the only known solid gold object by Paulus van Vianen, shows on the body of the cup two scenes of the story of Diana and Actaeon (Ovid, *Metamorphoses*, III, 138). One side shows Diana, recognizable by the crescent on her forehead, throwing water at Actaeon who had been spying on her while she was bathing with her maidens. As soon as he was touched by the water, Actaeon began to change into a stag, and antlers started growing on his head. On the other side of the cup, Actaeon, completely transformed now, is chased by his own companions and dogs, who no longer recognize him. These scenes return with minor modifications on a plaquette of 1612 (Utrecht, Centraal Museum) and on a basin of 1613 (Amsterdam, Rijksmuseum). The outside of the cover is decorated with three cartouches showing Venus and Cupid, Ceres, and Bacchus. The inside of the cover consists of a medallion with an embossed three-quarter-length figure of Heinrich Julius, Duke of Brunswick Wolfenbüttel Lüneburg and (Lutheran) Bishop of Halberstadt (1564–1613), who commissioned the cup. Heinrich Julius married Elisabeth, Princess of Denmark (1573–1625). Their daughter Sophia Hedwig (1592–1642), Consort of Ernst Casimir, Count of Nassau Dietz (1573–1632), inherited the cup after the death of Heinrich Julius. The cup stayed in the family of Nassau Dietz, and by inheritance in the House of Orange Nassau, until 1881 when it came into the possession of the Princes of Wied (see Prov).

On the medallion is the legend: HENRICVS IVLIVS. D[EI] G[RATIA] P[OSTU-LATUS] E[PISCOPUS] H[ALBERSTADTENSIS] D[UX] B[RUNSWIGENSIS] E[T] L[ÜNEBURGENSIS]. Heinrich Julius was a learned humanist, jurist, architect, and man of letters, who wrote many dramas. He was Chancellor of the imperial council at the court of Rudolf II (1552–1612) at Prague, where he died in 1613.

Paulus van Vianen worked as *Kammergoldschmied* to Rudolf II in Prague. Paulus van Vianen and his elder brother Adam (1565–1627) were the most important and famous Dutch silversmiths. In contrast to his brother, Paulus spent most of his life outside the Netherlands. From 1596 to 1601 he worked for the Dukes of Bavaria at Munich and from 1603 onwards at the imperial court at Prague. He also visited Italy (at an unrecorded date). According to Frederiks, "unlike his brother Adam, who developed himself more as a master of ornament than as a portrayer of scenes, the ornamental parts of Paul's works were not intended to be anything but a frame for his figure-subjects. He was one of the greatest masters in the art of embossing and chasing of scenes. His style was entirely pictorial, whereas Adam's became more and more plastic as time went on."

LIT: J. W. Frederiks, *Dutch Silver*, The Hague, I, 1952, 71, 111, 112, 150, 151, no. GG; Drossaers en Lunsingh Scheurleer, II, 93, no. 165; 207, no. 49; 253, no. 79
PROV: through inheritance to Sophia Hedwig (cf. no. 31), the second daughter of the first owner; in the collections of the House of Nassau Dietz; mentioned in inventories of 1681, 1696–1698, and 1702–1708; via Johan Willem Friso (1687–1711), Count of Nassau Dietz, after 1702 Prince of Orange, in the collections of the House of Orange Nassau; through inheritance by Maria, Princess of Orange Nassau (1841–1910), married to Wilhelm, Prince of Wied (1845–1907), in the collection of the House of Wied
FÜRST ZU WIED, NEUWIED, WEST GERMANY

31 SOPHIA HEDWIG, COUNTESS OF NASSAU DIETZ, PORTRAYED AS CARITAS, WITH HER THREE SONS

By PAULUS MOREELSE (Utrecht 1571 – 1638 Utrecht)
SIGNED AND DATED: PMoreelse 1621
Canvas: 140 x 122 cm
INSCRIBED (on the back): CHARITAS no. 154 SOPHIA HEDWICH GEB. H[ERZOGIN].V[ON]. B[RAUNSCHWEIG].G[RÄFIN].Z[U].N[ASSAU].HENRICH G[RAF].Z[U].N[ASSAU].... WILLEM FR[EDERIK].G[RAF].Z[U].N[ASSAU]. MAVRITS G[RAF].Z[U].N[ASSAU].

Sophia Hedwig (1592–1642), daughter of Heinrich Julius, Duke of Brunswick Wolfenbüttel (1564–1613), and Elisabeth, Princess of Denmark (1573–1625), was married in 1607 at age fifteen to Ernst Casimir, Count of Nassau Dietz (1573–1632), cousin of the Stadholders Maurits and Frederik Hendrik. In the year of her marriage, her husband became Fieldmarshal of the United Provinces of the Netherlands and Lieutenant Governor of the province of Gelderland, and three years later also Lieutenant Governor of Utrecht. In 1620 he was appointed Stadholder of Friesland and in 1625 of Groningen and Drente as well. Sophia Hedwig and Ernst Casimir had three sons: Hendrik Casimir I (1612–1640), on the right of his mother, as a boy of nine years; Willem Frederik (1613–1664), standing on the left of his mother, eight years old; Maurits (1619–1628), sitting in the foreground on a cushion. The painting was probably begun in 1620, the last year of Ernst Casimir's office in Utrecht, and finished in 1621.

Moreelse was active in Utrecht as a painter of portraits and genre pictures and also as an architect. He was a pupil of Michiel Jansz van Miereveld (1567–1641) (cf. no. 11 and no 14). In the monumental composition of this painting (so far as we know his only large group portrait) we see Italian influences. He had visited Italy about 1600. His colors are nevertheless typically northern. Represented as Caritas, Sophia Hedwig wears a quasi-oriental costume and jewelled headdress; the two eldest sons wear antique tunics. The costume of the youngest is also adapted to the allegorical theme of the picture; the two strings of pearls around his neck are also found in his earlier portrait by Moreelse (1619). In contrast to this group the figures in the background wear contemporary dress. They are a nurse and a baby thought to be Elisabeth Friso, born on 25 November 1620, perhaps added to the composition while Moreelse was working on the picture.

As part of an inheritance the painting went to Germany in 1698 and it returned to the Netherlands only in 1977 when it was bought by the Rijksmuseum Paleis Het Loo, Apeldoorn. In 1977 the picture was cleaned and the upper part of the headdress, the balcony, and the empty escutcheon over the entrance of the building in the background were re-discovered. These details were already known from the copy in the Royal Palace at Amsterdam and the version by Wybrand Symonsz de Geest (1592 – after 1667) at Leeuwarden, Fries Museum. In an 1726 inventory of the castle Oranienstein, near Dietz, West Germany, another copy is mentioned, this one by Louis Volders, active in Friesland from 1691 to 1700.

LIT: C. H. de Jonge, *Paulus Moreelse portret- en genreschilder te Utrecht 1517–1638*, Assen, 1939, 23, 24, 86, pl. III; cat. *Les plus belles oeuvres des collections de la Côte d'Or*, Dijon, Musée des Beaux-Arts, 1958, no. 30, fig. 6; Drossaers en Lunsingh Scheurleer, II, 109, no. 806; 208, no. 67; 371, no. 329
PROV: collection of Albertine Agnes, Countess of Nassau Dietz, Princess of Orange Nassau, to 1696; inherited by her granddaughter Albertine Johanette, Princess of Saxony-Eisenach (1693-1700). Later: coll. Carl Triepel, to 1874; St. Petersburg, Prince Paul Delaroff, to 1914; Madame D., to 1920; Dijon, Dr. G. Stefanovitch, to 1977; auction, Paris, Ader-Picard, 17 June 1977, no. 148; The Hague, Gallery Hoogsteder; purchased by Rijksmuseum Paleis Het Loo with aid of the Stichting 't Konings Loo, 1977
RIJKSMUSEUM PALEIS HET LOO, APELDOORN, INV. NO. RL451

32 CABINET ON STAND

Antwerp, about 1630
Mahogany with ebony veneer, mounted with silver: 166 x 122 x 44 cm
Thirteen painted panels by FRANS FRANCKEN II (Antwerp 1581 – 1642 Antwerp)

The doors open to a drop-front, which contains six drawers, and three small doors, hiding several small drawers. Cabinet doors, top lid, drawers, and small doors have inset painted panels, all signed, except one (bottom right): *D° Ffranck in f.* The cabinet is richly mounted with ornaments of unmarked embossed silver. The drop-front is decorated with Continental stumpwork panels, showing birds, deer, lions, flowers, and trees worked in gold and silver thread and colored precious stones, on silk.

The subjects illustrated on the panels are scenes from the life of Christ:

top lid (octangular): Mary Magdalen washing Christ's feet (32 x 77 cm)
left outer door (octangular): The multiplication of bread (50 x 38 cm)
right outer door (octangular): The marriage at Cana (50 x 38 cm)
top drawer left: Christ blessing the lame (10 x 24 cm)
top drawer right: The miraculous draught of fishes (10 x 24 cm)
small door left (heptagonal): Christ healing the blind (21 x 16 cm)
small door center (round-headed): Parable of the marriage feast (21 x 16 cm)
small door right (heptagonal): Raising of Lazarus (21 x 16 cm)
bottom drawer left: Christ and the Pharisees (10 x 24 cm)
bottom drawer center: Christ and the woman taken in adultery (10 x 24 cm)
bottom drawer right: Preaching at the seashore (10 x 24 cm)

Pieces like this were the specialty of Antwerp workshops, designed to house collections of jewels, shells, or other precious objects. They were exported all over Europe, and stands were not usually provided; these would be made locally in the country of destination.

Frans Francken II, the best-known artist of the Francken family, specialized in this type of art. From 1606 to 1616, when his father died, he signed his paintings "the younger Frans Francken"; then for ten years he used his own name only; and after that we find his signature "D°Ffranck," the old Frans Francken, to differentiate himself from his son, Frans Francken III.

The cabinet was presented to Queen Wilhelmina by the artist and collector Mr. Willem Hekking (1825–1904) in August 1902.

PROV: Amsterdam: coll. Mrs H. F. V. Usselino-Tollens, to 1866(?); coll. H. C. Tombergh; auction, Ed. Croese, Amsterdam, C. F. Roos & Co., 17 July 1877, no. 16, purchased by W. Hekking for fl3600.–

RIJKSMUSEUM PALEIS HET LOO, APELDOORN, INV. NO. L428
On loan from H. M. the Queen

STADHOLDER WILLEM II

Prince of Orange, Count of Nassau

WILLEM II, Prince of Orange, Count of Nassau, was born in 1626, the only son of Stadholder Frederik Hendrik (1584–1647) and Princess Amalia, who was born Countess of Solms (1602–1675). As a boy he was talented in mathematics and was trained by his father in the army. After lengthy negotiations, in 1641 Frederik Hendrik was successful in marrying Willem to Princess Mary Stuart (1631–1660), daughter of Charles I of England. Willem II succeeded his father in 1647 as Stadholder and Captain-General of the provinces of Holland, Zeeland, Utrecht, Gelderland, Overijssel, and Groningen and Drente. After the fall of his father-in-law in 1649, he tried to support the Stuarts in England. With the States-General, he was in favor of centralization and against the autonomy of the members of the Union, particularly of the most powerful province of Holland. Willem II acquired the hunting lodge Dieren near the Veluwe in Gelderland. After just four years of stadholdership, Willem died in 1650. His only son, William III, was born eight days after his death.

33 PLAN OF THE QUARTERS AT ASSENEDE, 1641, FROM A SKETCHBOOK OF THE FUTURE STADHOLDER WILLEM II

Title of the volume (written on the first folio): Eenige Quartiers en Slagorders onder den Prinsen Van Oranje 1622–1643 enz. [Some quarters and battle-orders of the Princes of Orange, 1622–1643, etc.]

BINDING: 18th-century pasteboard, calf spine with four raised bands, title on 2nd panel, gold on red morocco: VERSCHY[dene] LEGER QUARTI[ers]: 23.4 x 32.2 x 2 cm

CONTENTS: 63 folios: 7 folios with plans of quarters from 1640 to 1643; 8 folios with schematic plans of dispositions of troops; 11 folios with schematic plans of battle-orders from 1614 to 1637; 1 folio with title; and 36 blank folios

SHOWN HERE: folio 4ʳ, plan no. 3: Het Quartier tot Assenede Anno 1641 [The quarter at Assenede Anno 1641]

    Legend: A Huys van syn Hooheyt [His Highness' House, i.e., Prince Frederik
               Hendrik's house]
          B de Gaurdes [The guards]
          C Amonitie [Ammunition]
          D de France trou[pen] [The French troops]
          E de Engelsche tr [The English troops]
          F de Schotse tr [The Scottish troops]
          G baterien [Batteries]
          H Edelmanhuys [The manor house]

The annotations on the plan mention roads to Eselo and Selsaten, and dikes leading to 't Sas, Philippine, and Boucholt.

The first seven plans in the sketchbook, which concern the quarters of Prince Frederik Hendrik's troops in several villages in the period 1640–1643, were probably made on the spot by Prince Willem II. In 1637, when he was only eleven years old, his father sent for him to attend the siege of Breda, and from 1641 the young Prince permanently joined the campaigns. Yet Prince Frederik Hendrik never entrusted him with the supreme command, not even at the end of his life when he himself was too weak to take the command. As Willem II's training had been exclusively military, he was extremely frustrated after the establishment of peace in 1648. Assenede is one of the villages in the southwestern part of the Netherlands in which Frederik Hendrik quartered his troops several times after 1638, vainly attempting to besiege Antwerp.

LIT: *Supellectilem librariam sub sereness.is de stirpe Nassauia Arausii Principibus in ordines digessit Constantinus Hugenius*, 1686, 210, no. 1516 (manuscript, Royal Library, The Hague, 78D14)
PROV: Library of Stadholder Willem II
ROYAL LIBRARY, THE HAGUE, INV. NO. 128A17

34 THE FUTURE STADHOLDER WILLEM II AND HIS BRIDE, PRINCESS MARY STUART

Studio of ANTHONY VAN DYCK (Antwerp 1599 – 1641 London)
Canvas: 182 x 142 cm

This portrait of the young royal couple, standing hand-in-hand, was made on the occasion of their wedding on 12 May 1641. The nine-year-old Princess Mary (1631–1660), eldest daughter of King Charles I, wears the jewels given to her the day after the wedding. According to Gans, the brooch is described in a list of wedding presents of Willem II to his bride as "Une Boëtte de 4 Pierres et une Pendeloque tous diamans à facettes." This brooch was made by Gaspard Duarte (1582–1653), a Spanish emigrant living in Antwerp and court jeweller to Stadholder Frederik Hendrik. The ring is probably the one mentioned by Willem in a letter of 17 May 1641 to his father: "... apres cela je donez la bague à la Princesse; ce n'ettoit point la bague de diamant, mais une bague tout d'or simple, sans emalieuze quelquonque." The Prince, who is nearly fifteen years old, wears the costume made for the festivities by a London tailor.

The debate concerning the authorship of the painting has not been satisfactorily resolved until now. The design is without any doubt Van Dyck's, of whom it is known that he had to paint the wedding portrait. But, as Van Dyck died in the same year, 1641, it was probably finished, or perhaps completely executed, by another artist. As such the names of Adriaen Hanneman (1604–1671) at first and later Peter Lely (1618–

1680) were proposed, but both without convincing arguments for the authorship of this work.

The picture is mentioned 1667 in the palace Huis ten Bosch near The Hague, and as the chimney-piece in the gallery of paintings at Het Loo from 1713 to 1763. Other versions of the subject are known, as are paintings of the bride only and of the head of the Prince (cf. pp. 38–39).

LIT: cat. London 1950, no. 9; cat. London 1964, no. 12; M. H. Gans, *Juwelen en mensen. De geschiedenis van het bijou van 1400 tot 1900, voornamelijk naar Nederlandse bronnen,* Amsterdam, 1961, 96–99; Drossaers en Lunsingh Scheurleer, I, 282, no. 1188, and 677, no. 832; *idem,* II, 640, no. 20; cat. Rijksmuseum Amsterdam 1976, 209

RIJKSMUSEUM, AMSTERDAM, INV. NO. A102

35 MINIATURE OF STADHOLDER WILLEM II

By JEAN PETITOT (Geneva 1607 – 1691 Vevey)
Enamel, oval: 4.4 x 3.5 cm
On the back the crowned monogram WH and four times PO(?)

Petitot made this miniature after the figure of Willem II in the double portrait of him and his wife, Mary Stuart, by Gerard van Honthorst (1590–1656), dated 1647 (Amsterdam, Rijksmuseum, inv. no. A871). The Prince wears the blue ribbon of the Order of the Garter.

The Swiss enameller Jean Petitot worked from about 1636 for Charles I of England and his court. In this period he painted the miniature of Queen Henrietta Maria, signed and dated 1638, in the Dutch royal collection. From about 1644 he was active in Paris for Louis XIV, and for the French nobility. When Charles II of England stayed in Paris in 1651, he visited Petitot. During these years the miniature of Charles II's brother-in-law Willem II was probably painted. It may, however, have been ordered after the death of Willem II in 1650, which is suggested by the monogram WH of his son Willem (III) Hendrik on the back. The most likely explanation for the second monogram is that, composed of an interlaced O and two inverted P's, it stands for "P[rince of] O[range]." The same monogram appears on a medallion to the memory of Stadholder Frederik Hendrik, who died in 1647 (Amsterdam, Rijksmuseum). The signed companion piece of Princess Mary is also in the Dutch royal collection.

LIT: F. Lugt, *Le portrait-miniature illustré par la collection de S.M. la Reine des Pays-Bas,* Amsterdam, 1917, 38–40; M. H. Gans, *Juwelen en mensen. De geschiedenis van het bijou van 1400 tot 1900, voornamelijk naar Nederlandse bronnen,* Amsterdam, 1961, pl. 170
STICHTING HISTORISCHE VERZAMELINGEN VAN HET HUIS VAN ORANJE NASSAU

36 MINIATURE OF MARY STUART, WIFE OF STADHOLDER WILLEM II

Attributed to DAVID DES GRANGES (London 1611 – 1675 London)
Board, oval: 4.5 x 3.9 cm

The suggestion that this portrait was painted after an original by the Dutch painter Adriaen Hanneman (1604–1671) is not supported by any evidence. Judging from the age of the sitter the miniature could be dated around 1650 (regarding Des Granges, see no. 28).

LIT: cat. Rijksmuseum Amsterdam 1976, 754; cat. Mauritshuis The Hague 1977, 282
ROYAL CABINET OF PAINTINGS, MAURITSHUIS, THE HAGUE
On loan from the Rijksmuseum Amsterdam, inv. no. 4314

37 BABY-LINEN BASKET

By HANS COENRAADT BRECHTEL (Nuremberg 1608 – 1675 The Hague)
Marks: X [=1652]; HCB and a lily [H. C. Brechtel]; crowned stork [The Hague];
crowned V [19th-century tax mark]
Silver: 65 x 34 cm

Although a monogram is embossed in the center of the depression and engraved in the middle of each border, the original owner of this basket has not been identified. The same cypher may be found on a silver-gilt toilet service in The Hague (Gemeente Museum, Frederiks, IV, no. 174), dated 1665, and on a silver-gilt ewer in Amsterdam (Rijksmuseum), dated 1669(?), both made in The Hague. H. E. van Gelder reads the monogram as EBA and suggests that the basket and toilet service might have been presented in 1664 to Elisabeth van Nassau Beverweerd (1633–1681) who married Henry Bennet (1618–1685), created first Earl of Arlington in 1664. However, this solution is highly improbable. First of all, the monogram is surmounted by a ducal coronet; also the years of birth and marriage of Elisabeth van Nassau Beverweerd do not fit with the dates of the basket and toilet service. The possibility of the original owner being a duchess is confirmed by the letter D which can be discerned in the cypher.

Hans Coenraadt Brechtel was a Nuremberg silversmith who established himself in The Hague in 1640. Other important pieces by him are a silver-gilt cup and cover, 1641, presented by Elizabeth Stuart, Queen of Bohemia (1602–1675), to the city of Leiden because her sons had studied at the University of Leiden; the golden coronation cup, 1653, of Frederick III, King of Denmark (1609–1670); and the silver and silver-gilt clock, ca. 1660, from the collection of the Kings of Hanover, now in London (Victoria and Albert Museum). Baby-linen baskets, containing the linen given to the newborn child, were usually made of less costly materials like woven willow twigs. Another silver one, signed by the monogrammist GB and dated 1660 (Frederiks IV, no. 127), resembles the basket by Brechtel, showing the same type of floral ornament. In the bottom of this basket an orchestra of seven putti is depicted (Amsterdam, Rijksmuseum).

LIT: E. Voet en H. E. van Gelder, *Merken van Haagsche goud- en zilversmeden*, The Hague, 1941, 15, 16, pl. 5; 158, no. 11d; H. E. van Gelder, "Werk van Haagse zilversmeden," *Oud Holland*, 1950, 6–9, 127–128; J. W. Frederiks, *Dutch Silver*, IV, The Hague, 1961, 62–66, no. 135, pl. 145; no. 174, pls. 184–186; Th. H. Lunsingh Scheurleer a.o., "Enkele oude Nederlandse kraamgebruiken," *Antiek*, 1971/1972, 297–332; *Bulletin van het Rijksmuseum*, 1973, 133, pl. 5
PROV: presented by Queen Wilhelmina to Queen Emma
H. M. THE QUEEN

38 TWO ARMCHAIRS

Northern Netherlands, third quarter of the 17th century
(a) Walnut; arms and legs of spiral turning, stretchers decorated with spiral turning and knob turning in the middle, baluster-shaped arm supports; the ends of the arms and the lower junctions are carved with floral ornaments; modern upholstery: 87 x 61 x 54 cm
(b) Walnut; arms, legs, and arm supports of spiral turning, stretchers of spiral turning and knob turning in the middle; the ends of the arms are carved with lion's heads; modern upholstery: 91 x 57 x 54 cm

Spiral turning was in favor in the Netherlands from the second quarter until the end of the seventeenth century. The alternation of light and dark perfectly suited the baroque taste and many Dutch genre painters used the motif in their interior scenes. During the third quarter of the century chairs still had low backs, but walnut was used instead of oak which was normally used before 1650.

PROV: collection J. A. Völcker van Soelen, Castle Zoelen, the Netherlands
MRS. M. WITTOP KONING, 'S HERTOGENBOSCH

39 GOLD PALETTE, BRUSH-STICKS, AND MAULSTICK GIVEN TO DANIEL SEGHERS

By HANS COENRAADT BRECHTEL (Nuremberg 1608 – 1675 The Hague)
(a) (1) gold palette (brass and gilt "au mercure"); (2) five gold-mounted brush-sticks
(b) gold maulstick (an 18th-century replica)
(a) (1) 1649, palette on which are engraved the arms of the House of Orange and two laurel branches tied together: 23.5 x 17.5 cm; (2) 1649, five brush-sticks: each 22.5 cm long
INSCRIBED (along the edge): Danieli Seghers florum pictori et pictorum flori fragilem vitae splendorum, et huic supervicturam penicilli immortalis gloriam AMALIA DE SOLMS Princeps Auriaca Vidua hoc auro significatam voluit et hac lauro [To Daniel Seghers, painter of flowers and flower of painters. Amalia van Solms, Princess Dowager of Orange, wished through this gold and this laurel to make known the frail luster of the life and the fame of the immortal brush which will survive it]
(b) the original maulstick dated from 1652; this is a replica of before 1765 and without the

original top which was in the form of a skull wreathed with laurel: length 88 cm, diameter 12 mm
Mark (on back of palette): a "B" and a coat of arms, unidentified, but probably the coat of arms
of The Hague.

Three members of the House of Orange, Frederik Hendrik, Willem II, and Amalia
van Solms, together acquired at least seven paintings by the Antwerp Jesuit brother
and painter Daniel Seghers (1590–1661). None of them was paid for in money, but
instead Seghers was given valuables as "return" gifts. For an unidentifiable painting
of *Flowers in a Vase with Butterflies and Other Insects* he received from the Stadholder
Frederik Hendrik in 1645 a rosary with beads (decades) in the form of oranges and a
cross of solid gold in a red velvet case, which had an estimated value of 3,231 guilders,
but the goldsmith from The Hague Adriaen Rottermont (1579–1652), also mint-
master at Dordrecht, received 7 March 1645 only 1,369 guilders. For a *Garland of
Flowers* (on copper) around an antique bust of Flora (painted in grisaille by T. Willeboirts Bosschaert), Seghers received in 1646, also from Frederik Hendrik, a gold
cross weighing three pounds and three ounces. On 7 March 1645 the Prince had paid
1,369 Carolus guilders for a gold cross and a rosary with twelve beads, and on 15
March 1646 he had paid 2,142 Carolus guilders for a gold cross to Adriaen Rottermont, mint-master at Dordrecht (Archives of the Nassau Domains, no. 736, fols.
293 and 413). The painting of *Flora in a Garland of Flowers* is dated 1644 and is now in
the Boymans–van Beuningen Museum in Rotterdam (inv. no. 1800, 87.5 × 60 cm).

Frederik Hendrik's son, Willem II, acquired from Seghers a *Flower Piece* painted
on copper around "a standing image of the Virgin by Mr. Willeboerts" (=Willeboirts
Bosschaert). It is dated 1645; it later hung in the Huis ten Bosch as a chimney-piece
painting and is now in the Mauritshuis (inv. no. 256; 151 × 122.7 cm). This was the
picture for which Daniel Seghers was given as a "return" gift the "gold palette"
shown here, originally with "six gold brush-sticks" (a, 1 and 2). The palette and six
brush-sticks were delivered by The Hague silversmith H. C. Brechtel on 15 March
1649 and paid for on 24 March with 1,495 Carolus guilders and 10 stuivers.

After Willem II's death his mother, Amalia van Solms, ordered from Seghers a
Flower Piece "with lilies, thistles, and thorns" around a *Pietà* painted by Erasmus
Quellinus (canvas, 146 × 114 cm). This painting, which, along with sixty-five others,
later passed by inheritance to the Staatliches Museum Schloss Mosigkau, was lost in
the Second World War. For this lost *Flowerpiece around a Pietà* Daniel Seghers received in 1652 a "maulstick" surmounted by "his skull wreathed with laurel." The
"skull wreathed with laurel" is lost and the "maulstick" preserved only as the copy
exhibited here (b). This gift from Amalia van Solms was accompanied by a poem by
Constantijn Huygens the Elder explaining the symbolism. Seghers himself wrote the
same text as that to be read on the stick today in a letter of 24 February 1652 to his
cousin Dominicus Bocx, Prior of the Monastery of St. Bernard on the Schelde. In the
letter, which was in the possession of Count Geeraerd Le Grelle in 1858, is a note by
another hand to the effect that the stick weighed two pounds in gold, which at that
time amounted to a value of 2,370 guilders.

In addition to receiving princely gifts for his paintings, Daniel Seghers also brought it about, through his good relations with the Stadholders of the Northern Netherlands, that in 1648, among other things, seven Jesuits were given a safe-conduct through the occupied territory, and their estate, the still existing Rivierenhof at Deurne, was spared military molestation. According to M. Rooses (*Geschiedenis der Antwerpsche Schilderschool*, 1879, 545), Seghers did, on the other hand, refuse to do any painting for the Oranjezaal. However, Rooses gives no source for this and Seghers does not appear in the list drawn up by Constantijn Huygens in connection with that project.

Seghers left the gifts he had received from the Oranges to the Professed House of the Jesuits in Antwerp, where he had lived from 1618—with an interval of two years in 1625–1627 when he was in Rome—until his death in 1661. After the Jesuit church in Antwerp was burned down in 1718, the gifts were sold to pay for its rebuilding. According to the history painter Petrus Kremer (1801–1888), they came in 1724 into the possession of the Burgomaster of Antwerp, Pascal-Ignace van der Cruyse, and later in the eighteenth century into that of the Cornet family. In 1873 Kremer came upon these objects at the country house of Mrs. de Pret de Calesberg at Donck near Antwerp as the property of her grandson Count Cornet de Ways Ruart of Vonèche near Namur. The rosary with the gold cross and the large gold cross, which were still present at that time, have not yet come to light. According to Kremer, the palette was still accompanied then by twelve brush-sticks, and Cornelis de Bie (1661) also mentions twelve, although Brechtel was paid in 1652 for only six. According to a manuscript at Bornheim (fol. 193) referred to by Fr. Kieckens, which was written by a Benedictine monk in 1765, the maulstick was already a gilt copper copy by then, while it had lost "its crowned skull in token that Art also lives and flourishes after death" after 1718. The objects shown here were acquired in Brussels in 1930 (see under Prov) by Baron Georges Caroly, who presented them to the city of Antwerp. Since 1946 they have been kept in the Rubenshuis.

Seghers' princely gifts already acquired great fame during his lifetime. In addition to the poems in Latin and Dutch by Constantijn Huygens the Elder, which accompanied them, and in addition to the answers by Fathers Jacob Caters and Dominicus Bocx, there are poems by Joost van den Vondel, Jan Vos, Six van Chandelier, Simon Ingen, Florent de Rieu (1657), and Cornelis de Bie (1661). The gifts are also mentioned later by the historians Houbraken, Bullart, Weyerman, and others.

LIT: "Een handschrift van Daniel Seghers," by the editors, in *De Vlaemsche School*, 1858, 65–66; P. Kremer, "Geschencken van den prins en de prinses van Oranje aan Daniël Seghers," *De Vlaamsche School*, 1873, 122–123; Fr. Kieckens, S.J., *Daniel Seghers, de la Compagnie de Jézus, peintre de fleurs: Sa vie et son oeuvre, 1590–1661*, Antwerp, 1886; A. J. J. Delen, "Daniel Seghers en Het Huis van Oranje," *Op de Hoogte*, illustrated monthly, Haarlem, 1931, 343–349; reprinted in *Oude Kunst en Graphiek*, Antwerp, 1943, 73–102; D. F. Slothouwer, *De Paleizen van Frederik Hendrik*, Leiden, 1945, 336; J. G. van Gelder, "Hans Conrad Brechtel," *Oud Holland*, LXIII, 1948, 60–62 (for Brechtel see also no. 37 of the present catalogue); M. L. Hairs, *Les peintres flamands de fleurs au XVIIe siècle*, Paris and Brussels, 1955, 51–86, 160–177; second edition,

Brussels, 1965, 79–150, 402–411; M. W. Burke-Gaffney, S.J., *Daniel Seghers: A Tercentenary Commemoration*, New York, 1961, 30 and *passim*; W. Couvreur, "Daniël Seghers' inventaris van door hem geschilderde bloemstukken," *Gentse Bijdragen*, XX, 1967, 78–158

EXHIBITED: *Zeven Eeuwen Den Haag*, The Hague, Gemeente Museum, 30 July – 26 September 1948, no. 20

PROV: Daniel Seghers, to 1661; Professed House of the Jesuits, Antwerp, to 1724; for subsequent history see above; according to A. J. J. Delen, 1931 and 1943 (see under Lit above), sold at a sale of antiquities at Brussels in 1930 (no sale catalogue known) and acquired by Baron Georges Caroly, Antwerp; given by him to the city of Antwerp in 1930; placed in the Municipal Printroom, Antwerp; transferred to the Rubenshuis, Antwerp, in 1946

MUSEUM RUBENSHUIS, ANTWERP, INV. NO. A74 (palette); INV. NO. A74/1 (maulstick); INV. NO. A74/2 (5 brush-sticks)

WILLIAM & MARY

WILLEM HENDRIK, Prince of Orange, Count of Nassau, was born in 1650, the only and posthumous son of Stadholder Willem II and Princess Mary Stuart, daughter of King Charles I of England. He was educated by his mother and after her death by his grandmother, Princess Amalia, born Countess of Solms, widow of Stadholder Frederik Hendrik. In 1660 Willem's situation was changed by the fact that his uncle Charles II was restored to the English throne. In 1666 during the Anglo-Dutch war of 1665–1667, the States of Holland, being the most powerful of the United Provinces, took over his education and Willem was declared Child of State. This was *de facto* a recognition of his extraordinary position in the Netherlands, although his claims on the greatest offices in the Republic, viz., the stadholdership and the functions of Captain-General and Admiral, could be officially ignored for the reason that the offices were not hereditary. However, in 1672 when England joined with France and the Bishops of Münster and Cologne to attack the Dutch Republic by sea and land, Willem was finally nominated Stadholder of five of the seven United Provinces —Holland, Zeeland, Utrecht, Gelderland, and Overijssel, and Captain-General and Admiral of all the seven provinces. From this moment until the end of his life, his principal concerns were resistance to the increasing power of Louis XIV and the defense of the Protestant cause in Europe. In the wars against France, from 1672 to 1678 and from 1688 to 1697, he was ultimately successful in achieving his ends.

In 1677 Willem III married his cousin Princess Mary Stuart (1662–1695), eldest daughter of James, Duke of York (1633–1701), and Anne Hyde (1637–1671), daughter of the Earl of Clarendon. In 1685 her father ascended to the English throne as James II and Mary became heiress presumptive. When in 1688 a son was born to James II, who had joined the Roman Catholic Church and pursued a pro-French policy, the Protestants in England asked Willem III to intervene. After the landing at Torbay and the Glorious Revolution, Willem and Mary were crowned as King William III and Queen Mary II on 21 April 1689. After the death of Mary in 1695 William reigned alone until he died in 1702 in Kensington Palace at the age of fifty-two.

William and Mary both had a great passion for architecture and gardens. William bought the house Soestdijk, today the residence of Queen Juliana. Together with Mary he created the new country palace Het Loo in the Netherlands; in England they made important alterations at Kensington Palace and Hampton Court. In this context the royal orders to architects, sculptors, interior designers, portrait painters, cabinetmakers, tapestry weavers, factories of Delftware (a special interest of Mary), silversmiths, bookbinders, etc., for their splendidly furnished palaces were countless and prolific. William was also extremely interested in paintings, and he acquired a large collection of pictures of different schools for his galleries at Kensington Palace and Het Loo. Some aspects of these collections are discussed in one of the introductions to this catalogue.

40 WILLIAM III AS A CHILD

Studio of GERARD VAN HONTHORST (Utrecht 1590 – 1656 Utrecht)
Canvas: 109 x 89 cm

Portrait of William III as a child of three years with the insignia of the Order of the Garter, granted to him by his exiled uncle Charles II in 1653. In a fashion not unusual for princely children, William is represented as a hunter in a costume believed to be Roman, with a laurel wreath around his head like a young classical hero, in anticipation of his expected brilliant future.

Two variant versions of this portrait are in the collections of the Princes of Prussia, Castle Reinhartshausen near Erbach, West Germany, and, formerly, of the Princes of Dohna, Castle Schlobitten, East Germany (lost 1945).

LIT: A. Staring, "De portretten van den koning-stadhouder," *Nederlands Kunsthistorisch Jaarboek*, 1951, 164, fig. 5; C. Grommelt und C. von Merten, *Das Dohnasche Schloss Schlobitten in Ostpreussen*, Stuttgart, 1965, 121, 203, pl. VII; F. G. L. O. van Kretschmar, "Bij de aanwinsten uit de Cravencollectie," *Jaarverslag Vereniging "Oranje Nassau Museum" 1968*, The Hague, 1969, 9-12.
PROV: collection of Elizabeth Stuart, Queen of Bohemia (1596–1662), known as the Winter Queen; from 1662 at Combe Abbey, England, collection of the Earls of Craven to 1968; Sotheby sale, London, 27 November 1968
RIJKSMUSEUM PALEIS HET LOO, APELDOORN, INV. NO. A3619
On loan from the Vereniging Oranje Nassau Museum

41 MEDAL WITH A PORTRAIT OF THE FOUR-YEAR-OLD WILLIAM III

By PIETER VAN ABEELE (Amsterdam 1608 – after 1684 Amsterdam)
SIGNED in monogram: (obverse) PVA.F. (reverse) PVAB.F.
DATED on the obverse: 1654
INSCRIBED: (obverse) AN.WILHELMVS III D.G. PRINC.ARAVS.ETC. 1654; (reverse) TIME DEUM
Silver: diameter 6.4 cm

In the conclusion of the Peace treaty of 1654 between the Republic and England, Johan de Witt (1625–1672), Grand Pensionary of Holland, was forced by Oliver

Cromwell (1599–1658) to include the Act of Seclusion, which debarred members of the House of Orange from the highest offices in the province of Holland. The Act of Seclusion had been negotiated in secret and when it became publicly known it caused an angry protest and an Orangist movement. Some parties in Overijssel, for instance, appointed William III Stadholder of their province. This medal was probably made to commemorate the event. The appointment remained a point of debate in Overijssel until 1657 when it was decided to defer the matter until the coming of age of William III. The portrait of the Prince wearing a bonnet and a feathered hat is derived from a painting by Adriaen Hanneman (1604–1671). This portrait of William III as a boy was used many times on ceramics, glass, and medals (see no. 42). The reverse depicts the young Prince dressed in a Roman costume (see no. 40) with a marshall's staff. He stands in front of Minerva who is pointing at Jehovah.

LIT: N. Chevalier, *Histoire de Guillaume III*, Amsterdam, 1692, 7, 8; Van Loon, II, 388[1]
H. M. THE QUEEN

42 BLUE-AND-WHITE DELFTWARE DISH

Dutch, about 1655
Tin glazed earthenware painted in blue: diameter 39.5 cm

Five-year-old William III is depicted on his prancing horse, bearing a staff in his left hand. Over his head are the initials P[rince] W[illiam] and the coat of arms of Orange Nassau. The composition was copied after an engraving by Hendrik Rokesz (active 1650–1660 in Amsterdam) designed by Pieter Jansz (Amsterdam 1612–1672 Amsterdam). As the engraving is dated 1655, the dish must have been made shortly afterwards. Rider and horse are copied in detail, including the insignia of the Order of the Garter, granted in 1653, but the composition of the background has been simplified: the architecture of Het Binnenhof with the Hofvijver, the seat of the Stadholders and the Government, and also the coat of arms of the province of Holland, are replaced by simple brushwood.

LIT: D. F. Lunsingh Scheurleer, "Oranje-ceramiek in het Koninklijk Huisarchief,"
Nederlands Kunsthistorisch Jaarboek, 1970, 243, 244, figs. 1 and 2
H. M. THE QUEEN

43 SILVER BEAKER WITH PORTRAITS OF THE STADHOLDERS WILLEM I, MAURITS, FREDERIK HENDRIK, WILLEM II, AND WILLIAM III

Dordrecht, 1658
Silver, partly gilt: height 21.5 cm, diameter 13.5 cm
Marks: a rose [Dordrecht]; N [1658]; fleur-de-lis [unidentified maker]

The beaker is engraved with the portraits of the princes set in a type of auricular ornamentation and with a hunting scene at the bottom. The portraits were copied from contemporary prints and paintings. That of Prince Willem I is copied from a print by C. Visscher de Oude (1520–1586). The other engravings are derived from paintings by Michiel Jansz van Miereveld (1567–1641) (see no. 14), Gerard van Honthorst (1590–1656) (see no. 20), and Adriaen Hanneman (1601–1671). The portrait of William III is similar to that on the medal made in 1654 (see no. 41).

LIT: *Dordrechts goud en zilver*, Dordrecht (Museum Mr. S. van Gijn), 1975, no. 41; J. R. ter Molen, "Decoration on Silver: The Application of Prints in the Work of Seventeenth-century Dutch Silversmiths," *The Connoisseur*, October 1976, 94–103

RIJKSMUSEUM PALEIS HET LOO, APELDOORN, INV. NO. RL6

44 EMBLEMATIC DRAWING MADE BY WILLIAM III

Drawing in pen, on title page of book
BINDING: green morocco, gold-tooled: 21.9 x 16.3 x 1.9 cm; probably The Hague, ca. 1660
INSCRIBED: (written on flyleaf) Guillaume HP d'Orange; (written on title page) je maintiendray Nassau
CONTENTS: Balthazar Gerbier Douvilly, *Princely virtuous academicall discours, concerning military architecture, or fortifications* . . . , The Hague; illustrated with a portrait of Gerbier and plans of fortifications; printed dedication to Prince William III and a second dedication to Johan Boreel (1629–1691) and Frederik van Reede (1624–1666), friends of the Prince who held important positions in the army.

The emblematic drawing is traditionally ascribed to Prince William III as his signature in the book is written with the same ink; moreover, it is highly improbable that someone else would have made a drawing—without any comment—in a book specially bound for the Prince. William III was probably taught to draw by Abraham Raguineau (see p. 30).

The growing shoot in the drawing symbolizes the young Prince William, the only male descendant of Prince Willem I. At the same time the drawing recalls the device of Prince Maurits, *tandem fit surculus arbor* (compare no. 13). The volume consists of parts from different books by Gerbier.

LIT: *Supellectilem librariam sub sereniss.is de stirpe Nassauia Arausii Principibus in ordines digessit Constantinus Hugenius*, 1686, 211, no. 1787 (manuscript, Royal Library, The Hague, 78D14); *Catalogue des livres de la bibliothèque de S.A.S. Frédric-Henri, Prince d'Orange* . . . , The Hague, 1749, 101, no. 597; *De Oranje Nassau boekerij en de Oranje-penningen in de Koninklijke Bibliotheek en in het Koninklijk Penningkabinet te 's Gravenhage*, Haarlem, 1898, 40, no. 173; *150 jaar Koninklijk Kabinet van Schilderijen, Koninklijke Bibliotheek, Koninklijk Penningkabinet, Herdenkingstentoonstelling in het Mauritshuis*, The Hague, 1966, no. 48
PROV: Library of Prince William III

ROYAL LIBRARY, THE HAGUE, 138D6

45 EMBROIDERED PURSE GIVEN BY WILLIAM III TO HIS PROFESSOR, HENRICUS BORNIUS

Dutch, ca. 1665
Red velvet, silver and gold thread, seed-pearls, rubies: 14.5 x 8 cm
In the purse there is a piece of paper on which is written: *Stock beurs van Prins Willem de derde, present gegeven aen de Provesser Bornius doe zijn Hoogheit bij zijn E. studeerde* [Purse of Prince William III given to the Professor Bornius when his Highness was his student]

Henricus Bornius (ca. 1617–1678) was appointed Professor of Philosophy at Leiden in 1651. He opposed the theories of René Descartes. He was Prince William III's teacher of literature from 1659/60 until 1666, when William became "Child of State," that is, his education was put in the hands of a committee, appointed by the States-General. Afterwards Bornius acted as the steward of his estate.

PROV: collection Van Ittersum
RIJKSMUSEUM PALEIS HET LOO, APELDOORN, INV. NO. CIII
On loan from the Vereniging Oranje Nassau Museum

46 QUEEN MARY II

By CASPAR NETSCHER (Heidelberg 1639 – 1684 The Hague)
Canvas: 80.5 x 63.5 cm

Portrait of Queen Mary when Princess of Orange. The signed companion piece, representing William III standing in armor, can be dated about 1677 (according to Staring). The background is more elaborate than is usual in Netscher's portraits. This kind of small-size portrait of a figure in full length is typically Dutch, and was developed by Netscher's teacher Gerard Terborch (1617–1681). Netscher was born in Germany and came to the Netherlands in his youth. He was trained by Terborch around 1654. After 1662 Netscher was active in The Hague and became one of the most fashionable portrait painters of his day.

A version in three-quarter length is in the royal collection, on loan to the Rijksmuseum Paleis Het Loo, Apeldoorn. The head and shoulders were engraved by Jacob Houbraken (1698–1780).

LIT: F. Muller, no. 257ᶜ; Hofstede de Groot, no. 297; A. Staring, "De portretten van den koning-stadhouder," *Nederlands Kunsthistorisch Jaarboek*, 1951, 175, pl. 16
RIJKSMUSEUM, AMSTERDAM, INV. NO. CI95

47 MINIATURE OF QUEEN MARY II

By JOHAN VAN HAENSBERGEN (Gorinchem? 1642 – 1705 The Hague)
SIGNED: J.V.H.
Iron, oval: 13.3 x 10.4 cm

Johan van Haensbergen made this miniature after a portrait in three-quarter length of Mary when Princess of Orange by Willem Wissing (1656–1687) at Windsor Castle. This portrait was probably the one painted in Holland in 1685 by order of King James II. The portrait by Wissing, which was engraved by Robert Williams (active about 1680–1704), is known in several versions. In his early years Johan van Haensbergen was a painter of landscapes in the manner of Cornelis Poelenburgh (ca. 1586–1667); after 1669 he settled in The Hague and painted fashionable portraits.

LIT: O. Millar, *The Tudor, Stuart and early Georgian Pictures in the Collection of Her Majesty The Queen*, London, 1963, 139, no. 323

STICHTING HISTORISCHE VERZAMELINGEN VAN HET HUIS VAN ORANJE NASSAU

48 SILVER SNUFFBOX SET WITH A MOTHER-OF-PEARL MEDALLION OF WILLIAM III

Dutch(?), ca. 1690
Marks: A.I [unidentified master], dolphin [Dutch 19th-century tax mark]
Silver and mother-of-pearl: 7.7 x 5.2 cm

The portrait of William III does not provide a clue by which we can date the box, but the engraved decoration of floral ornaments and strapwork, related to the designs by Daniel Marot for watches and snuffboxes, suggests that it was made around 1690.

H. M. THE QUEEN

49 BINDING FROM THE LIBRARY OF WILLIAM III

Probably Queen's Binder D, ca. 1678
BINDING: red morocco, gold-tooled, with a frame and a symmetrical pattern made with small tools such as drawer-handle and pointillé tools; spine with five raised bands; the panels with tools in the center and corners, 2nd panel with title, 3rd panel with volume number: 25.8 x 20.3 x 6.7 cm
CONTENTS: Adam Littleton, *Linguae Latinae liber dictionarius quadripartitus. A Latin Dictionary, in Four Parts* . . . , London, printed for T. Basset, J. Wright and R. Chiswell, 1678; 2 volumes; engraved frontispiece by R. White; dedication to Prince William III written by the author on added leaf

The same book bound by the same binder with a dedication to Charles II is in the British Library (H. M. Nixon, *English Restoration Bookbindings*, London, 1974, no. 74).

This volume was probably given by the author to William III, shortly after his arrival in England in 1688.

LIT: *Supellectilem librariam sub sereness.is de stirpe Nassauia Arausii Principibus in ordines digessit Constantinus Hugenius*, 1686, 79, nos. 1238, 1239 (manuscript, Royal Library,

The Hague, 78D14); cat. London 1950, no. 317; *150 jaar Koninklijk Kabinet van Schilderijen, Koninklijke Bibliotheek, Koninklijk Penningkabinet, Herdenkingstentoonstelling in het Mauritshuis*, The Hague, 1966, no. 49

PROV: Library of Prince William III

ROYAL LIBRARY, THE HAGUE, INV. NO. 141C15,1

50 MEDAL FOR THE CORONATION OF WILLIAM III AND MARY, 1689

By GEORGE BOWER (London, active 1650–1690)
Signed on obverse: G.B.F.
DATED: (reverse) 1689
INSCRIBED: (obverse) GVLIELMVS.ET.MARIA.D.G.ANG.FRA.ET.HIB.REX.ET REGINA.
FID.DEF.&c.; (reverse) PRETIVMQ.ET.CAVSA.LABORIS
Gold: diameter 3.8 cm

The reverse of this coronation medal depicts Andromeda chained to a rock, the sea-monster and Perseus coming to her rescue. Andromeda symoblizes England under the reign of James II, the sea-monster represents the Roman Catholic Church, and Perseus, Prince William III. Various coronation medals were issued to be distributed among the people. The golden medal, however, would have been presented to courtiers who performed a special function during the coronation.

The text on the reverse is taken from Ovid, *Metamorphoses*, IV, 739.

LIT: E. Hawkins (edited by A. W. Franks and H. E. Grueber), *Medallic Illustrations of the History of Great Britain and Ireland*, London, 1885, I, 663, no. 26; N. Chevalier, *Histoire de Guillaume III*, Amsterdam, 1692, 102; Van Loon, III, 408, 2

PROV: presented by the Stichting 't Konings Loo, 1976

RIJKSMUSEUM PALEIS HET LOO, APELDOORN, INV. NO. KL93

51 SPOON, A SHOOTING TROPHY OF MATCHES HELD ON THE CORONATION DAY OF WILLIAM III AND MARY

Amsterdam, 1689
Marks: escutcheon of Amsterdam, lion, C (1689), unidentified master's mark
INSCRIBED (on the back of the bowl): Schuttersgift vant 3de corporael onder d'Hr Capitijn Joan Trip [shooting trophy of the 3rd corps of Mr. Captain Joan Trip]; William Rex Maria Regina gekroont den 21 April A 1689 binne Londe [William Rex and Mary Regina crowned in London on 21 April 1689]; Door Hollants Maght ter zee en lant—In veertigh winter Dagen—Heeft Willem door zijn kloek verstant—En sonder Slagh verslagen—Den Koningh die in quaat verbont—Met Lodewijck ons tegenstont—Om door sijn woeste bende—Godts Kerck en Staat te schende. I. Norel [Through Holland's might by sea and land—In forty winter days—Did William, by his brave intelligence—Beat without any

battle—The King who, in evil alliance—Banded against us with Louis—In order to
damage God's Church and State—with his riotous companions. I. Norel]; J. van Gastel;
(on the stem) Willem
Silver: 17.9 x 5.1 cm

J. van Gastel had probably won this prize in the shooting matches held by the corps
of Joan Trip (1662–1732) on the coronation day of William and Mary. In the previous
year Joan Trip had been appointed captain. Several spoons with the same stem and
figure, but holding a baton, are known. The oldest one dates from 1653 (Amsterdam,
Rijksmuseum). A similar one made in Rotterdam is dated 1688 (Frederiks, II, no.
594). The spoon shown here was adapted to William's new title by replacing the baton
with a scepter and adding a crown. The poem by Jan Norel (1635–1700) is also engraved on a spoon with the figures of both William and Mary (Frederiks, II, no. 253).

LIT: J. W. Frederiks, *Dutch Silver*, II, 1958, no. 594, pl. 298, no. 253, pl. 82; E. M. Ch. F.
Klijn, *Oude zilveren lepels*, Lochem, 1967, 42; M. Taupe, "De Noordnederlandse zilveren
lepel, vóór ca 1670," *Antiek*, XII, 433–443
H. R. H. PRINCESS MARGRIET OF THE NETHERLANDS

52 MARBLE MEDALLION PORTRAITS OF WILLIAM AND MARY

Ca. 1690
Marble, oval: each 22.5 x 19 cm
Gilded wooden frames

The anonymous sculptor who made these profile portraits must have been trained
internationally. They show a particularly close relation to the works of Jean Cavalier
(active 1683–1698/99), the French medallist and expert in portrait medallions in
ivory and wax, who worked in many courts of Europe, and during 1690–1691 in
London. The resemblance in these reliefs to Cavalier's portrait of Maria Anna Jo-
sepha, Electress Palatine (1654–1689), of about 1685–1690 is striking (Düsseldorf,
Stadtgeschichtliches Museum).

LIT: cat. London 1950, no. 101; cat. *De Stadhouder-koning en zijn tijd*, Amsterdam
(Rijksmuseum), 1950, no. 398; cat. *Europäische Barockplastik am Niederrhein: Grupello
und seine Zeit*, Düsseldorf (Kunstmuseum), 1971, no. 105, fig. 66
PROV: auction, Th. Stuart, Amsterdam, A. G. C. de Vries, 16 December 1930, no. 846
RIJKSMUSEUM PALEIS HET LOO, APELDOORN, INV. NO. A1248a,b
On loan from the Vereniging Oranje Nassau Museum

53 MEDAL COMMEMORATING THE CELEBRATION IN AMSTERDAM OF THE CORONATION OF WILLIAM III AND MARY IN LONDON

Dutch, 1689
INSCRIBED: (obverse) GVILHELMVS ET MARIA REX AT REGINA CORON. APR. 11/21 1689; (reverse) TER GEDAGTENIS.DAT.OP.DE.DAGH.DER.KRONING.DE. WAGHT.HAD.D.COMP.VAN.D.H.B.MVIKENS. [To commemorate the guard being held by the company of B. Muikens on the day of the coronation.]
Silver: diameter 5.8 cm

This medal was issued by the company of the guards of Amsterdam who were on duty on the day of the coronation of William and Mary. In Amsterdam it was celebrated with special decorations, a triumphal arch, and a model of the tower of London with fireworks. The reverse of the medal depicts three officers of the company on guard.

LIT: N. Chevalier, *Histoire de Guillaume III*, Amsterdam, 1692, 117; Van Loon, III, 419; E. Hawkins (edited by A. W. Franks and H. E. Grueber), *Medallic Illustrations of the History of Great Britain and Ireland*, London, 1885, I, 678, no. 54
H. M. THE QUEEN

54 MEDAL COMMEMORATING THE BATTLE OF THE BOYNE

English or Irish, after 1690
INSCRIBED: (obverse) POST.FUNERA.VIRTUS.MANET. (reverse) NOBIS.HAEC.OTIA. FECIT 1ᵗ OF. IULY 1690.
Gold: 5.2 x 4 cm

Hawkins suggests that this medal, with the portrait of William III as a Roman general, and a female figure on the reverse symbolizing freedom, was intended to be worn upon the anniversary of the battle of the Boyne and may have belonged to an Irish Orange club. This is the only golden specimen known; the others are of silver-gilt or silver.

LIT: E. Hawkins (edited by A. W. Franks and H. E. Grueber), *Medallic Illustrations of the History of Great Britain and Ireland*, London, 1885, I, 718 no. 140
PROV: presented by the Stichting 't Konings Loo, 1975
RIJKSMUSEUM PALEIS HET LOO, APELDOORN, INV. NO. RL316

55 DELFTWARE BUST OF WILLIAM III

SIGNED with the monogram of Louwys Victoorsz, factory De Dobbelde Schenckan, owned by Louwys Victoorsz, 1688–1713; or that of Lambertus van Eenhoorn, factory De

Metalen Pot, owned by Lambertus van Eenhoorn, 1691–1721
Delft, ca. 1690
Monogram: WR
Tin glazed earthenware painted in blue: 42 cm

Like the tulip-vase made by the same workshop (cf. no. 56), the bust bears the cypher of William as King of England, WR. The crown shows that the modeller was not familiar with the exact form of the English royal crown.

LIT: *De Stadhouder-koning en zijn tijd, 1650–1950*, Amsterdam (Rijksmuseum), 1950, no. 480; cat. London 1964, no. 224; D. F. Lunsingh Scheurleer, *Delfts Blauw*, Bussum, 1975, 76, pl. 85
PROV: coll. Loudon
RIJKSMUSEUM, AMSTERDAM, INV. NO. 12400–93

56 TULIP VASE WITH CYPHER AND BUST OF WILLIAM III

SIGNED with the monogram of Louwys Victoorsz, factory De Dobbelde Schenckan, owned by Louwys Victoorsz, 1688–1713; or that of Lambertus van Eenhoorn, factory De Metalen Pot, owned by Lambertus van Eenhoorn, 1691–1721
Delft, ca. 1690
Monogram: WR
Tin glazed earthenware painted in blue: 39.8 x 30 x 11 cm

Tulip vases were a favorite product of the ceramic industry at Delft in the seventeenth and eighteenth centuries. They were particularly appropriate for displaying the rare and expensive tulips which were very fashionable at that time. They were, however, used for other flowers as well. The form of the vase shown here is unusual and may have been specially designed. The lions with globes in their feet were also made as separate objects. The design on the back, derived from similar ones on Chinese porcelain, resembles the decoration of Delftware plaques. The vase may have belonged to the famous Delftware collection of Queen Mary. From an inventory dated 1712, we know that she had apartments containing Delftware in the cellar of Het Loo as she had also in the Water Gallery at Hampton Court.

LIT: Arthur Lane, "Delft Tiles from Hampton Court and Daniel Marot," *Bulletin van het Rijksmuseum*, 1959, 12–21; Joan Wilson, "A Phenomenon of Taste: The Chinaware of Queen Mary II," *Apollo*, XCVI, 1972, 116–123; Drossaers en Lunsingh Scheurleer, I, 658–659; Michael Archer, "Delft at Dyrham," *The National Trust Year Book*, 1975–1976, 12–18; Michael Archer, "Pyramids and Pagodas for Flowers," *Country Life*, January 1976, 166–169
PROV: Sotheby sale, London, 15 March 1940
RIJKSMUSEUM PALEIS HET LOO, APELDOORN, INV. NO. RL301

57 TWO HEXAGONAL DELFTWARE FLOWER PYRAMIDS

SIGNED with the monogram AK: Greek A factory, owned by Adriansz Koex (or Kocks) from 1687 to 1701, his son Pieter Adriansz to 1703, and Pieter's widow to 1722
Tin glazed earthenware painted in blue: each pyramid consists of seven parts; one part has been renewed: 131 x 35 cm

At the end of the seventeenth century the Delft earthenware factories frequently experimented with new forms of objects. In this period large vases were made in the forms of pyramids and pagodas, which were meant to stand on the floor. They are made up of tiers of self-containing, tapering sections with nozzles at the corners, which are placed on a straight base without nozzles. As it was a common practice to use different elements from the same range of moulds to make fresh combinations, the nozzles like the mouths of monsters occur also on other pyramids (Hampton Court; San Francisco, de Young Museum). However, so far as it is known, the vases shown here have the unique feature of nozzles in a spiral form.

The pyramid form recurs in pedestals made for china in the porcelain rooms of the same period. As at Het Loo, where two pyramids were placed in Queen Mary's dairy in the basement of the palace, the flower pyramids and pagodas would have belonged in porcelain rooms. When filled with flowers they would have been colorful, eye-catching elements among the mainly blue-and-white earthenware and porcelain.

All marked pyramids bear the monogram AK. The factory was owned by Adriansz Kocks until his death in 1701. His son Pieter died in 1703 and the factory was continued by his widow until 1722. It was quite customary in Holland for a widow to take over the concern of her late husband, as women were often trained in management. Benjamin Franklin met with this phenomenon when, after the death of one of his agents, his widow, born in Holland, was able to continue the concern until her son was old enough to take over. He was so impressed by it that he recommended Americans to follow the Dutch example.

LIT: Drossaers en Lunsingh Scheurleer, I, 658, nos. 289, 292 (cellar of Her Majesty at Het Loo, inventory 1713: 2 Delft pyramids, five small flower pyramids); and see no. 56
COLONIAL WILLIAMSBURG FOUNDATION, WILLIAMSBURG, INV. NO. 1936–2123 1,2

58 ARMORIAL TAPESTRIES OF WILLIAM III AND MARY STUART

Workshop of Jerome LeClerc (active 1677–1717), Brussels; ca. 1690
(a) Not signed; silk and wool: 273 x 235 cm
(b) Signed: LECLERC (lower right-hand edge) and two B's separated by the shield of Brussels; silk, wool, gold, and silver: 274 x 230 cm

The two tapestries bear the coat of arms of William III and Mary as King and Queen of England, surrounded by ornaments related to them and symbolizing their reign. At present about fifteen tapestries with similar decoration are known. They can be divided into two groups: the ones with the standing figures of Apollo and Hercules, the others with Mars and Minerva sitting on both sides of the escutcheon. The signatures J. LeClerc, J. van der Borght, J. Cobus, and J. Coenot, appearing on various pieces of these series, correspond with those in a document in the archives of the city of Brussels dated 15 June 1700 referring to a series of eight armorial tapestries made by these weavers for the English King. Possibly the six tapestries mentioned in the inventory of 1702 of the palace Noordeinde in The Hague and described as "six tapestries with figures, all kinds of flowers, and the coat of arms of His and Her Highnesses," formed part of this set. The designs are definitely the work of Daniel Marot (1663–1752), the French Huguenot who became architect for William III. He made designs for interiors and for parts of the garden of Het Loo as well as for the royal palaces in England. His work was published in the first quarter of the eighteenth century, and covered the whole area of applied arts, including beds, clocks, garden urns, parterres, tiles, fabrics, etc. It had an enormous impact on Dutch architecture and interior decoration in the first half of the eighteenth century.

LIT: H. Göbel, *Wandteppiche I: Die Niederlande*, Leipzig, 1923, 372, 375; H. H. Mulliner, *The Decorative Arts in England*, London, 1923, pl. 181; J. G. Phillips, "An Armorial Tapestry," *Bulletin of the Metropolitan Museum*, New York, 1936, 122–124; cat. London 1964, no. 140; A. M. L. E. Erkelens, "Wapentapyten van Willem III naar ontwerp van Daniel Marot," *Bulletin van het Rijksmuseum*, 1967, 43; Drossaers en Lunsingh Scheurleer, I, 489
PROV: (a) bought by King Willem III 1890; (b) collection Mazaros-Riballier, Paris
(a) RIJKSMUSEUM PALEIS HET LOO, APELDOORN, INV. NO. PL242A
On loan from the Stichting Historische Verzamelingen van het Huis van Oranje Nassau
(b) METROPOLITAN MUSEUM OF ART, NEW YORK, SAMUEL D. LEE FUND, 1936

59 THE LANDING OF WILLIAM III IN 1691 ON HIS RETURN FROM ENGLAND TO THE NETHERLANDS

By LUDOLF BACKHUYSEN (Emden 1631 – 1708 Amsterdam)
SIGNED AND DATED: L Bakhuis 1691
Canvas: 51 x 66.5 cm

On 16 January William III left Kensington Palace in London and set sail on the 28th, at Gravesend, under convoy of twelve warships. After a very dangerous crossing with a heavy fog and unfavorable winds, William left his ship on 30 January for a sloop. Then after drifting for many hours he landed on the 31st on the isle of Goeree in the southern part of the province of Holland. In the painting, William III is represented leaving the sloop accompanied by his intimate friend Hans Willem Bentinck, Earl of Portland (1649–1709).

LIT: see next number
PROV: Kunsthandel Nystad, Lochem, The Hague, 1956
RIJKSMUSEUM PALEIS HET LOO, APELDOORN, INV. NO. A3035a
On loan from the Vereniging Oranje Nassau Museum

60 THE RETURN TO THE NETHERLANDS IN 1691 OF STADHOLDER WILLIAM III AS KING OF ENGLAND

By LUDOLF BACKHUYSEN (Emden 1631 – 1708 Amsterdam)
SIGNED AND DATED: L Bakhuis 1692
Canvas: 53.5 x 67.5 cm

After the landing at Goeree, shown in the previous number, William III proceeded by ship to the Oranjepolder on the mainland of the province of Holland. He arrived at The Hague the same evening. On 5 February, he made his famous triumphal entry into this city. In contrast to no. 59, the King is painted here as the courageous hero. The Earl of Portland is riding at his side and behind him are his English guards. The painting belongs (with no. 59) to a series of three. The third one, representing another scene of the landing, is in the same collection as no. 59. Unlike the others, the present painting belonged to the collection of Stadholder Willem V and is mentioned in 1757 as being at Het Loo and in the gallery of Willem V at The Hague ca. 1770. A drawing for this painting is at Windsor Castle (inv. no. 85, as by Jan de Bisschop). The marine painter Ludolf Backhuysen, who also made portraits, was active in Amsterdam from 1649 on. These paintings are unusual examples of contemporary reporting in pictures.

The eventful crossing of the North Sea contributed to the heroic reputation of William III.

LIT: Hofstede de Groot, no. 23; A. W. J. Mulder, "De landing van de Stadhouder-Koning Willem III in de Oranjepolder op 31 januari 1691," *Jaarverslag Vereniging "Oranje Nassau Museum," 1956*, The Hague, 1956, 12–13; Drossaers en Lunsingh Scheurleer, II, 641, no. 40; *idem*, III, 206, no. 14; D. P. Snoep, *Praal en Propaganda. Triumfalia in de noordelijke Nederlanden in de 16de en 17de eeuw*, Alphen aan de Rhijn, 1975, 92–95; cat. Mauritshuis The Hague 1977, 34
SCHILDERIJENZAAL PRINS WILLEM V, THE HAGUE
On loan from the Royal Cabinet of Paintings, Mauritshuis, The Hague, inv. no. 6

61 EXOTIC ANIMALS

By MELCHIOR D'HONDECOETER (Utrecht 1636 – 1695 Amsterdam)
SIGNED: M d'Hondecoeter
Ca. 1692
Canvas: 169 x 156.8 cm

This painting shows an Indian elephant, a moufflon, the North African bubalis, various other exotic antelopes, gazelles, rams, and different kinds of ducks. It is mentioned in 1713 and 1757 as a chimney-piece at Het Loo in the private cabinet of the Stadholders at the corner of the inner western pavilion, finished about 1692, which gives out on the garden. The traditional nineteenth-century title, *The Menagerie of William III at Het Loo*, is not tenable. As Evers already wrote in 1912 and 1914, no menagerie existed at Het Loo before 1695, the year Hondecoeter died. The first *Indian* animals are mentioned only in 1705. Moreover, there were no elephants in the Stadholder's zoos before 1786, when two specimens from Ceylon arrived at Het Loo.

Melchior d'Hondecoeter, pupil of his father, Gysbert (1604–1635), and Jan Baptist Weenix (1621–1660), was one of the most highly regarded painters of birds and mammals of his day. William III had six pictures by him at Het Loo, four of them chimney-pieces and two over-door paintings.

LIT: G. A. Evers, "De menagerieën op Het Loo," *Gelre*, 1912, 533, 534; idem, "De menagerie van prins Willem V op Het Loo," *Gelre*, 1914, 203; cat. London 1950, no. 13; cat. London 1964, no. 24; Drossaers en Lunsingh Scheurleer, I, 667, no. 536; *idem*, II, 607, no. 143; cat. Mauritshuis The Hague 1977, 115

SCHILDERIJENZAAL PRINS WILLEM V, THE HAGUE
On loan from the Royal Cabinet of Paintings, Mauritshuis, The Hague, inv. no. 60

62 BINDING WITH COAT OF ARMS AND CYPHERS OF WILLIAM III AND MARY STUART

London, ca. 1693–1695
BINDING: blue morocco, both covers gold-tooled with the coat of arms of William III and Mary Stuart as King and Queen of England, with the insignia of the Order of the Garter and the English royal device: DIEU ET MON DROIT; the monograms of William and Mary, WR and MR, are placed on both sides of the crest; spine with five raised bands; the panel gold-tooled with a rosette in the center and small tools in the corners: 15.9 x 9.4 x 1.7 cm
CONTENTS: [William] Sherlock, *Reflexions sur la mort ou l'on presse la nécessité de bien vivre, pour bien mourir, traduit par un refugié*. Londres, N. Griffin et D. de Chemin 1693

As the cover bears the cypher of Queen Mary, the binding must have been made before her death, 7 January 1695. Usually William III continued to use the Dutch device, *Je Maintiendrai*, instead of the English royal device.

ROYAL LIBRARY, THE HAGUE, INV. NO. 144F4

63 LONG CASE CLOCK MADE FOR WILLIAM III

By THOMAS TOMPION (Ickfield Green, Bedfordshire 1639 – 1713 London)
SIGNED (on the dial): THO.TOMPION LONDINI FECIT
Burl walnut with gilded mounts: 293.4 cm

On the top of the clock the goddess Minerva stands with the head of Medusa on her shield. On the base of this statuette is the monogram WR for William Rex. The gilded chased ornaments of the open-work dial corners, friezes, and side panels are very finely elaborated. The same applies to the gilded metal foot—the ebonized base is not authentic—with cupids, garlands, and volutes. There is only one other Tompion clock on a metal foot: the clock made in 1703 for Prince George of Denmark (1653–1708), consort to Queen Anne. Like the other identical mounts on these two royal clocks, the feet are also cast in the same moulds.

According to Symonds, the clock has a two-train striking movement of three-month duration and a rare perpetual calendar which makes allowance for leap year. In the dial are two calendar slots: the upper for the name of each month and its number of days; the lower one for the day of the month, actuated by the perpetual calendar mechanism. The dial itself is one of Tompion's earliest examples of using half-quarter marks, here in the form of a little cross.

It is traditionally thought that the clock was made for William's bedchamber at Hampton Court. As Symonds argues, this should be an indication that Tompion made the clock in or after 1699 because the extending and refurnishing of Hampton Court after the death of Queen Mary was begun only in that year.

LIT: R. W. Symonds, *Thomas Tompion: His Life and Work*, London, 1969, 270, 271, figs. 30, 31, 33, 35, 37, 56, 77, 78; *The Williamsburg Collection of Antique Furnishings*, Williamsburg, 1973, 113

PROV: Queen Victoria (1819–1901); George, Duke of Cambridge (1819–1904); coll. Percy Webster, 1904; coll. George Dunn, Woolley Hall, Maidenhead, until 1914; coll. Percy Webster, 1914; coll. D. A. F. Wetherfield, Blackheath, until 1928; Mallet & Son, London, 1928; coll. Francis P. Garvan until 1934; coll. J. S. Sykes until 1956

THE COLONIAL WILLIAMSBURG FOUNDATION, WILLIAMSBURG, INV. NO. 1956-436

64 BRASS-BOUND TRAVELLING COFFER-ON-CHEST

English, ca. 1690
Ebonized woods, seaweed marquetry of sycamore on a ground of walnut: 126 x 73.5 x 42 cm

This type of marquetry with patterns resembling stylized seaweed was fashionable in England about 1690. One of the finest examples of this art is the writing table made for Queen Mary by Gerreit Jensen in 1690 (he was a Dutch cabinetmaker who worked in London from ca. 1680). The chest of drawers is a typically English piece of furniture, but the combination with a coffer is unusual.

In the inventory of the palace in Leeuwarden made in 1688/1694 a "van allerhande couleurde haut ingelegt Engelisch cabinet met drij groote en twe cleine laayes, staat ob vier knopen" (a cabinet inlaid with all kinds of coloured wood with three big and two small drawers, standing on four knobs) is mentioned. Unfortunately one cannot prove that this description and the "Engelish cofferttjen beschlagen met eiser ver-guldene bandes" (an English coffer mounted with iron-gilt bands), mentioned in the same inventory, refer to the displayed coffer-on-chest, as too little is known about its provenance.

LIT: R. Edwards, *The Shorter Dictionary of English Furniture*, London, 1964, 553–555, pl. 6; Drossaers en Lunsingh Scheurleer, II, 154, nos. 537, 540

H. M. THE QUEEN

65 TWO CHAIRS IN THE MANNER OF DANIEL MAROT

Dutch, last decade of the 17th century
Walnut, richly carved painted and gilt, caned seat: 123.5 x 43.5 x 51 cm
(a) partly restored, flower in cresting replaced by fleur-de-lis
(b) part of seat-rail missing; painting and gilding renewed

The chairs with richly carved backs, intended mainly for decorative use, were fashionable in the last quarter of the seventeenth century. Although no designs by Daniel Marot for carved chairs are known, many were made in his style. The design of the chairs shown here is rather unusual. Generally the carved part of the back is enclosed by straight uprights and the back is not joined directly to the seat to leave space for a cushion. Six identical, but unpainted chairs, now in the Dutch State Collections may belong to the same set.

LIT: C. H. de Jonge, *Holländische Möbel und Raumkunst*, The Hague, 1922, pl. 320; A. C. A. W. van der Feltz, "Belangrijke meubelen uit het tijdperk van Stadhouder–Koning Willem III in de Stichting 'Hannema–de Stuers Fundatie'," *Antiek*, 1979, 397–407

STICHTING HANNEMA–DE STUERS FUNDATIE, HEINO

66 CHANDELIER MADE FOR WILLIAM III

By DANIEL GARNIER (France, active London, ca. 1684–1700)
London, 1691–1697
Marks: DG and crowned fleur-de-lis on inner ends of seven arms
Silver, 10 arms: 86.6 x 83.8 cm

The chandelier bears only the maker's mark. This suggests that it was made for royal or ambassadorial use, since plate made for the King or his ambassadors was not obliged to be sent to the Goldsmiths' Hall for full marking. The mark was used by Daniel Garnier from 1691 to 1697, and the chandelier dates from this period. The chandelier was first mentioned in the inventory of 1721 where it was placed "At St. James / In the Lodgings."

The silversmith Adam Loofs (The Hague, ca. 1660–1710) made a list of gold and silver objects belonging to William III; from this we know that William had several silver chandeliers in Holland. Three chandeliers with eight arms, are mentioned: one was brought from England in 1677, probably a part of Mary's dowry or as a wedding present; one was made by a Mr. Van Rheenen (both Jan Arentz and Pieter van Rheenen, father and son, were silversmiths in The Hague); and the third was supplied by Adam Loofs on 30 December 1686. A note in the margin says that this chandelier was placed in Het Loo. Although no silver chandeliers are mentioned in the inventories of the palace, we know from a description (dated 1693) by a visitor that there was one in the dining room. The date of delivery suggests that Adam Loofs made the chandelier for the Stadholder's newly completed country house Het Loo. As the dining room, designed by Daniel Marot, was built only in 1692, the chandelier must have been originally placed in another room.

LIT: A. E. Bolhuis, *Journaal van een reis naar 't Loo in 1693* (manuscript, Groningen, Rijksarchief); Drossaers en Lunsingh Scheurleer, I, 415, nos. 71, 73, 75; J. D. Davis, *English Silver at Williamsburg*, Williamsburg, 1976, 13–15, no. 1; for further literature see J. D. Davis
PROV: English royal collections, sold 1808(?); Sneyd family, Staffordshire, sold 1924; William Randolph Hearst, sold 1938
THE COLONIAL WILLIAMSBURG FOUNDATION, WILLIAMSBURG, INV. NO. 1938–42

67 FOUR SILVER SCONCES WITH THE CYPHER OF WILLIAM AND MARY

London, ca. 1670
Marks: originally unmarked; only the second arms by ROBERT GARRARD (London 1793 – 1881 London) added in 1856/57 are marked
Silver: 47–49.5 x 29.8–33 x 21.4–23.5 cm

These sconces were made for royal use during the reign of Charles II; the crown and the cypher of William and Mary must have been added between 1689 and 1695. The holes above and below the festoons suggest that the alterations also included the removal of some ornaments. There are remnants of swags of leaves and acorns which would have originally extended the full length of the sides of the back plates. Four similar sconces with these swags are in the collection of H. M. the Queen of England. Also, the numbers 1, 2, 3, 5, 6, 8, 11, and 12 on the back plates of the Williamsburg series indicate that the set originally consisted of twelve pieces. The use of monograms was very fashionable in the days of William and Mary and their cyphers may be noted on nearly every important object in their collections.

LIT: J. D. Davis, *English Silver at Williamsburg*, Williamsburg, 1976, 15–17, no. 2; for further literature see J. D. Davis
PROV: English royal collections, sold 1808(?); Sneyd family, Staffordshire, sold 1924; William Randolph Hearst, sold 1938
THE COLONIAL WILLIAMSBURG FOUNDATION, WILLIAMSBURG, INV. NO. 1938–34

68 TWO SILVER SCONCES WITH THE ENGRAVED MONOGRAM OF WILLIAM III

By PHILIP ROLLOS (France, active London, ca. 1698–1704)
Marks: RO [Philip Rollos], lion's head, Britannia, "e" [1700/1701]
Silver: 40 x 11.4 x 21.6 cm

This type of sconce in the form of a truss or console was probably introduced in England by Huguenot silversmiths. Also certain details of these sconces betray the French origin of Philip Rollos, for instance, the hand and fleur-de-lis on both sides of the crown, being the upper terminals of scepters used in France, and the enrichments of the undersides of the saucers. The crown with four arches instead of two shows that Philip Rollos was not familiar with the English crown. The engraved monogram surmounted by the correct crown was possibly added by someone of the royal household. As the sconces are fully marked, they were probably not commissioned by William III.

Philip Rollos came to England at the end of the seventeenth century and was admitted to the "freedom" in 1697. William III patronized him, but he also supplied the court after William's death, as we know from objects made by him for Queen Anne (1665–1714) and King George I (1660–1727). The list of William's silver and gold objects in Holland (see no. 66) mentions several sets of silver and silver-gilt sconces. At least four of them, belonging to a series of fourteen, hung in Het Loo.

The Williamsburg sconces belong to a set of four, the other two now being in a private collection.

LIT: J. F. Hayward, *Huguenot Silver in England, 1688–1727*, London, 1959; Drossaers en Lunsingh Scheurleer, I, 415, no. 70; J. D. Davis, *English Silver at Williamsburg*, Williamsburg, 1976, 17–19, no. 3; for further literature see J. D. Davis
PROV: English royal collections, sold 1808(?); Sneyd family, Staffordshire, sold 1924; William Randolph Hearst, sold 1938
THE COLONIAL WILLIAMSBURG FOUNDATION, WILLIAMSBURG, INV. NO. 1938-35

69 DESIGN FOR A SET OF FURNITURE FOR HET LOO

By DANIEL MAROT (Paris 1661 – 1752 The Hague)
SIGNED AND DATED: D. Marot fecit ala Haye ce 28 dec. 1700 et elle on est cé acheveé et possé den le mois d'oust 1701 a Loo.
INSCRIBED on the verso: 1701, table et miroir doré pour Loo ce 17 Sep., sa sculpteur coute 400 fl.
Pen: 40.4 x 24.5 cm

Marot's designs and inventions not only concerned the interior decoration of Het Loo but extended also to its furniture, even to that in the garden, where, except for the parterres-de-broderies, he designed garden "furniture" such as vases. The present design, one of the two known furniture drawings by Marot, represents a side table, a mirror, and one of a pair of stands, forming a suite very much in favor during the last quarter of the seventeenth and the first quarter of the eighteenth centuries in northwest Europe. Such suites were executed in various costly materials, like marquetry, laquered or gilded wood, or in wood mounted with silver and also gold (cf. no. 70). The inscription on the recto of the drawing informs us that the table should have a white marble top, and the inscription on the verso indicates that the set has been gilded. Marot also showed in his drawing how it would be possible to adapt the wall panelling for the large mirror.

The set can be identified with the one described in the traveller's diary from 1705 of M. van Bolhuis and an inventory of 1713 as being in the King's antechamber of the inner western pavilion looking out on the gardens. The description of 1713 reads: *Een marmre tafel met een vierkante voet, gesnede werk met beelden en festoenen verguld, twee dito geridons, alles bekleed met groene houses. En groote spiegel met een vergulde lijst.* (A marble table with square support, carved with figures and garlands, gilded; two similar stands, all with green covers. A large mirror with gilded frame.) The Rijksmuseum in Amsterdam in 1972 acquired a pair of stands which closely resembles the one on this drawing by Marot.

LIT: M. van Bolhuis, *Reisverslag in 1705* (manuscript, Groningen, Rijksarchief); M. D. Ozinga, *Daniel Marot: De schepper van den Hollandschen Lodewijk XIV–stijl*, Amsterdam, 1938, 69, pl. 8; cat. London 1950 no. 65; R. C. Smith, "Five Furniture Drawings in Siena," *Furniture History*, III, 1967, 5, 6 pl. 7; Drossaers en Lunsingh Scheurleer, I, 667, nos. 528, 530; F. Liefkes, "Twee gueridons in de stijl van Marot," *Bulletin van het Rijksmuseum*, Amsterdam, 1975, 103, 104; P. Thornton, *Seventeenth-century Interior Decoration in England, France, & Holland*, New Haven, 1978, 44, fig. 51

RIJKSPRENTENKABINET, RIJKSMUSEUM, AMSTERDAM, INV. NO. 1898A1945

70 SILVER FURNITURE

By JOHANN I BARTERMANN (†1732 Augsburg)
SIGNED on each piece: I.B. with a pineapple for Augsburg
Silver and silver-gilt on oak and walnut: table 77 x 95.5 x 64.5 cm; mirror 145 x 88 cm; stands 91.5 x diameter 28 cm

The wooden core of this set of furniture, to be dated shortly after 1700, is covered with silver sheets on which embossed ornaments in silver are fixed with nails. Part of the ornaments of the mirror are gilt, including the central cartouche, the two acanthus volutes on the hood, and the decorations on the frame. Lunsingh Scheurleer suggests that the engraved table top represents a scene from the story of Endymion: the moment when he meets Ismene, who helped him to find his beloved Diana.

The top is the only engraved one known on an Augsburg silver table, other known pieces from Augsburg having embossed table tops. Similarity to a Dutch table top (London, Victoria and Albert Museum) caused Lunsingh Scheurleer to suggest that the present top, being part of a lost Dutch table, was perhaps added to the Augsburg table later. However, the close resemblance of the engraving on the table top to the engraving on an Augsburg basin of about 1690 by Johann Christoph I Treffler (coll. S. J. Phillips, London, 1975) leads us to presume that the table top could have been made in Augsburg as well as the base.

Johann I Bartermann (possibly a native of Danzig who married in 1693 in Augsburg) is known to have made another complete set of silver furniture about 1720: Rosenborg Castle, Copenhagen, in the collection of the Danish Crown.

Although many pieces of silver furniture (also a set, comprising table, mirror, and stands, of ebony mounted with gold; in the collection of William III) are mentioned in the inventories of the House of Orange from the early seventeenth century to the second half of the eighteenth century, it seems that the present set entered the royal collection only in the nineteenth century, perhaps as part of the dowry of one of the German Queens.

LIT: J. W. Frederiks, *Dutch Silver*, III, The Hague, 1960, no. 439, pl. 327; Th. H. Lunsingh Scheurleer, "Silver Furniture in Holland," *Opuscula in Honorem C. Hernmark*, Stockholm, 1966, 141–158; H. Kreisel, *Die Kunst des deutschen Möbels*, II, Munich, 1977, 129, figs. 326–329

RIJKSMUSEUM PALEIS HET LOO, APELDOORN, INV. NO. L420a, L420b, L421, L422
On loan from H. M. the Queen

71 MARBLE BUST OF WILLIAM III

By JAN BLOMMENDAEL (Breda or The Hague ca. 1650 – 1702 The Hague)
SIGNED AND DATED: J. Blommendael.F.1699.HAGAE.COMITIS.
Marble: 80 x 52 x 34 cm

The King wears the royal robes and the chain of the Order of the Garter. Blommendael, probably a pupil of Rombout Verhulst (1624–1698), had already made in 1676 a marble statuette of William III (The Hague, Mauritshuis), closely resembling the former statues of the four Stadholders Willem I, Maurits, Frederik Hendrik, and Willem II made in 1646 by Francesco Dieussart (ca. 1600–1661), for the castle Honselaersdijk. However, in this monumental bust, Blommendael is directly influenced by contemporary French baroque portrait sculpture. The bust has been identified as being in the collections of the Stadholders Willem IV and Willem V, respectively, in 1731 and 1764. In the accounts concerning Het Loo it is indicated that Blommendael also made two marble vases for the gardens.

LIT: E. Neurdenburg, *De zeventiende eeuwse beeldhouwkunst in de Noorderlijke Nederlanden*, Amsterdam, 1948, 227–230; cat. London 1950, no. 93; cat. *De Stadhouder-koning en zijn tijd*, Amsterdam (Rijksmuseum), 1950, no. 576; A. Staring, "De portretten van den koning-stadhouder," *Nederlands Kunsthistorisch Jaarboek*, 1951, 190, 191; cat. London 1964, no. 130; cat. *Europäische Barockplastik am Niederrhein: Grupello und seine Zeit*, Düsseldorf (Kunstmuseum), 1971, no. 199; Drossaers en Lunsingh Scheurleer, I, 682; *idem*, II, 407, no. 546; *idem*, III, 54, no. 610

ROYAL CABINET OF PAINTINGS, MAURITSHUIS, THE HAGUE, INV. NO. 361

72 WILLIAM III

By JEAN HENRI BRANDON (Sedan ca. 1660 – 1714 Utrecht)
Canvas, oval: 84.5 x 70.5 cm

The attribution of this portrait from the collection of Castle Amerongen to Brandon is based on the direct affinity in all details to Brandon's portrait of William III, ordered in 1699 for the town hall of Alkmaar, today in the collection of the Stedelijk Museum of this city. In the same period (that is, ca. 1693) Brandon also made a portrait of Margaretha Turnor, Baroness of Reede, Lady of Amerongen (1613–1700). It is known that there were friendly relations between William III and the owners of Amerongen. William visited Amerongen several times. The Amerongen portrait of William III may be dated about the same year as the one in Alkmaar. The French emigrant Brandon was active in The Hague from 1688 and painted other portraits of William, and also of Mary, some of them widely distributed in engravings by Pieter Stevensz van Gunst (1659 – ca. 1724). The rich and ornate frame, decorated with the English crown, the royal cypher WR, the royal shieldbearers of the lion and unicorn, scepter, military attributes, and the Orange Nassau device, *Je Maintiendray*, is carved after designs by Daniel Marot (1661–1752) through combining some engravings from his *Nouveau Liure d'Ornements*, *Pour Lutillitée des Sculpteurs, et Orfevres*, all etched by Marot himself and dated ca. 1700. The frame was originally part of an interior decoration, probably a chimney-piece or an over-door painting. It may have been taken from a room in Castle Amerongen when it was modernized, or from some other house of the owners of Amerongen.

LIT: P. Jessen, *Das Ornamentwerk des Daniel Marot*, Berlin, 1892, pl. 171; cat. London 1950, no. 50; A. Staring, "De portretten van den koning-stadhouder," *Nederlandsch Kunsthistorisch Jaarboek 1950–1951*, The Hague 1951, 190, fig. 31

CASTLE AMERONGEN, AMERONGEN

73 MINIATURE OF WILLIAM III

Ca. 1700
Parchment, oval: 6.4 x 5.1 cm

The unknown miniaturist followed the type created by Sir Godfrey Kneller (1646?– 1723), Principal Painter and Gentleman of the Privy Chamber to William and Mary. In facial expression the miniature is very close to Kneller's portrait of William III on horseback (1701) at Hampton Court.

STICHTING HISTORISCHE VERZAMELINGEN VAN HET HUIS VAN ORANJE NASSAU

74 WILLIAM III STAG-HUNTING

By DIRCK MAAS (Haarlem 1656 – 1715 The Hague)
Canvas: 59.5 x 86.5 cm

Dirck Maas, painter of horses and battles who was influenced by Philips Wouwerman (1619–1668), travelled to England in the army of William III and painted the battle of the Boyne on 1 July 1690 (collection of the Duke of Portland, Welbeck Abbey). About 1700 William III ordered Maas to paint a chimney-piece representing a *herte-jacht* (a deer or stag hunt) for his small hunting lodge Merwel near Het Loo. This painting may have been moved afterwards to Het Loo and therefore identified as the present picture. The castle in the plain in the background is situated like, and has contours very similar to, Het Loo. Composition and execution are closely related to the big *Boar Hunt* of William III by Maas, signed and dated 1693, which also belongs to the collection at Het Loo.

From Het Loo inventories of 1713 and 1757, it is evident that Maas painted the figures in a series (now lost) of seven hunting scenes in which the landscapes were made by Johannes Glauber (1646–1726) and Aalbert Meijering (1645–1714). The same teamwork is preserved in two ceilings of the royal palace Soestdijk.

LIT: Drossaers en Lunsingh Scheurleer, I, 647, 656, no. 230; *idem*, II, 618, no. 377
RIJKSMUSEUM PALEIS HET LOO, APELDOORN, INV. NO. PL242
On loan from the Stichting Historische Verzamelingen van het Huis van Oranje Nassau

75 ROBERT CHESEMAN, COURTIER OF KING HENRY VIII OF ENGLAND

By HANS HOLBEIN THE YOUNGER (Augsburg 1497/8 – 1543 London)
Panel: 59 x 62.5 cm
INSCRIBED: Robertus Cheseman ..etatis suae. XLVIII. anno . DM..M.D.XXXIII.

Robert Cheseman was a member of an old English county family, and not, as was formerly supposed, a falconer of King Henry VIII. (The salary of a falconer at the King's court was modest, at least too small to be able to commission a private portrait.) Holbein, who had his workshop in Basel from 1515 til 1526, after a stay of two years in England, returned to Basel from 1528 to 1532, and finally settled down in London for the rest of his life. It was in 1533, at the beginning of his second stay in London, that Cheseman was portrayed. The three-quarter turn of the face to the left is neutralized by his right arm, lightly touching the falcon on his left gloved arm. Cheseman's hairdress follows the fashion of the time, i.e., cut short at the front and long over the temples, ears, and back of the head. Shortly afterwards, in 1535, the fashion changed by order of King Henry VIII: a beard no longer should be shaved, and hair should be clean cut.

The portrait of Cheseman is one of the paintings of the English royal collection which William III brought to Het Loo. After William's death Queen Anne reclaimed these works, but they did not return to England. A seal on the back is evidence that later on it was part of the collection of Johan Willem Friso, Prince of Orange after 1702 and heir of William III.

LIT: P. Ganz, *Hans Holbein*, Basel, 1950, no. 72; R. Salvini and W. Grohn, *Das gemahlte Gesamtwerk von Hans Holbein der J.*, Milan, 1971, 101, no. 82; Drossaers en Lunsingh Scheurleer, I, 679, no. 887; 697, no. 35; *idem*, II, 639, no. 9; *idem*, III, 215, no. 60
PROV: English royal collections; coll. William III at Het Loo; coll. Prince Johan Willem Friso, 1712, 1713; coll. Stadholder Willem IV at Het Loo, 1734; coll. Stadholder Willem V, The Hague, to 1795
ROYAL CABINET OF PAINTINGS, MAURITSHUIS, THE HAGUE, INV. NO. 276

76 IVORY CARVED HANDLE WITH THE FIGURES OF WILLIAM AND MARY

Dutch or English, ca. 1700
Ivory: 9.7 x 3 x 2.5 cm

The King and Queen are dressed in the royal robes. The King wears the English crown and both the King and Queen bear a scepter. A fork with the same carving is in the collection of the Cutler's Company in London (collection of the Cutler's Company, London, no. 39). Two ivory handles in the Victoria and Albert Museum, one with two figures symbolizing Hope and Faith, the other with Justice and Abundance, are carved in exactly the same way and must have been made by the same artist. A bone knife-handle with figures of William and Mary in the Gemeente Museum in The Hague (inv. no. OH12–1959) is probably copied from the ivory carving by a less capable hand.

LIT: C. T. B. Bailey, *Knives and Forks*, London and Boston, 1927, fig. 35; Gertrud Benker, *Alte Bestecke*, Munich, 1978
PROV: Sotheby sale, London, 18 December 1978, no. 38
RIJKSMUSEUM PALEIS HET LOO, APELDOORN, INV. NO. RL526

77 SPOON AND FORK WITH WILLIAM III AND MARY IN CORONATION ROBES

(a) Spoon by JOHANNES ENNEMA (Franeker, active ca. 1724)
Marks: J E [Johannes Ennema]
INSCRIBED: L.H. and unidentified crest with a lion and arrows
Silver: 17.5 x 4.9 cm
(b) Fork by BERNARDUS RIENKS JELGERHUIS (Leeuwarden 1692 – 1766 Leeuwarden)
Marks: B I [Bernardus Jelgerhuis], unidentified mark, dolphin [19th-century tax mark]
Silver: 18 cm

Until well into the eighteenth century, spoons and forks were surmounted by the figures of William and Mary in their coronation robes. Although there are quite a number of commemorative spoons (given on special occasions, mostly at births), only a few forks of this type are known.

LIT: E. M. Ch. F. Klijn, *Oude zilveren lepels*, Lochem, 1967; E. Voet, *Merken van Friese goud- en zilversmeden*, The Hague, 1974, nos. 196 and 459
(a) RIJKSMUSEUM PALEIS HET LOO, APELDOORN, INV. NO. RL458
(b) H. M. THE QUEEN

STADHOLDER JOHAN WILLEM FRISO

Prince of Nassau Dietz, after 1702 Prince of Orange Nassau

JOHAN WILLEM FRISO was the son of William III's cousin Hendrik Casimir II (1657–1696) and Amalia, Princess of Anhalt Dessau (1666–1726). After the death of his father he became Stadholder of the province of Friesland, but due to his youth his mother acted as regent until his coming of age in 1707. In 1708 he was appointed Stadholder of the province of Groningen as well. He was General in the army of the Dutch Republic and fought in the battles of Oudenaarde (1708), Malplaquet (1709), and Douai (1710). He married Marie Louise, Landgravine of Hesse Kassel (1688–1765) in 1709.

William III made him his heir; however, this inheritance—as well as the possessions which went with the title of Prince of Orange—was challenged by King Frederick I of Prussia, a grandson of Stadholder Frederik Hendrik. On his way to negotiations about his inheritance in 1711, Johan Willem Friso was drowned in the Hollandsch Diep near Moerdyk.

78 PAIR OF FLINTLOCK PISTOLS FOR STADHOLDER JOHAN WILLEM FRISO

By GERRIT PENTERMAN THE ELDER (active 1673–1720, Leeuwarden)
SIGNED: (on lock) PENTERMAN (on barrel) LEEUWAERDEN and a mark with a heart under an open crown
French walnut stocks; barrels, locks, and mounts carved in bright steel against a gilt fish-roe ground: length overall 51.6 cm; barrel (length) 33.2 cm; bore 1.55 cm

According to A. Hoff, this pair of pistols is the most brilliant work by Gerrit Penterman. They must have been made for Stadholder Johan Willem Friso as they bear his coat of arms. However, it is not known when this pair was commissioned. They were probably presented to him at the time of one of his appointments during his military career. The carvings on the barrels, locks, and mounts are of classical figures, including Terpsichore (beneath a canopy suspended from a mask), Flora, and Victory. The French walnut stocks have raised carving of animals and plants framing the metal parts. On the escutcheons are the arms of Johan Willem Friso surmounted by a ducal coronet and supported by lions.

Both Gerrit Penterman the Elder and Gerrit Penterman the Younger worked in Leeuwarden, the capital of Friesland. Gerrit Penterman the Elder moved from

Utrecht to Leeuwarden in 1684, where he died, probably in 1720. Gerrit Penterman the Younger learned the craft from his father and would have become his partner. The Gerrit Penterman, master of the arsenal, who died in 1727 is likely to have been Gerrit Penterman the Younger. As this pair, which must been made in the first decade of the eighteenth century, still has some seventeenth-century characteristics, like the round forms and the boldly moulded ramrod pipes, A. Hoff suggests that it was made by Gerrit Penterman the Elder, who had also worked for the father of Johan Willem Friso, Stadholder Hendrik Casimir II.

According to eighteenth-century inventories, several pistols made by members of the Penterman family were in the possession of Johan Willem Friso and Stadholder Willem V. However, the descriptions are too brief to relate this pair to any one of the entries in the inventories.

LIT: C. A. Hartmans, "De geweermakersfamilie Penterman," *Livrustkammaren*, V, 1949–1951, 49–63; Drossaers en Lunsingh Scheurleer, II, 297, no. 1115; 298, no. 1132, 1134; 755, no. 103, 111, 115; 756, no. 150; A. Hoff, *Dutch Firearms*, London, 1978
PROV: acquired by Henry Walters from Sangiorgi, Rome
WALTERS ART GALLERY, BALTIMORE, INV. NO. 51.454/55

STADHOLDER WILLEM IV

Prince of Orange Nassau

HE WAS born in 1711 after the death of his father, Johan Willem Friso (1687–1711), heir of William III, Prince of Orange and Stadholder of the northern provinces of Friesland, Groningen, and Drente. Until 1731 under the regency of his mother, Marie Louise, Landgravine of Hesse Kassel (1688–1765), Willem IV succeeded his father in Friesland and was nominated in 1718 Stadholder of Groningen and in 1722 of Drente and Gelderland. In 1734 he married the Princess Royal, Anne (1709–1759), daughter of King George II of England. In 1747 he was proclaimed as first member of the House of Orange a hereditary Stadholder of all United Provinces of the Netherlands.

Willem IV extended the palace Huis ten Bosch near The Hague (by Daniel Marot) during the years 1734–1736. In 1733 he bought Rembrandt's *Simeon's Song of Praise* of 1631 for the picture gallery at Het Loo (today Mauritshuis, The Hague); it was the first painting by this master for the collections since all the works acquired by Stadholder Frederik Hendrik from Rembrandt himself had passed out of the possession of the House of Orange. Among the other pictures purchased by Willem IV are the famous *Bull* (1647) by Paulus Potter (1625–1654), also today in the Mauritshuis, The Hague, and several paintings representing different events related to the history of his family. He as well collected coins and ancient objects. After his death in 1751 Princess Anne formed ethnographic and natural-historical collections.

LIT: Th. H. Lunsingh Scheurleer, "De stadhouderlijke verzamelingen," *150 jaar Koninklijk Kabinet van Schilderijen, Koninklijke Bibliotheek, Koninklijk Penningkabinet,* The Hague, 1967, 18–22; Drossaers en Lunsingh Scheurleer, II, 643, no. 88; 652m, 730

79 TWO SNUFFBOXES OF AMETHYST QUARTZ

Germany(?), ca. 1750
(a) Gold mounted amethyst quartz, eyes of almandine: 5 x 6 cm
(b) Gold mounted amethyst quartz, eyes of brilliants, collar set with brilliants and amethyst: 6 x 8 cm

Both snuffboxes are mentioned as being among the many owned by members of the Stadholder's family in the eighteenth century. That of a lap dog lying down appears in the inventory of the inheritance of Princess Anne, the wife of Prince Willem IV. The box in the form of a dog's head and adorned with a deer (lying on the lid) belonged to her son, Willem V.

LIT: Drossaers en Lunsingh Scheurleer, II, 713, no. 26, 772, no. 62
H. M. THE QUEEN

80 PART OF A PORCELAIN AND VERMEIL SOLITAIRE

Meissen and Augsburg, ca. 1723
Porcelain by JOHANN GEORG HÖROLDT (Jena 1696 – 1775 Meissen)
Vermeil by ELIAS ADAM (? – 1745 Augsburg) and PAUL SOLANIER (married 1666 – 1725 Augsburg)
Marks: Porcelain unmarked, except for numbers in gold, vermeil; mount of jug: E.A
[Elias Adam]; knife, spoon, and fork: P.S. [Paul Solanier], Augsburg pineapple
jug: 24.5 x ca. 14 cm; broth cup and cover (cover restored): 12 x 18 cm; saucer: diameter
18 cm; beaker with cover (restored): 17 x 10.2 cm; knife: length 23 cm; fork: length
17.5 cm; spoon: length 18.1 cm

The travel service, consisting of vermeil-mounted porcelain, glass, and vermeil cutlery kept in a black leather case, is said to have belonged to Prince Willem IV. The decoration of the porcelain, with a white background and a low horizon for the landscape, is typical of the early period of Johann Georg Höroldt. Höroldt became manager in the Meissen factory in 1720 and worked in Meissen until his retirement in 1765. He is particularly famous for his fine chinoiserie paintings.

LIT: M. Rosenberg, *Der Goldschmiede Merkzeichen*, Frankfurt am Main, 1922, I, no. 648;
O. Walcha, *Meissner Porzellan*, Dresden, 1973, 54–71, pl. 65
H. M. THE QUEEN

81 PART OF A CHINESE ARMORIAL TEA SERVICE WITH THE ARMS OF STADHOLDER WILLEM IV

China, ca. 1747
INSCRIBED: VIVAT ORANYE
Porcelain enamelled in turquoise, gold, black (originally silver?), and red; teapot: 15 x 19.7 x 11
cm; tea caddy: 13.5 x 7.8 cm; milk jug (ear restored): 12.5 x ca. 9 cm; plate: diameter 15.6 cm;
hexagonal tray: diameter 13 cm; cup: 4 x 7.5 cm; cup with handles: 6.5 x 8.5 cm;
saucer: diameter 11.5 cm
The service consists of a teapot, a tea caddy, a milk jug, an hexagonal tray, a sugar bowl, a
bowl, two plates, six cups, six cups with handles, and twelve saucers

The motto underneath the arms indicates that the service was not commissioned by a member of the Stadholder's family. It was probably ordered by a supporter of the Orangist party in about 1747. The type of escutcheon is derived from prints made in the second quarter of the eighteenth century. Parts of another Chinese armorial tea set, commemorating Willem IV's elevation to Stadholder, but with the coat of arms of Willem III when Prince of Orange, are in the collection of H. M. the Queen, the British Museum, and in Delft, Museum Het Prinsenhof. A service with the arms of Prince Willem IV and his wife, Princess Anne of England, is in the collection of the Earl of Harewood.

LIT: D. F. Lunsingh Scheurleer, "Oranje-ceramiek in het Koninklijk Huisarchief," *Nederlands Kunsthistorisch Jaarboek*, 1970, 251, 152, pl. 9; D. S. Howard, *Chinese Armorial Porcelain*, London, 1974, 797, 798
RIJKSMUSEUM PALEIS HET LOO, APELDOORN, INV. NOS. RL516, 517, 518, 520, 522, 523, 524

82 COMMEMORATIVE PLATE WITH THE PORTRAIT OF STADHOLDER WILLEM IV, 3 MAY 1747

Chinese porcelain: diameter 21.5 cm
INSCRIBED: Willem Karel Henrik Friso Prinse van Oranien en Nassau &c.&c.&c.
Stadhouder Admiraal en Capitein Generaal over de Seve Provincien in de Nederlanden.
den 3 Maÿ 1747

The portrait and the inscription are exact copies of an etching by Philip Endlich (Amsterdam, active 1731–1748), made after a painting by Philip van Dijk (Amsterdam 1680 – 1753 The Hague). The plate is one of the many souvenirs commemorating the proclamation of Willem IV as hereditary Stadholder of the United Provinces of the Netherlands. Until recently it was assumed that Chinese porcelain adorned with European scenes, portraits, or escutcheons was painted in China. However, W. B. Honey and D. F. Scheurleer suggest that Chinese porcelain was also decorated in Delft. On the one hand, the inscription, in perfect Dutch script, and the portrait without any Chinese features indicate a European artist; but, on the other hand, the very clumsy way Dutch commemorative china was generally painted does not seem in keeping with the high quality of the decoration. A comparable plate is in the collection of the Museum Boymans–van Beuningen, Rotterdam. A plate with the same portrait and text in black and white, on the art market at present, fits the description in the inventory of Maria Amalia, Princess of Nassau Dietz (1689–1771), an aunt of Prince Willem IV.

LIT: W. B. Honey, "Dutch Decorators of Chinese Porcelain," *Antiques*, 1932; D. F. Lunsingh Scheurleer, *Chinese Export Porcelain: Chine de Commande*, London, 1974, 180–181, pl. 250; Drossaers en Lunsingh Scheurleer, III, 174, no. 469
PROV: coll. R. May, Amsterdam; coll. J. J. Post, Amsterdam
RIJKSMUSEUM PALEIS HET LOO, APELDOORN, INV. NO. RL515

83 GOLD AND SILVER MINIATURES OF STADHOLDER WILLEM IV AND PRINCESS ANNE

By JEREMIAS STAGMAN (Erfurt 1699 – 1762 Amsterdam)
Marks: boarhead [re-mark used beginning 19th century]
Gold, silver, and diamonds: 13.5 x 11.4 cm
INSCRIBED (on the base and the banderole of the miniature representing Willem IV):
IN SPEM CONCORDIA PACESQUE VENIT EN UTRAQUE ADEST [He comes in hope of
concord and peace; behold both are present] and ANNO WILHELMUS IV PRINC.AURAS
1748 [Willem IV Prince of Orange 1748]
INSCRIBED (on the base of that showing Princess Anne): ANNA REGIA MAGNAE BRITTANIA
PRINCEPS CELSISSIMI GULIELMI IV [Anne, Princess Royal of Great Britain,
Consort to the illustrious Willem IV]

The bust of Willem IV, represented as Captain-General of the United Provinces of
the Netherlands and with the insignia of the Order of the Garter, is surrounded by
war trophies and green- and orange-lacquered branches of the orange tree. The bust
of Anne, decorated with three diamonds, is surrounded by a royal crown, musical
instruments, attributes of the art of painting, and the lacquered branches of the
orange tree. Jeremias Stagman, who is known as a specialist in miniature busts in
gold and silver, made several similar pairs of these profile busts, dating from 1747
until Willem's death in 1751: two signed pairs in Amsterdam (Rijksmuseum and
Stedelijk Museum), and one pair, only dated, at Castle Amerongen in the collection
of the descendants of the original owners, the Earls of Athlone. According to the
inventories of 1759, one pair belonged to Stadholder Willem V (that is, the pair today
in the Rijksmuseum, Amsterdam).

According to the legend on the base and the banderole of the Prince, the miniature
busts are made to commemorate the elevation of Willem IV to the stadholdership in
1747 and the Peace of Aachen in 1748. They were probably commissioned by the
Stadholder as presents to men of special merit.

LIT: Drossaers en Lunsingh Scheurleer, II, 721, nos. 5 and 6; A. M. L. E. Erkelens,
"Miniatuur-borstbeelden van Prins Willem IV en Prinses Anna van Hannover,
Jeremias Stagman (1699–1762)," *Vereniging Rembrandt, Verslag over 1977*, 29–33
PROV: coll. Mrs. Greta S. Heckett, Pittsburgh; Sotheby sale, New York, 16 February 1977,
no. 554
RIJKSMUSEUM PALEIS HET LOO, APELDOORN, INV. NO. RL417a and b

84 BINDING WITH PAINTED COATS OF ARMS OF STADHOLDER WILLEM IV AND PRINCESS ANNE

Kantrol-bindery (active 1748 – ca. 1754), Amsterdam, 1748
BINDING: red morocco, gold-tooled; central panel pasted on (gold, beige, and silver),
painted in oil; spine with five raised bands: 20 x 11.8 x 2.8 cm
CONTENTS: Gerard van Loon, *Historisch bewys dat het graafschap van Holland, sedert het
begin der Leenen tot den afgezwooren Philips den II toe, altyd een Leen des Duytschen Ryks*

geweest is, Te Leiden, by Pieter vander Eyk, 1748 [Historical proof that the county of Holland always has been a feudal tenure of the German Empire from the beginning of the fiefs until the abjuration of King Philip II]; printed dedication to Willem Karel Hendrik Friso (Stadholder Willem IV)

The form of the central panel, a kind of elongated quatrefoil, was used during the period 1740–1750.

LIT: J. Storm van Leeuwen, "Eenige ontwikkelingen in de stijl van platbestempeling bij Nederlandse boekbanden uit de 18e eeuw," *Documentatieblad werkgroep 18e eeuw*, 1977, 14, 15
ROYAL LIBRARY, THE HAGUE, INV. NO. 343 H15,1

85 FOB SEAL WITH THE PORTRAIT OF PRINCESS ANNE

Dutch(?), 2nd quarter of the 18th century
Rock-crystal with gold handle: 3.5 cm

The Princess Royal, Anne (1709–1759), daughter of George II, married Prince Willem IV in 1734. This seal of her portrait was inherited by her son Prince Willem V; it appears on a list of valuables belonging to him.

LIT: Drossaers en Lunsingh Scheurleer, II, 714, no. 69
H. M. THE QUEEN

86 MOURNING RING OF STADHOLDER WILLEM IV

Dutch(?), 1751
INSCRIBED: (outside) W.K.H.FRISO.PRINS.V.ORAN.NAS.; (inside) Nat. 1 Sep. 1711 Denat. 22 Oct. 1751
Gold, black enamel, diamonds, carnelian: diameter 1.9 cm

The character of the ring is emphasized by being adorned with symbols of Death, an hourglass and a scythe. The carnelian represents an orange, symbol of the House of Orange. In the Netherlands, unlike England, the custom of bequeathing mourning rings to relatives and friends was not common. Although some rings with monograms mentioned in the inventories of the family of Orange might have been mourning rings, this one, with those of William and Mary, are the only ones known which belonged to a member of the House of Orange in the eighteenth century.

LIT: Charles Oman, *British Rings, 800–1914*, London, 1974; Drossaers en Lunsingh Scheurleer, II, 25, no. 61; 263, no. 75; *idem*, III, 160, nos. 18–20
RIJKSMUSEUM PALEIS HET LOO, APELDOORN, INV. NO. RL310

87 TOILET MIRROR WITH THE COAT OF ARMS OF STADHOLDER WILLEM IV

Augsburg, 1734/35
Marks: A surmounted by a pineapple [Augsburg 1734/35]; B [unidentified master]
Silver-gilt: 29.5 x 18 cm

The mirror is surmounted with the coat of arms of Prince Willem IV with the insignia of the Order of the Garter and is crowned by a German princely coronet. It probably belonged to one of the (now lost) silver-gilt toilet sets mentioned in the inventories of the Stadholder's family.

LIT: M. Rosenberg, *Der Goldschmiede Merkzeichen*, Frankfurt am Main, 1922, I, no. 238
H. M. THE QUEEN

STADHOLDER WILLEM V

Prince of Orange Nassau

ONLY SON of Stadholder Willem IV and Princess Anne of England, he was born in 1748. When three years old he succeeded to his father's offices under the regency of his mother and, after her death, of Ludwig Ernst, Duke of Brunswick Wolffenbüttel (1718–1788). In 1766 he was installed as reigning Stadholder of the United Netherlands, and the next year he married Wilhelmina, Princess of Prussia (1751–1820), niece of Frederick the Great. In the early eighties his position became controversial, and only by Prussian intervention were his rights re-established. During the French Revolution he had to flee with his family to England. From 1801 he lived in Germany, where he died in Brunswick in 1806.

Willem V collected an important group of pictures, continuing his father's purchases of paintings. His promising activities as a collector were, however, limited to his early years. His first acquisition was made in 1760 when he was only twelve years old, and his last, at the sale of Gerrit Braamcamp in 1771, when he was twenty-three years of age. His most important contribution was the entire collection of forty-one paintings formed by Govert van Slingeland, bought in 1768 (cf. nos. 95–97). Like many collectors of that time, Willem was mainly interested in Flemish and Dutch painting of the middle and second half of the seventeenth century. French and Italian masters were rarely bought; nor were contemporary pictures. Parts of the collections of William III and Willem IV were transferred from other palaces to The Hague, and, after enlarging his own collection, in 1773–1774 he built a special gallery where about 200 paintings were hung, which was open to the public until the beginning of the French Revolution. In 1795 all of the contents of this gallery were transferred to Paris, but they were, for the most part, returned in 1815. In 1822 the paintings were removed from the gallery to the Mauritshuis, where to this day they form the heart of the collection. The gallery itself was restored in 1977 and has since been used for exhibiting a number of the original paintings and other pictures in the State Collections. Besides paintings, Willem V collected drawings, prints and historical objects, and he also made additions to the natural-historical and mineralogical collections. The greater part of these were later incorporated by his son King Willem I in the State Collections.

LIT: Th. H. Lunsingh Scheurleer, "De stadhouderlijke verzamelingen," *150 jaar Koninklijk Kabinet van Schilderijen, Koninklijke Bibliotheek, Koninklijk Penningkabinet*, The Hague,

1967, 22–30; C. W. Fock, "De schilderijengalerij van Prins Willem V op het Buitenhof te Den Haag," *Antiek*, 1976, 113–137; B. Brenninkmeyer–De Rooy, "De schilderijengalerij van Prins Willem V op het Buitenhof te Den Haag," *Antiek*, 1976, 138–176; cat. *De schilderijenzaal Prins Willem V te 's-Gravenhage*, The Hague, 1977 (with English summaries)

88 GOBLET ENGRAVED WITH THE COAT OF ARMS OF STADHOLDER WILLEM V

German(?), 3rd quarter of the 18th century
INSCRIBED: VIVAT PRINTZ VON ORANIGEN [the N's are mirror images]
Glass: 21.7 cm

The German inscription may indicate that the glass was engraved in that country. The coat of arms of Prince Willem V is identical to that of his father. However, the type of decoration and the form of the glass suggest that the glass was made after the death of Willem IV.

PROV: presented by the Stichting 't Konings Loo, 1976
RIJKSMUSEUM PALEIS HET LOO, APELDOORN, INV. NO. RL320

89 MINIATURE OF STADHOLDER WILLEM V

By ROBERT MUSSARD (Geneva 1713 – 1777 Paris)
Parchment: 5.3 x 7.1 cm

Willem V, born on 8 March 1748, is represented in front of a chair, upon which a princely crown is placed. The chair bears some resemblance to the Stadholder's chairs used on official occasions. According to the inscription on another version in the same collection, but in inferior condition, where the boy holds a baton and crown on a table beside him, the miniature was painted in or shortly after September 1751: "R. Mussard pinxit agé de 3 ans e-demi dans l'année 1751" (The Hague, Mauritshuis; on loan from the Rijksmuseum, Amsterdam, inv. no. A4340). Judging by the official character of the portraits, the miniatures were probably ordered after the death of Willem IV on 22 October 1751. Although the signature is now lost, we know from a description that the companion piece, representing Willem's sister, the Princess Carolina (1743–1787) (*idem*, inv. no. A4342), was originally signed "R. Mussard."

In 1768 Mussard, whose works are rare, also painted a miniature of Princess Wilhelmina of Prussia (1751–1820), wife of Willem V; it was originally in the Stadholder's collection (Amsterdam, Rijksmuseum, inv. no. A4341).

PROV: Royal Cabinet of Rarities, The Hague
ROYAL CABINET OF PAINTINGS, MAURITSHUIS, THE HAGUE
On loan from the Rijksmuseum, Amsterdam, inv. no. A4343

90 PENDANT OF THE ORDER OF THE GARTER

English(?), ca. 1752
INSCRIBED: HONI SOIT QUI MAL Y PENSE
Onyx cameo, gilt and blue enamelled mount, gold suspension hook (probably a later
addition): length 8.5 cm

The back of the pendant has another figure of St. George and the dragon, chased in gold.

The Order of the Garter was bestowed on the four-year-old Prince Willem V on 5 June 1752. The decorations of the order were offered to him in the Huis ten Bosch in The Hague. A print designed by T. P. C. Haag (1737–1812), the art master of Prince Willem V and the future custodian of his picture gallery, depicts this event. The pendant was worn on a blue sash on the right hip, as is seen on some portraits of Willem V by Benjamin Samuel Bolomey (Lausanne 1739 – 1819 Lausanne) (Hoorn, West Fries Museum; The Hague, The Binnenhof, Government collection).

The pendant shown here fits the description on the list of valuables of Willem V made in 1759: *Nogh een George, gesneden in witte onyx* (another George, cut in white onyx). In addition to this pendant, four other decorations of the Order of the Garter are mentioned in the list: a large eight-pointed star of diamonds, a great George with twelve big diamonds, a link set with an even bigger diamond, the Garter of the Order set with diamonds from one end to the other, and an enamelled George with gold letters and six diamonds.

LIT: F. Muller, no. 4048; Drossaers en Lunsingh Scheurleer, II, 715, nos. 88–92
H. M. THE QUEEN

91 VELVET BINDING WITH COAT OF ARMS OF STADHOLDER WILLEM V

Dutch, ca. 1756(?)
BINDING: dark-red velvet, embroidered with gold and silver thread and paillettes, appliquéd with silk; smooth spine embroidered with rococo ornament: 21.7 x 12.9 x 4.7 cm
CONTENTS: *Les Pseaumes de David. Mis en vers François. Revus et approuvés par le Synode Walon des Provinces-Unies.* Nouvelle edition, A Amsterdam, chez Z. Chatelain & Fils. 1756

Both covers bear the embossed coat of arms of the Prince of Orange, designed in a rococo style, in the center. The same kind of escutcheon may be seen on contemporary pottery and engravings, for example, on the title page of the printed funeral procession of Princess Anne (*Convoi-funèbre de Son Altesse Royale Anne, Princesse Royale de la Grande Bretagne . . . 23 Fevrier 1759*, dessiné par P. C. la Fargue, gravé en cuivre par Simon Fokke, La Haye chez Pierre Grosse, 1759).

ROYAL LIBRARY, THE HAGUE, INV. NO. 140F7

92 BINDING AND TOOL WITH THE COAT OF ARMS OF STADHOLDER WILLEM V

First Stadholder's Bindery, The Hague, 1760
BINDING: red morocco, both covers gold-tooled with two ornamental frames and the crowned coat of arms of the Prince of Orange in the center. Spine with five raised bands, second panel with title on black leather, the others gold-tooled in the center and the corners: 20.6 x 15.7 x 2.5 cm
CONTENTS: Thymon Boey, *Bedenkinge over de oudheyt mitsgaders korte schets van het aansien en gezag van den Hove van Holland, Zeeland en Vriesland . . .*, 's Gravenhage by Mattheus Gaillard, 1760 [Thoughts on the Age, and a Short Description of the Importance and Authority of the Courts of Holland, Zeeland, and Friesland]; printed dedication to Prince Willem V and the Presidents of the Councils of Holland, Zeeland, and Friesland
TOOL, brass: 7.8 x 8.2 x 1.6 cm

The tool used for this binding and three others with the same coat of arms still exists and belongs to the collection of H. M. the Queen. They were probably commissioned by Prince Willem IV, but were in the possession of the binder. Two of the tools were used by the so-called First Stadholder's Bindery (active ca. 1725–1793) in The Hague. This bindery bound most of the dedication copies, and also re-bound the manuscripts and books originally in the libraries of the Princes of Orange in the seventeenth century, which were bought by Prince Willem IV in 1749 from King Frederick II of Prussia. The two other tools still in the possession of the Queen were used by the binder Johan Georg Berg (ca. 1746–1807). Most of the deluxe bindings from the collections of the Stadholders Willem IV and Willem V are dedication copies and were commissioned by the authors. Usually the author presented the specially bound copy to the Stadholder personally. The Stadholder was expected to give the author a monetary reward in return. Through such rewards the Stadholder stimulated the publication of books.

LIT: J. Storm van Leeuwen, *De achttiende-eeuwse Haagse boekband in de Koninklijke Bibliotheek en het Rijksmuseum Meermanno-Westrenianum*, The Hague, 1976, 479–481, no. 86
PROV: Library of Prince Willem V
Tool: H. M. THE QUEEN
Binding: ROYAL LIBRARY, THE HAGUE, INV. NO. 138C11

93 TWO PAINTED GLASS ALLEGORIES ON THE MARRIAGE OF PRINCESS WILHELMINA OF PRUSSIA TO WILLEM V, STADHOLDER OF THE NETHERLANDS

By C. F. HAEGELIN
Each one signed and dated: *Fait par C. F. Haegelin, Vitrier de la cour du Roy de Prûsse. Berlin le 4me October 1767*

Painted glass: 25 x 16.5 cm, inset on either page of a pseudo book, 29 x 18.5 cm
In a calf binding: 30 x 20 x 2.4 cm
Binding and blue satin flyleaves are gold-tooled
The glass plates are framed in blue satin and lined with silver thread

Apparently the otherwise unknown artist offered the plates as a wedding present to the Princess, as is apparent from the inscription at the bottom of the second plate: "à S.A.R. Madame la Princesse Wilhelmina de Prusse à l'occasion de son très heureux mariage." On the first plate, fitted in an elaborate rococo framework, the branch of an orange tree with two blossoms, two leaves, and an orange has a two-fold significance, being a symbol of fertility (bearing blossom and fruit at the same time) but also alluding to the House of Orange Nassau. In the center stands an altar on which are heaped two flaming hearts and seven arrows (symbol of the Seven United Provinces of the Netherlands) bound together by an orange ribbon. Small forget me nots decorate the bottom cartouche.

Again inside a rococo framework, decorated with olive branches as symbols of peace, the other glass plate presents an allegory concerning the Princess. Seated with Amor at her side, and regally dressed, she gestures imperiously to a small round temple, a common symbol for the true religion of Christianity. A rather exotic town is seen in the background, suggesting the walls and towers of Babylon as symbols of the art of architecture. A palette with brushes, a lute in her left arm, and the sheet of music, a bust, the books, and the globe hint at the arts and the knowledge in which the Princess excelled. Even the palm tree refers to a special desirable attribute, since it is a symbol of resistance to obstacles. The columns symbolize stability. The cartouche on top, with a royal crown, bears the monogram FSW, for Frederika Sophie Wilhelmina, flanked by the Prussian black eagle and the Dutch lion. The whole book is preserved in a calf slip-case, probably Dutch.

RIJKSMUSEUM PALEIS HET LOO, APELDOORN
On loan from the Royal Library, The Hague, inv. no. 1306A4

94 HYMNAL PRESENTED TO STADHOLDER WILLEM V AND PRINCESS WILHELMINA OF PRUSSIA BY THE JEWISH PARISH IN AMSTERDAM, 1768

Dutch, 1768
BINDING: painted silk: 22 x 12.5 cm
CONTENTS: printed on silk, *Vreugde lof en dankbaarheid gecelebreerd by de Hoogduitsche Jooden. In der selver synagoge ten dage dat hunne Doorluchtige en Koninklijke Hoogheden de Prince en Mevrouw de Princesse van Oranje en Nassau de stad met een bezoek hebben vereerd* [Liturgy of the public worship celebrated by the German Jews in their synagogue on the day their Serene and Royal Highnesses graced Amsterdam with a visit]

Prince Willem V married Princess Wilhelmina of Prussia in 1767 in Berlin. The next year he paid an official call in Amsterdam, which was his first visit to the capital as reigning Stadholder. The festivities lasted six days. A set of prints by Simon Fokke (Amsterdam 1712 – 1784 Amsterdam) and Reinier Vinkeles (Amsterdam 1741 – 1816 Amsterdam) depicts several of the events (F. Muller, no. 4210). The upper cover of the hymnal offered by the Amsterdam Jews is painted with the coats of arms of the Prince and Princess surrounded by Amsterdam's town hall, figures symbolizing Peace, Fame, and Charity, with putti. The lower cover is decorated with Hope, Concord, and Constancy, an escutcheon with a palm tree, a sailing ship, and a reading man (probably referring to history).

The hymnal is printed in Hebrew.

H. M. THE QUEEN

95 A YOUNG LADY COMPOSING MUSIC

By GABRIEL METSU (Leiden 1629 – 1667 Amsterdam)
SIGNED: G. Metsu
Panel: 57.5 x 43.5 cm

Metsu, belonging to the Leiden school of so-called "refined" painters, left his native town in 1650, and settled in Amsterdam. As a painter of genre pieces (as they were later known), he depicted the daily life of distinguished citizens. While his earlier work shows influences of Rembrandt and Frans Hals, the beginning of the sixties is marked by stronger coloring, especially red, blue, and yellow, which derives from the work of Vermeer and De Hooghe. Metsu turns to Terborch for subject matter congenial to his own involvement with the importance and place of women, but he does not follow Terborch's brilliant treatment of textures.

For the present painting Metsu borrowed Terborch's familiar device of a standing figure looking over the shoulder of a lady who was sitting at a table, here with a sheet of music in front of her. Behind the table and backed by a big fireplace, a second woman strums on a lute. The young lady keeping time to the music with her right hand symbolizes Moderation (the lute being a common attribute of Temperance), and the watchful little dog in the lower right hand corner is usually a symbol of Fides (Fidelity). Together, the symbols indicate the emblematic message of the panel as a Mirror of Virtue. The contrast is provided by the painting over the fireplace showing a shipwreck on a turbulent sea, which symbolizes "a disappointing love."

The picture which belonged to the collection of Govert van Slingeland was acquired by Stadholder Willem V in 1768 (cf. nos. 96, 97).

LIT: Hofstede de Groot, no. 162; cat. *Gabriel Metsu*, Leiden (Stedelijk Museum De Lakenhal), 1966, no. 41; E. de Jongh, *Zinne- en minnebeelden in de schilderkunst van de zeventiende eeuw*, Amsterdam, 1967, 52–53; S. J. Gudlaugsson, "Kanttekeningen bij de ontwikkeling van Metsu," *Oud Holland*, 1968, 34; F. W. Robinson, *Gabriël Metsu*, New York, 1974, 39, 200

ROYAL CABINET OF PAINTINGS, MAURITSHUIS, THE HAGUE, INV. NO. 94

96 A BOY BLOWING BUBBLES

By Frans van Mieris the Elder (Leiden 1635 – 1681 Leiden)
SIGNED AND DATED: M.DC.LXIII. F.van Mieris.fec[i]t. Lugd[unum].Bat[avorum].
Panel: 25.5 x 19 cm

This is an allegory of the relativity of human life, disguised in a genre scene. The soap bubble was in the sixteenth and seventeenth centuries a well-known allusion to the transitoriness of life, an illustration of the Latin expression *Homo bulla* (The life of man is like a bubble). The snail, in this context a symbol of earthly life, will not withstand death, as the bubble is not resistant to the air.

The picture must have been very popular. According to Plietzsch, seven versions by the painter himself are known, six of them dated 1663 and one 1666. Frans van Mieris, pupil of Gerard Dou (1613–1675), was renowned by the collectors of his own day, among them Leopold Wilhelm, Archduke of Austria (1614–1662), Stadholder of the Southern Netherlands; Johann Wilhelm, Elector Palatine (1658–1716); and Cosimo III, Grand Duke of Tuscany (1642–1723), who visited (when hereditary prince) the artist in his studio in 1667 and 1669.

The present painting was acquired in 1768 by Stadholder Willem V as part of the collection of Govert van Slingeland (cf. nos. 95, 97).

LIT: Hofstede de Groot, no. 229; E. Plietzsch, *Holländische und Flämische Maler des XVII. Jahrhunderts*, Leipzig, 1960, 50, 52; E. de Jongh, *Zinne- en minnebeelden in de schilderkunst van de zeventiende eeuw*, Amsterdam, 1967, 81; Drossaers en Lunsingh Scheurleer, III, 220, no. 90
ROYAL CABINET OF PAINTINGS, MAURITSHUIS, THE HAGUE, INV. NO. 106

97 SELF-PORTRAIT AS A YOUNG MAN

By Rembrandt Harmensz van Rijn (Leiden 1606 – 1669 Amsterdam)
Panel: 37.5 x 29 cm

This self-portrait, which may be dated around 1629, is one of the first portraits by Rembrandt which is not primarily concerned with the study of different expressions. In contrast to the sharp division of light and shadow on the faces of his previous portraits, Rembrandt here uses a softer *clair-obscur* in relation to a more modest and individual expression. An etching of 1629 resembles this painting. A drawing for this painting is in the British Museum, London.

The picture, with two other early works of Rembrandt—the Susanna of 163(7?) and a self-portrait of the mid-thirties, both also today in the Mauritshuis, The Hague —belonged to the renowned collection of forty-one pictures formed by Govert van Slingeland. Among them were also three paintings by Rubens and three by Van Dyck. The collection was acquired as a whole by Stadholder Willem V in 1768.

LIT: Hofstede de Groot, no. 544; A. Bredius, *The Paintings of Rembrandt*, London, 1937, no.

6; H. Gerson, *Rembrandt Paintings*, Amsterdam, 1968, no. 39; Drossaers en Lunsingh Scheurleer, III, 228, no. 132

ROYAL CABINET OF PAINTINGS, MAURITSHUIS, THE HAGUE, INV. NO. 148

98 VIEW OF THE NEW CHURCH IN DELFT

By HENDRICK CORNELISZ VAN VLIET (Delft 1611 – 1675 Delft)
SIGNED: HvVliet
Canvas: 100 x 91 cm

Through a frame which is partly painted on the canvas and partly real is seen the interior of the church. It is flanked on the right hand by a green illusionistic painted curtain. In the seventeenth century these curtains were often used as protection against daylight. In this painting the curtain conceals most of the mausoleum of Prince Willem I of Orange, the architectural and sculptural masterpiece of Hendrick de Keyser (1565–1621). Of the four allegorical figures, Freedom, Religion, Strength, and Justice, only the statue of Justice (holding scales) and part of the baldachin crowned with a large obelisk are visible. Under orders of the States-General, De Keyser began in 1614 to work from his model of the mausoleum; when he died in 1621 the work had to be completed by his son Pieter de Keyser (1595–1676). The tomb is in the middle of the choir between large white columns with the usual boards of coats of arms and of mourning. The black and white tiles and the iron gate depicted by Van Vliet are not there today.

Van Vliet, as a follower of Gerard Houckgeest (ca. 1600–1661) and Emanuel de Witte (ca. 1617–1692), started architectural painting after 1650. Before this date only portraits and genre paintings by him are known. A painting by Houckgeest of the same subject, showing the tomb of William the Silent, was purchased by Stadholder Willem V in 1774 (now in the Mauritshuis, The Hague).

LIT: H. Jantzen, *Das niederländische Architecturbild*, Leipzig, 1910, 101–107; E. Neurdenburg, *De zeventiende eeuwsche beeldhouwkunst in de Noordelijke Nederlanden*, Amsterdam, 1938, 49–54, ill. 18–28

STEDELIJK MUSUEM, HET PRINSENHOF, DELFT, INV. NO. NK2433
On loan from the State Collections

99 PART OF THE MEISSEN DINNER SERVICE PRESENTED TO STADHOLDER WILLEM V

Meissen, ca. 1772
INSCRIBED: black enamel on the bottom of the tureen: *'t Huis Marquette op te linkerzijde* [The house Marquette from the left side] and *'t Prinsenhof te Medenblik* [The Prince's Court at Medemblik]; on the cover: *Vriesche Poort te Alkmaar* [The Frisian gate in Alkmaar] and *Kennemer Poort te Alkmaar* [The Kennemer gate in Alkmaar]; oval tray:

Het Huis op Zigt Rijk in perspectief [The house Zigt Rijk (the country seat of the Governor-General in Java), in perspective]; sauce boat: *Loenen, van het Dorp op de syde van de Groote Laen te sien* [The house Loenen, seen from the main drive] and *Loenen met haere Vleugels van agteren te sien* [Loenen garden-front]; leaf-shaped tray: *De vergader plaats van de Heeren Staaten van Holland en West Friesland* [The Assembly hall of the States of Holland and West Friesland]
Marks: all pieces: crossed swords with point, blue, under glaze; tureen and sauce boat: J, over glaze; leaf-shaped tray: impressed K.; tureen: 15.5 x 23 cm; oval tray: 26.7 x 35.8 cm; sauce boat: 9.8 x 22.6 x 19 cm; leaf-shaped tray: 21 x 26 cm

The tureen, sauce boat, and trays shown here belong to a dinner service decorated with views of the Netherlands and Java, originally consisting of at least 435 pieces. It was supposed to have been presented by the directors of the Dutch East India Company to Stadholder Willem V who was Commander-in-Chief of the company. This theory is confirmed by the appearance on the service of many views of Java and the company's offices in Dutch cities. The only known eighteenth-century notice of the service is a remark by Johann Joachim Kaendler (Fischbach 1706 – 1775 Meissen) about the delivery of a lion for the "Servic vor den Stadthalter nach Holland bestellet." His description of the lion, sitting, with a bundle of arrows in his right paw, and bearing a crown with the words "Ostindianische Compagnie," corresponds with the lions surmounting the large tureens now in New York (Metropolitan Museum) and Washington (Smithsonian Institution), except that brass crowns replace the original porcelain ones. The service was probably dispersed during the French Revolution. In 1823 a part of the service was sold in the auction of the collection of William Beckford (1759–1844) at Fonthill Abbey. The description in the sale catalogue is as follows: "A matchless and extensive DINNER and Desert SERVICE of the rare OLD DRESDEN PORCELANE, elaborately enamelled in Views of all the principal Sea Ports and Towns of Holland, painted expressly for the PRINCE of ORANGE, comprising...." Pieces belonging to it are today in museums in the U.S.A. (Brooklyn, Hartford, New York, Philadelphia, Toledo, and Washington), in Europe (London and various Dutch museums), and in private collections. The Rijksmuseum Paleis Het Loo has been very fortunate in recently acquiring ninety-one pieces, which, together with sixty-five on loan from H. M. the Queen and H. R. H. the Prince of the Netherlands, now make up 156 parts of the service. Although the views and the inscriptions have been copied from Dutch prints sent to Meissen, only a few of these have as yet been traced. The house of Zigt Rijk, painted on the oval tray, also appears on a tray in the collection of the Metropolitan Museum; the views of Loenen, painted on the sauce boat, are also on one of the sauce boats in Washington (Smithsonian Institution).

LIT: A. L. den Blaauwen, "Eetservies van Stadhouder Willem V, Meissen ca 1772," *Vereniging Rembrandt, Verslag over 1975*, 47–49; auction, William Beckford, Fonthill Abbey (Phillips), 9 September 1823, nos. 762–765
PROV: coll. J. A. Völcker van Soelen, Castle Zoelen, the Netherlands
RIJKSMUSEUM PALEIS HET LOO, APELDOORN, INV. NOS. RL305, 425, 307, 347

100 TORTOISE-SHELL SNUFFBOX DECORATED WITH GOLD PIQUÉ POSÉ AND MOTHER-OF-PEARL

Dutch(?), ca. 1750
Marks: N.I.(?)
INSCRIBED: BIBL SA-CRA; HONI SOIT QUI MAL Y PENSE
Tortoise shell, mother-of-pearl, gold: 5 x 8.2 x 6.3 cm

The allegorical scene with the Dutch virgin reclining on the coat of arms of the Prince of Orange and four putti with various attributes, one of them painting HONI SOIT QUI MAL Y PENSE, may allude either to Willem IV's elevation to Stadholder or to the bestowing of the Order of the Garter on Willem V in 1752. Possibly the description in the inventory of the clothes of Willem IV, which was made in 1750, refers to the displayed box: "1 tabatière d'écaille dont le dessus est incrusté d'or et de nacre, représentant plusieurs figures emblématiques sur la paix; présent de Monsr. Benois." In that case the scene may suggest the Peace Treaty of Aachen in 1748.

Piqué posé is a technique of inlaying gold or silver in tortoise shell, ivory, or leather. A small hole is made in the shell and by the stroke of a hammer the shell is warmed and the gold is inlayed. When the shell cooled down, it shrank and held the gold. When the patterns are made of small golden balls, the technique is called piqué point.

LIT: Drossaers en Lunsingh Scheurleer, II, 466, no. 240; H. C. Dent, "Piqué: A Beautiful Minor Art," *The Connoisseur*, LXI, 1921, 87–95, no. 242; Clare le Corbeiller, *European and American Snuff-Boxes*, London, 1966
PROV: Prince Hendrik of the Netherlands (1820–1879)
H. M. THE QUEEN

101 SILVER SNUFFBOX WITH EQUESTRIAN PORTRAIT OF STADHOLDER WILLEM V

By PETRUS STAGMAN (Amsterdam, active ca. 1770)
INSCRIBED (on the back of the lid): Wilhelmus de Vde Prins van Oranje Erfstadhouder, Capitein en Admiraal Generaal der Vereenigde Nederlanden.
SIGNED (on the back of the lid): P. Stagman fecit.
Marks: M.P.B. [unidentified master, active ca. 1770], crowned coat of arms of Amsterdam, W [1781], crowned a [tax mark, 1795, Dordrecht]
Chased gold and silver figure, on black velvet, mounted in silver and mother-of-pearl box: 3.5 x diameter 7 cm

Two other boxes with the same portrait of Prince Willem V, made by Petrus Stagman, son of Jeremias Stagman (see no. 83), are known. Probably the chased figure dates from about 1766, the year of Willem V's inauguration, and was mounted only in 1781. We know from a catalogue of the Orange Nassau exhibition held in 1880, in which a snuffbox with the same portrait and inscription is described as having been presented by the Stadholder to one of the parents of the owner, that the Stadholder used these boxes as presents.

LIT: *Catalogus der tentoonstelling van voorwerpen betrekking hebbende op het Vorstelijk Stamhuis Oranje Nassau* ..., The Hague, 1880, no. 2986; C. H. C. A. van Sypesteyn, *Geschiedkundige verzamelingen, de prinsen van Oranje in 's Gravenhage, penningen, medaillons, draagtekens, linten, miniaturen enz.*, The Hague, 1901, pl. 1, no. 27; 78, no. 27; K. A. Citroen, *Amsterdamse zilversmeden en hun merken*, Amsterdam, 1975, nos. 554, 555
H. M. THE QUEEN

102 STIPPLED GLASS WITH THE PORTRAIT OF STADHOLDER WILLEM V

By DAVID WOLFF ('s Hertogenbosch 1742 – 1798 The Hague)
SIGNED AND DATED: D. Wolff, 1784
Glass with stippled engraving: height 13 cm

The technique of stipple engraving on glass is almost exclusively Dutch. The earliest glasses engraved in this manner were made by Frans Greenwood (1680–1761). Other engravers who used this technique were Gilles Hendrik Hoolaart, Jacobus van der Blijk, and Aart Schouman. The most prolific artist, however, was David Wolff. He did not choose his subjects for political reasons since he also made glasses for the patriotic party which was the opponent of Willem V.

METROPOLITAN MUSEUM OF ART, NEW YORK, MUNSEY FUND, 1927

103 FIVE SILHOUETTES REPRESENTING STAD-HOLDER WILLEM V, HIS WIFE, PRINCESS WILHELMINA OF PRUSSIA, PRINCESS LOUISE, HEREDITARY PRINCE WILLEM, AND PRINCE FREDERIK

Five silhouette portraits painted on paper: each 9.5 x 7.5 cm
In oval gilt frames decorated with a Louis XVI knot, fixed on an orange velvet panel: 35.5 x 35.5 cm, in a gilt frame

When we compare these with Tischbein's portrait group of 1789 showing the children of Willem V, Louise (1770–1819), Willem (1772–1843), and Frederik (1774–1799) (cf. no. 105), we may reasonably date the silhouettes about four years before, ca. 1785, particularly if we take into account the childlike profile of the younger Prince. The hairstyles and hats of the Princesses are fashionable and exuberant.

RIJKSMUSEUM PALEIS HET LOO, APELDOORN, INV. NO. PL963
On loan from H. M. the Queen

104 PRINCESS LOUISE AND HEREDITARY PRINCE WILLEM

By their mother, PRINCESS WILHELMINA (Berlin 1751 – 1820 Apeldoorn)
INSCRIBED (on the back): *Peint d'après nature par S.A.R. Madame La Princesse d'Orange 1788*
Ivory: 7 x 6.7 cm

The Princess Louise is shown with a portrait of her eldest brother, the later King Willem I, wearing the insignia of the Order of the Black Eagle of Prussia. Princess Wilhelmina was a dilettante-painter. She made miniatures—especially portraits of the members of her family—copies after pictures in the collection of her husband, and decorative paintings. A description of Het Loo of 1773 mentions a room with white taffeta hangings painted "in the manner of Peking" by the Princess herself.

LIT: B. Tideman, *Apeldoorn in zijn opkomst*, Apeldoorn, 1885, 16; cat. Rijksmuseum Amsterdam 1976, 767
STICHTING HISTORISCHE VERZAMELINGEN VAN HET HUIS VAN ORANJE NASSAU

105 THE CHILDREN OF STADHOLDER WILLEM V

By JOHANN FRIEDRICH AUGUST TISCHBEIN (Maastricht 1750 – 1812 Heidelberg)
SIGNED AND DATED: Tischbein.p. 1789
Canvas: 100 x 129 cm

This group portrait shows the only daughter of Willem V and Wilhelmina of Prussia, the nineteen-year-old Princess Louise leaning against the seventeen-year-old hereditary prince, the later King Willem I, who wears the star of the Prussian Order of the Black Eagle. Sitting at a writing table is Prince Frederik, age fifteen. On the writing table is a gilded bust of William the Silent (very close to no. 9) with the inscription "W[illem]. I. P[rince]. O[range].," and, in the middle of the rear wall, an oval marble profile portrait of Frederick the Great of Prussia, the most eminent member of their mother's family, with the legend FREDERICVS.II.BORVSSORVM.REX.

Friedrich (as he was called) Tischbein, the outstanding member of a large German family of artists, was the son of the portrait painter Johann Valentin Tischbein (1715–1768), who worked for Stadholder Willem IV in 1735 and stayed in the Netherlands in 1750 and the years following. Friedrich became about 1770 the protégé, and, in 1780, court painter to Frederic, reigning Prince of Waldeck (1743–1812), and, in 1796, to Leopold III, Prince of Anhalt Dessau (1740–1817). After studies in France and Italy, he travelled in Germany and the Netherlands, where, also as a portrait painter, he found his clientele at the princely courts and in rich bourgeois and intellectual circles.

The composition and many details of the present picture are so closely related to a portrait group of Louis Gohin (the Parisian merchant of artist's colors and the inventor of Prussian blue) and his family by Louis Léopold Boilly (1761–1845), painted two years earlier in 1787 (Paris, Musée des Arts Décoratifs), that Tischbein must in all probability have known this painting directly or indirectly from an engraving. The resemblance is most remarkable in the attitude of the two standing figures in combination with the boy at the writing table, and, moreover, in the movement of the figures against the rectilinear patterns of walls and floor. Notwithstanding these probable borrowings, Tischbein's painting has his own delicate and refined expression in design and color and also the balance between the three figures and the space around them is his own creation.

Another signed version exists, also in the royal collection, at Palace Huis ten Bosch. A mezzotint by John Raphael Smith (1752–1812) after the painting was published in 1790 in London by A. C. de Poggi.

LIT: Van Someren II, no. 573*; M. Praz, *Conversation Pieces: A Survey of the Informal Group Portrait in Europe and America*, London, 1971, 92, fig. 55; A. Staring, *Johann Friedrich August Tischbein's Hollandse Jaren*, Zutphen, 1978
RIJKSMUSEUM PALEIS HET LOO, APELDOORN, INV. NO. PL201
On loan from the Stichting Historische Verzamelingen van het Huis van Oranje Nassau

KING WILLEM I

ELDEST SON of Stadholder Willem V and Princess Wilhelmina of Prussia, he was born in 1772. After studies at Leiden University, he was nominated in 1790 General of the Dutch Infantry. He fought against France until 1795, when he had to flee to England with his family. From 1802 to 1806 he was given the principality of Fulda in Germany as compensation for his father's loss of the stadholdership. After the fall of Napoleon he was inaugurated in 1813 as Willem VI, Sovereign Prince of the Netherlands. In 1815 he became King and reigned as Willem I. Willem I worked at first successfully on the unification of the Northern Nertherlands (territory of the Dutch Republic until 1795) and the Southern Netherlands, which were under Austrian government until 1795. He had a great interest in economy and opened the country to trade and industry. He could not face the fact that after the Revolt of 1830–1831 the Southern Netherlands became the independent Kingdom of Belgium. He abdicated in 1840 at Het Loo and died in 1843.

In 1815–1816 after the return of most of his father's collections, taken during the French Revolution, Willem I partly presented these collections and partly put them at the disposal of the newly created State museums. The collection of paintings of Stadholder Willem V was transferred to the Royal Cabinet of Paintings, the Mauritshuis. He supported the museums with special funds under his control and also made some personal purchases for them, most notably, in 1822, *The View of Delft* by Vermeer in the Mauritshuis, The Hague.

LIT: Th. H. Lunsingh Scheurleer, "De stadhouderlijke verzamelingen," *150 jaar Koninklijk Kabinet van Schilderijen, Koninklijke Bibliotheek, Koninklijk Penningkabinet*, The Hague, 1967, 36–42; cat. Rijksmuseum Amsterdam 1976, 15–21; cat. Mauritshuis The Hague 1977, 13, 14

106 KING WILLEM I WHEN HEREDITARY PRINCE

By JOHN HOPPNER (London 1758? – 1810 London)
Canvas: 76.5 x 64 cm

The attribution here made to Hoppner is based on the strong similarity of execution, particularly of face and hair, and the use and gradation of colors, which one finds in his paintings. This portrait of the Hereditary Prince, wearing the star of the Prussian Order of the Black Eagle, was in all probability painted about 1799, when Hoppner (possibly by order of the Prince of Wales, the later King George IV) made the portraits of Willem's parents, the Stadholder Willem V and Princess Wilhelmina of Prussia, also in the Dutch royal collection at Het Loo. Until recently the picture of the Prince remained almost unknown, in contrast to those of his parents, of which engravings by Pierre Condé (active 1806–1840) were published in London in 1804, and of which small copies exist in the English royal collection at Buckingham Palace. John Hoppner, of German origin, from 1785 on painted several portraits of members of the English Royal Family and also executed many portraits of prominent personages, commissioned by Kings George III and George IV. By 1793 he was the official painter of the latter when Prince of Wales.

LIT: O. Millar, *The Later Georgian Pictures in the Collection of Her Majesty the Queen*, London, 1969, 56

RIJKSMUSEUM PALEIS HET LOO, APELDOORN, INV. NO. PLI172
On loan from the Stichting Historische Verzamelingen van het Huis van Oranje Nassau

107 SWIVEL SEAL WITH THE COAT OF ARMS OF KING WILLEM I

By ERNST SIMON (Warmbrunn 1817 – 1894 Warmbrunn)
SIGNED: SIMON
Carnelian matrix, gold mount: 5.5 x 4.2 cm

The matrix is engraved with the arms of the King or reigning Queen of the Netherlands, which Willem I had designed after his inauguration in 1815. The coat of arms is that of Nassau surmounted by a royal crown. The order engraved on the seal is the "Militaire Willems-Orde." This order was instituted by Willem I on 30 April 1815 and is the principal order of the Netherlands, bestowed, as the motto says, for courage, conduct, and loyalty.

H. M. THE QUEEN

108 TWO ARMCHAIRS

By FRANÇOIS HONORÉ GEORGES JACOB-DESMALTER (Paris 1770 – 1841 Paris)
Ca. 1805–1808
Mahogany, ormolu mounts: 89 x 71 x 70 cm

In 1806 Louis Napoleon (1778–1846), younger brother of Napoleon, became King of Holland. He moved his residence from The Hague to Amsterdam and confiscated the famous City Hall of the capital to turn it into a palace. Although he ordered most of the furniture from Dutch cabinetmakers and upholsterers, the set in his bedchamber was made by the prominent French cabinetmaker of the period Jacob-Desmalter. The set was originally placed in the bedchamber of Queen Hortense (1783–1837) in the palace in Utrecht. The difference of the chairs and armchairs from the rest of the suite is explained by a label on one of the armchairs, which states that the chair was made for Caroline Bonaparte (1782–1839), wife of Joachim Murat (1771–1815), for the Elysée Palace at Paris which was furnished by Jacob-Desmalter in 1805–1808: "S.A.S. le Prince Murat / à l'Elisée / Petit Apt. della Princesse / au rex de chaussée / Chambre à coucher / de la Princesse." During his four-year reign Louis Napoleon re-built and re-furnished five palaces: the palaces Huis ten Bosch, Soestdijk, and Het Loo, formerly owned by the Stadholder's family; the City Hall of Amsterdam, and a group of houses he transformed into a palace in Utrecht in 1795. The palaces Soestdijk, Huis ten Bosch, and Het Loo were completely stripped of furniture since the belongings of the Stadholder's family had been confiscated and sold by the new Bataafse Republic.

As was the custom in France, Louis Napoleon had the furniture of his palaces marked.

Except for the palace in Utrecht, Willem I, when he became King of the Netherlands, took possession of the palaces furnished by Louis Napoleon, and many pieces of his furniture are still in the Dutch royal palaces.

LIT: Th. H. Lunsingh Scheurleer, "De inrichting van het koninklijk paleis te Amsterdam onder Lodewijk Napoleon," *Publikaties van het genootschap voor Napoleontische studiën*, 1953, 256–258, fig. 6

ROYAL PALACE, AMSTERDAM, INV. NOS. AP63-3, AP63-4

109 COMMODE

By FRANÇOIS HONORÉ GEORGES JACOB-DESMALTER (Paris 1770 – 1841 Paris)
SIGNED: Jacob.D. R[ue]. Meslee
Ca. 1806
Mahogany with ormolu mounts: 97 x 136 x 56 cm

The commode also belonged originally to the furniture of the bedchamber of Queen Hortense in Utrecht and was afterwards placed in the bedroom of King Louis Napoleon in the Palace of Amsterdam.

LIT: see no. 108
ROYAL PALACE, AMSTERDAM, INV. NO. 52-321-8

KING WILLEM II

KING WILLEM II, the eldest son of King Willem I and Queen Wilhelmina, was born in 1792. During the Napoleonic wars he was at the military academy in Berlin. From 1809 to 1811 he studied law at Oxford University. As aide-de-camp of Wellington he fought in Spain against Napoleon, and, after Napoleon's return in 1815, Crown Prince Willem was Commander of the First Army Corps of the British-Dutch Army and Commander-in-Chief of the Dutch forces.

In 1816 he married the Grand Duchess Anna (1795–1865), daughter of the Russian Emperor Paul I (1754–1801). In 1831 he was Commander-in-Chief of the "Ten-Days' Campaign" during the Belgian Revolt. He ascended the throne in 1840 and died in 1849.

Willem II was greatly interested in architecture and was one of the first to introduce the neo-gothic style to the Netherlands. Between 1840 and 1848 he was his own architect for his neo-gothic residence in the heart of The Hague. This vast palace contained a huge hall for his private collection of paintings, and, leading to this hall, a gallery specially designed for the display of his collection of drawings, including many by Raphael and Michelangelo. Only the hall, modelled on the one of Christ Church, Oxford, has been preserved. Almost all of his famous collection of paintings were sold (in 1850 and 1851) after his death. Among the pictures were works of Jan van Eyck, Memling, Bouts, Quinten Metsys, Rubens, Van Dyck, Jordaens, Teniers, Rembrandt, Wouwerman, Ruysdael, and Hobbema; works of many Italians, among them Leonardo da Vinci (attributed), Titian, Raphael, Del Sarto, Annibale Carracci, Ludovico Carracci, Domenichino, Guercino, and Reni; and Spanish artists like Velásquez and Murillo. From his large collection of drawings, only a few still remain in the royal collection; the greater part was also sold at the time of the other sales.

LIT: *Gravure aux traits, d'apres les tableaux, de la Galerie de Sa Majesté, le Roy des Pays-Bas,* dessinées et gravées par A. L. Zeelander, The Hague, 1847–1848; H. E. van Gelder, "De kunstverzameling van Koning Willem II," *Maandblad voor Beeldende Kunsten,* 1948, 137–148; H. W. M. van der Wyck, "Koning Willem II als bouwheer," *Opus Musivum. Een bundel studies aangeboden aan Professor Doctor M. D. Ozinga,* Assen, 1964, 415–438

110 THE FUTURE KING WILLEM II

By JOHN SINGLETON COPLEY (Boston 1738 – 1815 London)
SIGNED AND DATED: J. S. Copley R.A.pinx. London 1813
Canvas: 90 x 60 cm

1. King Willem II sitting in the Gothic gallery, 1848.
   Painting by Jean Baptist van der Hulst (1790–1862).

2. Gothic hall with the collection of paintings of King Willem II—
   in the background the gallery with the drawings, 1842.
   Watercolor by Bartholomeus Johannes van Hove (1790–1880).

The future King Willem II is shown in his uniform of aide-de-camp to Wellington and as Commander-in-Chief during the Napoleonic war in Spain. He is wearing the Peninsular Gold Medal. After the victory of Vittoria in June and the battle of the Pyrenees in August 1813, the Prince returned to London with messages from Wellington to the Prince Regent and the British Government. This portrait is a preliminary study for the painting of Wellington and the Prince of Orange at the battle of the Pyrenees, now in Boston, Museum of Fine Arts.

According to a letter of 3 September 1813 from London to his mother, Princess Wilhelmina of Prussia, the Prince was sitting in those days for Copley who had been active in London since 1774. Prince Willem wrote: "Je vais dans ce moment donner une séance à Mr. Copley qui veut representer Lord Wellington à cette dernière bataille des Pyrenées dont j'ai été le porteur c.à.d.: de la nouvelle."

In the painting in Boston the pose of the Prince is different from that in this preliminary study: the Prince does not hold his bare saber before him, greeting his commander, but holds it down towards the right. On 4 December 1813 Charles Turner (1773–1857) published an engraving after the study of the Prince, one week before the announcement of his engagement to Princess Charlotte (1796–1817), heir to the English throne. This alliance was broken off the next year. Other versions of this painting are at Buckingham Palace and the Wellington Museum at Apsley House, London.

LIT: Van Someren, II, no. 647; J. D. Prown, *John Singleton Copley in England*, Cambridge, Mass., 1966, II, 381–382, 428, 436; O. Millar, *The Later Georgian Pictures in the Collection of Her Majesty The Queen*, London, 1969, 20; E. Pelinck, "Portretten van de Koningen Willem I en Willem II tussen 1808 en 1813," *Bulletin van het Rijksmuseum*, Amsterdam, 1971, I, 13–15
RIJKSMUSEUM PALEIS HET LOO, APELDOORN, INV. NO. PL277
On loan from the Stichting Historische Verzamelingen van Het Huis van Oranje Nassau

III LETTER WRITTEN BY KING WILLEM II, WHEN CROWN PRINCE, IMMEDIATELY AFTER THE BATTLE OF WATERLOO

DATE: [19 June 1815]
TEXT: Victoire! Victoire! Mes tres chers Parens Nous avons eu une affaire magnifique ce jour contre Napoleon qui'est venus nous attaquer dans notre position en avant de bois de Soignies, c'est mon corps qu'a principalement donné et a qui nous devons la victoire, mais l'affaire a été entierement decidée par l'attaque que les Prussiens ont fait sur la droite de l'Empereur, je suis blessé d'une balle qui m'a traversé l'epaule gauche mais c'est peu de chose. A vie et a mort tout a vous   Guillaume   2 h A nuit   Bruxelles
Size: 20 x 13 cm

During the battle of Waterloo, at about half past seven, the Prince was shot in his left shoulder and was forced to retire. He was brought to Brussels where he wrote this letter to his parents. His condition permitted him to give only a short description of the course of the battle; however, this was not devoid of chauvinism.

H. M. THE QUEEN

112 SABER BORNE BY KING WILLEM II, WHEN CROWN PRINCE, DURING THE BATTLE OF WATERLOO

Turkish(?), ca. 1810
Ivory handle, bronze, metal sheath upholstered with velvet: length 92 cm

Crown Prince Willem was Commander of the First Army Corps of the British-Dutch Army and Commander-in-Chief of the Dutch forces during the battle of Waterloo. Two days before the actual battle of Waterloo on 18 June he had an encounter with the enemy at Quatre-Bras.

For his courage during the battle, King Willem I bestowed upon him the first grand cross of the newly instituted Militaire Willems-Orde (see no. 107). The Dutch people showed their gratitude by giving him the title "Hero of Waterloo" and presenting him with the enlarged Palace Soestdijk. Willem II was very attached to the Waterloo saber and even in his official portraits when King of the Netherlands he used to bear it.

H. M. THE QUEEN

113 BRACELET WITH THE PORTRAIT OF KING WILLEM II, COMMEMORATING HIS MARTIAL EXPLOITS

Miniature by JEAN BAPTISTE JOSEPH DUCHESNE (Gisors 1770 – 1856 Paris)
SIGNED: Duchesne fe.
DATED: 1822 Paris
INSCRIBED: Waterloo 1815, 7 October 1840 Hasselt Leuven 1831; (on back of miniature): Quatre Bras Waterloo 16 18 juin 1815 WO [in monogram]; (on links): Cindad, Rodrigo, Badajos, Salamanca, Vittoria, Pampeluma, Nivelli, 1811 1812 1813 1814
Gold mounted enamel miniature, seven gold links: length 17.5 cm

The bracelet probably originally consisted of the miniature and the links with the names of the battles of the Peninsular War. The miniature may have been reset so as to add the names of Hasselt and Leuven, cities taken during the "Ten-Days' Campaign" against the Belgian rebels in 1831, and the date of Willem II's inauguration.

J. B. J. Duchesne was a favorite miniature and enamel painter of royalty in the first half of the nineteenth century. His portrait of Napoleon was given to the Empress Marie Louise in 1810 as a wedding present. Queen Victoria commissioned him to paint a set of enamel miniatures of the English Royal Family after portraits by William Charles Ross (London 1794–1860 London).

LIT: M. H. Gans, *Juwelen en mensen*, Amsterdam, 1961, 151, pl. 192
H. M. THE QUEEN

114 CAMEO WITH THE PORTRAIT OF KING WILLEM II

By N. JULIN, ca. 1840–1848
SIGNED: N. Julin
Cameo, gold frame enamelled in green, red, white, and blue: 8 x 6 cm

The cameo set in a frame with the royal crown and a red, white, and blue ribbon would have been made after the inauguration of Willem II.

PROV: Castle Raçot, Silesia
H. M. THE QUEEN

115 CROWNED GOBLET WITH THE PORTRAIT OF KING WILLEM II

By DOMINIK BIMANN (Harachsdorf-Neuwelt, Bohemia, 1800 – 1857 Cheb near Franzensbad)
SIGNED: B
Glass: 34 cm

As Ritsema van Eck indicated, the glass was probably engraved in Franzensbad where Dominik Bimann made many glasses for the important guests staying there to take the water. Although he mainly engraved portraits from life, this one is copied after the well-known lithograph by Carel C. A. Last (1808–1876). This lithograph was based on the painting of 1831 by Jean Baptist van der Hulst (1790–1862); Last, however, changed the costume to that of the military uniform in another portrait of Willem II by Van der Hulst of ca. 1828, both at the Palace Soestdijk.

The goblet may be dated at about 1840, since Bimann used the same unusual signature on two glasses dated 1840, and the engraving is very similar to that on his goblet with the portrait of Franz Karl, Archduke of Austria, also dated 1840.

Glass crowns are rare and are added to goblets only in the case of royal sitters.

LIT: P. C. Ritsema van Eck, "Een onbekend Oranje-portret door Dominik Bimann," *Jaarverslag Vereniging "Oranje-Nassau Museum" 1976*, The Hague, 1977, 14–21; *idem*, "Een onbekend Oranje-portret door Dominik Bimann," *Antiek*, October 1977, 173–180
PROV: probably presented by King Willem II to D. Westenberg (1771–1846); in the possession of his descendants until 1976
RIJKSMUSEUM PALEIS HET LOO, APELDOORN, INV. NO. A3835
On loan from the Vereniging Oranje Nassau Museum

116 QUEEN ANNA PAVLOVNA

By Jean Chrétien Valois (The Hague 1809 – 1894 The Hague)
signed and dated: J. C. Valois fc. 1845
Watercolor: 60.5 x 42.5 cm

The Queen is represented in Russian court robe and *kokochnik* with tulle veil which, in adapted form, was in use for court ceremonies in St. Petersburg until the end of the empire. Robe and *kokochnik* are ornamented with many of the Queen's fabulous jewels.

Jean Chrétien Valois, son of the landscape painter Jean François Valois (1778–1853), painted portraits and miniatures of several members of the Royal Family in the 1840's (cf. no. 122).

Stichting Historische Verzamelingen van het Huis van Oranje Nassau

117 CHALICE OF QUEEN ANNA PAVLOVNA

By Alexej Ivanov Ratkov (active 1777–1821), 1816
inscribed: IPI, IMF, AP, EA, KP, AF, NP, AP, AP, MP, EP
Marks: St. George killing the dragon [Moscow hallmark]; A.P [Alexej Ivanov Ratkov], 8+
Gold with white enamel medallions painted in gold; one medallion lost: 18.5 x 9 cm

This vessel was formerly described as a salt cellar; however, since Queen Anna Pavlovna ordained that after her death the vessel should be given on loan to the Russian Orthodox Church in The Hague, and since the salt cellars usually were smaller in this period, it seems more reasonable that it is a chalice. As such it is found on the list of Anna Pavlovna's dowry, in which it is described as "Une calice avec des images en email" belonging to the gold objects for the church. Anna Pavlovna remained Russian Orthodox after her marriage, and a Russian Orthodox Church was established for her in The Hague. The cyphers on the medallions are those of her parents and her brothers and sisters: IPI and IMF, Emperor Paul I (1759–1801) and Empress Maria Feodorovna, formerly Sophy of Württemberg (1759–1828); AP and EA, Alexander Pavlovich (1777–1825) and his wife, Elizabeth Alexevna, formerly Marie Louise of Baden (1779–1826); KP and AF, Konstantin Pavlovich (1779–1831) and his first wife, Anna (1781–1860), formerly Juliane, daughter of Franz, Duke of Sachsen Coburg Saalfield; NP, Nicholas Pavlovich (1796–1855); AP, Alexandra Pavlovna (1783–1801); AP, Anna Pavlovna (1795–1865); MP, Michael Pavlovich (1798–1849); and EP, Elena Pavlovna (1784–1803). The lost medallion may have been painted with the monogram either of Catharina Pavlovna (1788–1819) or of Maria Pavlovna (1786–1859). The last one is the more probable as Anna and Catharina were not on speaking terms.

The Empress Maria Feodorovna may have painted the monograms. She wrote, when describing an octagonal amber and ivory alter: "I have painted all the ciphers of the children in roses and myrtle; mine is in little blue flowers."

Alexej Ivanov Ratkov was one of the best silver- and goldsmiths of that period. Other members of his family were as well silversmiths.

LIT: *Inventaire des effects de la dot de Son Altesse Imperiale Madame la Grande Duchesse, Anna Paulowna*, manuscript, Royal Archives, The Hague; *In the Russian Style*, edited by J. Onassis, London, 1977, 87
H. M. THE QUEEN

118 PORTRAIT OF A BOY

By ANNIBALE CARRACCI (Bologna 1560 – 1609 Rome)
INSCRIBED (on verso of lining in pencil in 19th-century hand): *Domenichino*
Red chalk: 29.4 x 22.4 cm
Watermark: three hillocks surmounted by an *F*, within a shield (Briquet 11938)

The identity of the boy whom the artist honored with this striking life-size portrait will perhaps never be known. His sober countenance and unblinking gaze are depicted with extraordinary directness and consummate mastery of draughtsmanship. Could he have been Antonio Carracci, the son of Agostino Carracci, born most probably in 1589 in Venice, but possibly as early as 1583? Was he a studio apprentice seen in a mood of unwonted sobriety as he was called upon to pose for his master, perhaps by candlelight in the evening? Does he bear any resemblance to the youth seen at the side of Annibale Carracci in his self-portrait, the painting in the Brera, Milan (Donald Posner, *Annibale Carracci*, London, 1971, II, pl. 25)? The drawing can be compared with the likeness of the lute player Mascheroni in the Albertina (Otto Benesch, *Meisterzeichnungen der Albertina*, Salzburg, 1964 [English ed. 1967], pl. 46), a study for Annibale's painting in Dresden (Posner, II, pl. 76). Likewise in red chalk, the Albertina drawing, though more finished, is similarly unerringly modeled with passages of feathery cross-hatching that give shape and form to the features.

At the same time, one cannot dismiss a certain similarity in execution to the *Portrait of a Woman*, also in strict frontality, in the collection of the late Curtis O. Baer, a drawing assigned to Annibale's older brother Agostino (*Drawings from New York Collections, II: The Seventeenth Century in Italy*, exhibition catalogue by Felice Stampfle and Jacob Bean, The Metropolitan Museum of Art, The Pierpont Morgan Library, New York, 1967, no. 5, repr.). If the attribution of the sheet to Annibale is disputed in favor of Agostino—who as an engraver was accustomed to make use of regularly hatched shading—the drawing could only be regarded as a singularly inspired achievement of the older brother and perhaps one owed to a relationship with the model. Although the drawing carries the stamp of Sir Thomas Lawrence, it cannot have been among the 160 drawings by the three Carracci exhibited at the Lawrence Gallery in 1836 by Samuel Woodburn, these having been sold *in toto* to Lord Francis Egerton, later the first Earl of Ellesmere, and eventually dispersed at auction in 1972. It may be that Sir Thomas attributed the drawing to Domenichino, a follower of the Carracci, whose name is written on the back of the drawing in a nineteenth-century hand. (In the sale of 12 August 1850 of Willem II, one or the other of two drawings might have referred to the present sheet: "No. 93. Annibale Carrachi, Étude de tête d'homme, à la sanguine" [bought in by Roos for 45 florins], or "No. 236. Domenichino [d'après]. Étude de tête; à la sanguine" [bought in by Brondgeest for 15 florins].) There is a red chalk portrait, formerly in the Ellesmere collection (lot 30 of the Sotheby sale of 11 July 1972) and now in the Art Institute of Chicago, which, according to an old inscription, is a likeness by Agostino of his son Antonio, but it may well be studio work.

PROV: Sir Thomas Lawrence (Lugt no. 2445); King Willem II; King Willem III; Queen Wilhelmina

H. M. THE QUEEN

119   ST. FRANCIS OF ASSISI

By GIOVANNI FRANCESCO BARBIERI, called IL GUERCINO (Cento 1591 – 1666 Bologna)
Red chalk (light foxing; losses at lower left corner and upper right margin): 24 x 19.1 cm
Watermark: illegible design within a circle

This devotional image of the saint shows him in his hooded habit kneeling before a rectangular stone that serves as a kind of altar table; his expressive countenance is seen in slightly less than three-quarter view as he meditates on the crucifix held in his left hand. The artist represented St. Francis at his devotions before a crucifix in various other drawings, but none more movingly than this one which was a favorite of Queen Wilhelmina and hung in her drawing room. Among the other depictions representing the saint are the red chalk drawings in the Uffizi (inv. no. 3665) and the British Museum (inv. no. F.f.2–129), and a pen-and-wash study in the Royal Library at Windsor Castle (inv. no. 2582). The latter is a study for the painting of 1645 in the Church of San Giovanni in Monte at Bologna. The success of that painting, which was the first of Guercino's works to be placed in a Bolognese church, led to other commissions in that city. Possibly this drawing was among them either as an independent work or as a study for a painting though none is known at this time. The present drawing and that in the British Museum were once together in the collection of Jonathan Richardson, Sr.

PROV: Jonathan Richardson, Sr. (Lugt no. 2184); fragment of his press mark on verso, . . . *24/JH* (linked); Thomas Hudson (Lugt no. 2432); Charles Rogers (Lugt no. 624); his sale, London, T. Philipe, 15 April 1799, lot 336; Sir Thomas Lawrence (Lugt no. 2445); King Willem II; his sale, The Hague, 12 August 1850, lot 228, "St. François; dessin à la sanguine" (bought in by [Jean Albert] Brondgeest, one of the directors of the sale, for 20 florins); King Willem III; Queen Wilhelmina

H. M. THE QUEEN

120 STUDY OF A MALE NUDE

By PETER PAUL RUBENS (Siegen 1577 – 1640 Antwerp)
INSCRIBED (in pen and brown ink in lower right corner): *Rubens*
Black chalk heightened with white chalk on gray-brown paper; some water stains at upper
left and several scattered small losses. The paper of the drawing has been extensively
trimmed on the diagonal at the right corners and then laid down on another sheet of
paper regularizing the right corners: 48.9 x 31.5 cm. The paper of the drawing measures
48.9 cm at the left margin; 25.5 cm at the upper margin; 16.6 cm at the lower edge;
and 11.3 cm at the right margin
Watermark: partially legible, fragment of hunting horn?

One of Rubens' most important commissions after his return to Antwerp from Italy
late in 1608 was the execution of the *Raising of the Cross* (1610–1611) for the Church
of St. Walburga, the monumental triptych now in the Antwerp Cathedral. His prepa-
rations for the painting began with the oil sketch of the composition now in the Louvre,
followed by the execution of numerous drawings for the individual figures, studied
after the living model. This powerful rendering of the muscular body of a young man,
tautly stretched in a strong diagonal, defined the final position of the Roman soldier
helping to elevate the cross at the left of the scene in the central panel of the triptych.
In the painting he is clad in armor and the position of his head is altered slightly
from the strict profile view of the drawing. It will be noted that the artist tried two
positions for the legs and feet, choosing finally the lower one, and further that he did
not bother to complete the figure's right arm which he realized would be obscured
by the adjoining figure in the painting. The shaft of the cross is perhaps suggested by
the short diagonal at the upper right in the area of the figure's left hand, which likewise is incomplete. In the painting the hand actually rests against the upstretched
arm of the Christ rather than the cross itself. The short diagonal may also indicate
the wand which the studio model held as he posed. Among the other life studies for
the great triptych are the following: *Studies for the Figure of Christ* (2), Fogg Art
Museum, Harvard University, Cambridge, Mass.; *Nude Male Torso*, Ashmolean
Museum, Oxford; *Crouching Nude Man*, now in the possession of the heirs of Chr.
P. van Eeghen, Amsterdam; *Two Studies for Hands*, Albertina, Vienna; and three
fragments of *Studies of a Man Holding a Shaft of the Cross* scattered among the Musée
Bonnat, Bayonne, the Seilern Collection, London, and the Metropolitan Museum,
New York.

This sheet has been mistakenly associated with the drawing in *The Lawrence Gallery, First Exhibition*, 1835, under no. 27: "A Study for the figure of a soldier in the
picture of the Raising of the Cross: black chalk and bistre wash. Size, 18¼ inches
×12½. From the Verstegh Collection." The Lawrence Gallery drawing is the Van
Eeghen drawing.

LIT: Alfred Scharf, "An Exhibition of Flemish Drawings," *Burlington Magazine*, XCI, 1949,
138, fig. 13; Julius S. Held, *Rubens: Selected Drawings*, London, 1959, 129, no. 76, pl. 87, 126,
under no. 70; Justus Müller Hofstede, review of "Julius S. Held: *Rubens: Selected Drawings*,"
Kunstchronik, XV, 1962, 134, no. 76; L. Burchard and R.-A. d'Hulst, *Rubens Drawings*,

Brussels, 1963, 96, no. 56, pl. 56, 95, under no. 55; Justus Müller Hofstede, review of "Burchard-d'Hulst: *Rubens Drawings*," *Master Drawings*, IV, 1966, 445, no. 56; David Rosand, "Rubens Drawings," *Art Bulletin*, XLVIII, 1966, 245; Justus Müller Hofstede, "Aspekte der Entwurfzeichnung bei Rubens," *Stil und Überlieferung*, III, 1967, 114; Justus Müller Hofstede, "Eine Kreidestudie von Rubens für des Kreuzaufrichtungsaltar," *Pantheon*, XXV, 1967, 40, note 4; Justus Müller Hofstede, "Rubens in Rom 1601–02: Die Altargemälde für S. Croce in Gerusalemme," *Jahrbuch der Berliner Museen*, XII, 1970, 94; J. J. Kusnetzov, *Risunki Rubensa*, 1974, pl. 30; Marianne Bernhard, *Rubens: Handzeichnungen*, Munich, 1977, 202. [The completeness of this bibliography is owed to the courtesy of Mrs. Anne-Marie S. Logan.]

EXHIBITED: Rotterdam, Museum Boymans, *Teekeningen van Peter Paulus Rubens*, 1939, no. 63 (Supplement), repr.; Rotterdam, Museum Boymans, *Tekeningen van Jan van Eyck tot Rubens*, 1948–49, no. 113a; Brussels, Palais des Beaux-Arts, *De Van Eyck à Rubens: Dessins de maîtres flamands*, 1949, no. 83; Paris, Bibliothèque Nationale, *De Van Eyck à Rubens: Les maîtres flamands du dessin*, 1949, no. 86; London, Wildenstein and Co., *A Loan Exhibition of Works by Peter Paul Rubens*, catalogue by L. Burchard, 1950, no. 58; Antwerp, Rubenshuis, *Tekeningen van P. P. Rubens*, catalogue by L. Burchard and R.-A. d'Hulst, 1956, 48–49, no. 35, repr. pl. XII; Antwerp, Royal Museum of Fine Arts, *P. P. Rubens: Paintings-Oilsketches-Drawings*, 1977, 299, no. 131, repr.

PROV: Prince of Orange, later King Willem II; possibly his sale, The Hague, 12 August 1850, lot 303, "Rubbens (P.P.) Figure académique d'un homme. Dessin largement exécuté à la pierre d'Italie; d'un beau faire" (bought in by [Jean Albert] Brondgeest, one of the directors of the sale, for 35 florins); King Willem III; Queen Wilhelmina

H. M. THE QUEEN

121 GARDEN FRONT OF THE PALACE HET LOO

By ANDREAS SCHELFHOUT (The Hague 1787 – 1870 The Hague)
SIGNED: A. Schelfhout f.
Panel: 84.5 x 113.5 cm

The palace is seen from the back. Only the main building and the two pavilions at either side are visible: the wings are hidden by the groves. On the left in the foreground, a *troika* with unidentified occupants. The palace shows the alterations which had been made by King Louis Napoleon in 1807–1809: white plastered walls, empire windows, and a landscaped garden. As Pelinck has indicated, the painting was commissioned by Queen Wilhelmina (1774–1837) about 1837–1838 as a present to Princess Mary (1776–1857), daughter of King George III of England, who was married in 1816 to William Frederic, Duke of Gloucester (1776–1834). Long before her marriage, Princess Mary had been the idol of Prince Frederik (1774–1799), youngest son of Stadholder Willem V, who had arrived in England in 1795 as an exile with his family. A marriage was ruled out by George III. After Frederik's death in 1799 in Padua when Commander-in-Chief of the Austrian army in Italy, Princess Mary remained on friendly terms with the House of Orange. In 1836 she visited the Dutch Royal Family and stayed at Het Loo. As a souvenir of this occasion, the Queen ordered two views of Het Loo. The second one, perhaps representing the façade of the palace or the mediaeval castle The Old Loo, is now unknown. The account (in German) reads as follows: "14 juli 1838: Dem Maler A. Schelfhout im Haag für zwey Gemälde, Ansichten aus dem Park vom Loo vorstellend, welche noch von weiland Iher Majestät der Königin bestellt und zu einen Geschenke für Ihre Königl. Hoheit die Herzogin von Gloster bestimmt worden, einschlieslich der reich verzierten goldenen Rahmen *f* 6400.—"

Schelfhout, one of the most esteemed landscape painters of his time, was also in high favor with the Royal Family. He visited Het Loo several times. A watercolor with a preparatory drawing of the garden front is in the collection of H. M. the Queen in the Royal House Archive; a matching pair of watercolors of façade and garden front is in a Dutch private collection.

LIT: E. Pelinck, "Het Koninklijk Paleis Het Loo geschilderd door Andreas Schelfhout," *Jaarverslag Vereniging "Oranje Nassau Museum" 1967*, The Hague, 1968, 9–14
PROV: coll. Mary, Duchess of Gloucester; Christie's sale, London, 21 January 1966, no. 112; London, Patterson & Shipman, 1966; The Hague, Kunsthandel P. A. Scheen, 1966; Vereniging Oranje Nassau Museum, 1967
RIJKSMUSEUM PALEIS HET LOO, APELDOORN, INV. NO. A3633
On loan from the Vereniging Oranje Nassau Museum

KING WILLEM III

ELDEST SON of King Willem II and Queen Anna Pavlovna, he was born in 1817. In 1839 he married his cousin Sophie, Princess of Württemberg (1818–1877). She bore him three sons who all died before him: Willem (1840–1879), Maurits (1843–1850), and Alexander (1851–1884). He married in 1879 the young Princess Emma of Waldeck Pyrmont (1858–1934), whose daughter succeeded him as Queen Wilhelmina (1880–1962).

Willem III was more a military man than a politician. He had a passion for Het Loo, where in 1873 he built a gallery for his collection of contemporary art. He invited a number of artists to stay at Het Loo, for example, Andreas Schelfhout (1787–1870), Charles Rochussen (1814–1894), and Nicolaas Pieneman (1809–1860). Willem III also had a great interest in music. He died in 1890 at Het Loo.

122 KING WILLEM III

By JEAN CHRÉTIEN VALOIS (The Hague 1809 – 1894 The Hague)
SIGNED (on the back): Valois
Watercolor, oval: 32.2 x 27.7 cm

The King is represented as a lover of music: his left hand rests on a score of the "Romance d'Jago" from the opera *Otello* by Gioacchino Rossini, 1816. Behind stands a volume of the comic opera *Zampa ou La Fiancée de Marbre* by the French composer Louis Hérold, of which the first performance took place at Paris in 1831.

Willem III was deeply interested in music. He gave scholarships to young students and invited renowned musicians and composers to his court.

The watercolor must be dated before November 1849 when it was presented by the King to his aide-de-camp, A. C. A. Schönstedt. Jean Chrétien Valois made other portraits of the Royal Family in these years (cf. no. 116).

H. M. THE QUEEN

123 MINIATURE OF QUEEN SOPHIE

After NICAISE DE KEYSER (Santvliet 1813 – 1887 Antwerp)
Ca. 1845
Ivory, oval: 5 x 4.1 cm

Nicaise de Keyser, painter of historical tableaux, genre pieces, and portraits, made several state portraits of King Willem II, Queen Anna Pavlovna, and Queen Sophie. The miniature was painted by an anonymous artist after De Keyser's picture of

Sophie made in 1845 (The Hague, Sophia Stichting, Nederlandsch Zeehospitium), which was engraved by Charles Billion (1813–1869). The well-known diadem of Queen Sophie was added by the miniaturist.

LIT: Van Someren, II, no. 742; cat. *Rondom een album van Koningin Sophie*, Delft (Stedelijk Museum Het Prinsenhof), 1977, 9, fig. 1
PROV: presented by Queen Sophie to her secretary Wilhelm C. A. von Weckherlin (1807–1872), Counselor of the state of Württemberg; by inheritance in the collection of the family De Marez Oyens; coll. Mrs. R. Voskuil-Horna until 1975
RIJKSMUSEUM PALEIS HET LOO, APELDOORN, INV. NO. RL303

124 SET OF THREE GOLDEN BRACELETS OF QUEEN SOPHIE WITH PORTRAITS OF HER SONS

Bracelet I with portrait of Crown Prince Willem (1840–1879)
Miniature by EDOUARD DE LATOUR (Brussels 1817 – 1863 Brussels)
SIGNED AND DATED: Edouard de Latour 1842
Miniature, in ivory, oval: 2.7 x 2.2 cm

Bracelet II with portrait of Prince Maurits (1843–1850)
Ca. 1847
Miniature, in ivory, oval: 3.5 x 2.7 cm

Bracelet III with portrait of Prince Alexander (1851–1884)
Miniature by HENRI PHILIPPE HEIDEMANS (Amsterdam 1804 – after 1864 London?)
SIGNED AND DATED: H. P. Heidemans 1853
Miniature, in ivory, oval: 2.8 x 2.4 cm
H. M. THE QUEEN

125 SEAL OF WILLEM, PRINCE OF ORANGE

Dutch(?), 3rd quarter of the 19th century
White agate matrix, red coral hand, gold, blue enamelled pistol: height 3.5 cm

The seal, engraved with a crowned W in gothic style, belonged to Willem (1840–1879), eldest son of King Willem III and Queen Sophie, who as Crown Prince held the title of Prince of Orange.

H. M. THE QUEEN

126 DESK SEAL OF QUEEN SOPHIE

Dutch(?), 3rd quarter of the 19th century
Gold mounted malachite handle, silver lion, amethyst matrix: height 5.3 cm

The matrix is engraved with the coats of arms of the Netherlands and Württemberg, the native country of Queen Sophie. Before the investiture of Willem III, Sophie bore the coat of arms of the Princess of Orange; therefore the seal must be dated after 1848.

H. M. THE QUEEN

127 DESK SEAL WITH THE COAT OF ARMS
OF QUEEN SOPHIE

Dutch(?), 3rd quarter of the 19th century
Heliotrope jasper matrix, handle of agate and various kinds of jasper, chased gold mounts:
height 7 cm

The coat of arms is placed on the royal robe and surmounted by a crown.

H. M. THE QUEEN

128 SOUVENIR ALBUM OF QUEEN SOPHIE

Ca. 1855
BINDING: by J. H. BOUSCHOLTE, The Hague; black leather, tooled, partly gold-tooled;
tooled on upper cover and back: ALBUM: 41 x 57 cm
CONTENTS: 46 watercolors and designs, by different artists, commissioned and collected by
Queen Sophie, with notes in her own handwriting. On the first flyleaf the following note:
Apres ma mort à remettre à monsieur de Beyerman Aide-de-Camp de S.M. le Roi des Pays-Bas,
en Souvenir de la Reine ma soeur Sophie † 3 Juin 1877 et de mes bien-aimés neveux les
deux Princes d'Orange Guilaume † 11 Juin 1879 et Alexandre † 21 Juin 1884. Ceci ma
dernière volonté! Stouttgart 25 d'Avril 1885[.] Marie Princesse de Wurtenberg.
SHOWN HERE: page 33, drawing room of Queen Sophie in palace Noordeinde, The Hague; watercolor: 343 x 445 cm, unsigned; since the portrait of the eldest son, Prince Willem, on the left wall,
painted by Nicolaas Pieneman is dated 1855 and since the Queen vacated the room in the same
year, the watercolor may be dated 1855.

Albums like these were in vogue in the nineteenth century. Queen Sophie, who loved
travelling and often stayed at the courts of England, France, and Germany, made the
album for her private purpose, preserving pictures of palaces, rooms, towns, and
lakes, as a visual souvenir.

Most of the watercolors are of palaces where the Queen once lived. Of remarkable
documentary value are the interior scenes of the private rooms in the Württemberg
palace in Stüttgart and in the Queen's palaces in The Hague. Most of the furniture
and the works of art depicted in these rooms are preserved.

LIT: cat. *Rondom een album van Koningin Sophie*, Delft, Stedelijk Museum Het Prinsenhof,
1977
PROV: Queen Sophie of the Netherlands; 1877, Prince Alexander of the Netherlands; 1884,
Princess Marie of Württemberg (1816–1887); 1887, H. Beyerman (1836–1913), former aide-de-
camp of Prince Alexander; 1926, Vereniging Oranje Nassau Museum
RIJKSMUSEUM PALEIS HET LOO, APELDOORN, INV. NO. A2340
On loan from the Vereniging Oranje Nassau Museum

129 RIDING WHIP WITH A HANDLE IN THE FORM
OF A FALCON ON A WOMAN'S HAND

Black plaited whip with a golden handle set with diamonds, turquoise, and pearls: 80 cm

The riding whip was part of Queen Sophie's costume for the Royal Hawking Club 't Loo. This Club originated with a small group of English and French noblemen who in 1839 obtained permission from King Willem I to go hawking on the grounds of Het Loo. The hunt was extremely successful and the Royal Princes Willem and Alexander became interested in it. The next year the Royal Hawking Club 't Loo was founded under the patronage of King Willem II; Prince Alexander (1818–1848) was elected chairman.

Among the royal members of the international club were Prince Frederik (1797–1881), brother of King Willem II; Prince Willem, the future King Willem III; and his brother, Prince Hendrik (1820–1879). They followed the example of their ancestor William III, who was a devotee of hawking, and had a falconry built at Het Loo. The Prince of Wales and the Duke of Cambridge were honorary members. Some years after the foundation of the club Queen Sophie became the first and only female member, assuming the title of Patroness. An equestrian portrait by Henry Auguste d'Ainecy, Comte de Montpezat (Paris 1817 – 1859 Paris), dated 1849, depicts her wearing the club's costume, a green velvet dress and a gray hat with an aigrette of heron feathers, and holding a hawk on her left hand (Apeldoorn, Rijksmuseum Paleis Het Loo, on loan from the Vereniging Oranje Nassau Museum, inv. no. A12).

LIT: J. M. P. van Oorschot, *Vorstelijke vliegers en valkenswaarde valkeniers sedert de zeventiende eeuw*, Tilburg, 1974, 226–246

H. M. THE QUEEN

130 FRANZ LISZT AT HET LOO

By CHARLES ROCHUSSEN (Rotterdam 1814 – 1894 Rotterdam)
INSCRIBED: *au chateau du Loo – 6 Mai 1875.*
Pencil and pen: 21.5 x 27.7 cm

Franz Liszt stayed with King Willem III at Het Loo in 1875, where he gave a recital on 6 May. On this occasion he was asked by the King also to hold an audition for young girls, called "pensionnaires," who had followed a course in piano, elocution, and embroidery. The drawing represents the moment when the "pensionnaires" were presented to Liszt, before they competed for the prize which the King awarded each year to the best performer. The traditional attribution to Rochussen is quite acceptable. In a signed watercolor in the royal collection, Rochussen depicted the King and Liszt in the park of Het Loo.

Charles Rochussen, painter of historical and military scenes, was frequently invited by the King to stay at Het Loo, where he recorded many events in watercolors and drawings which are preserved in the royal collection.

PROV: given to F. R. H. R. Baron Fagel (1828–1890), Superintendant of Het Loo; by inheritance to the present owner

RIJKSMUSEUM PALEIS HET LOO, APELDOORN
On loan from Jonkheer Leopold Quarles van Ufford, New York

HENDRIK

Prince of the Netherlands

THIRD SON of King Willem II (1792–1849) and Queen Anna Pavlovna (1795–1865), he was born in 1820. He married twice: (1) Amalia, Princess of Saksen Weimar (1830–1872), in 1853; and (2) Maria, Princess of Prussia (1855–1888), in 1878. He died in 1879 and had no children.

Prince Hendrik became a naval officer in 1833 and Commander-in-Chief of the Dutch Royal Navy in 1852. His interest in navigation caused him to be called "Prince Hendrik the Seafarer."

In 1850 King Willem III appointed him as his Stadholder of the Grand Duchy of Luxembourg, the personal possession of the King of the Netherlands after 1815, and hereditary only in the male line. In 1865, after the death of his mother, Queen Anna Pavlovna, he inherited the palace of Soestdijk.

131   ST. MARTIN'S CATHEDRAL OF UTRECHT: INTERIOR OF THE CHOIR TO THE WEST

By PIETER JANSZ SAENREDAM (Assendelft 1597 – 1665 Haarlem)
SIGNED AND DATED (in pen and brown ink at lower right corner): *Int Jaer ghe* (a line drawn through *ghe*)./*1636/den 17 Septem*[ber]/*Pieter Saenredam*; inscribed (at lower left edge),
Ste Maertens Doms Kerck, Binnen uijttrecht
The vanishing point (⊙) is indicated in the niche at the right
Pen and brown ink, black chalk and some red and orange, stumped: 37.9 x 31.1 cm
Watermark: fragment of a fleur-de-lis

According to information received from the Royal Family, this fine drawing came into the royal collection through "Prince Hendrik the Seafarer."

Saenredam, the famous painter of church interiors, "the first portraitist of architecture," painted and drew more churches in Utrecht than in any other town in the Netherlands. He spent almost half a year there in 1636, drawing the various churches both from the exterior and the interior. Seven of his more than fifty drawings of the churches of Utrecht are devoted to St. Martin's, the most important gothic cathedral of the Netherlands which was begun in 1254; it is now the property of the Dutch Reformed Church. With the exception of the present drawing and one in the Bibliothèque Nationale in Paris, the attribution of which is not universally accepted, all the other drawings (five) of the Cathedral are in the Municipal Archives of Utrecht, where, in fact, the greater part of the artist's known drawings are preserved. On 3 September 1636, he drew—or finished drawing, for the plotting of the perspective and the meticulous execution of these drawings must have taken considerable time—the interior of the nave and choir as seen from the west; on 15 September, the interior from the south arm of the transept to the north; and on 17 September he executed the present drawing. In the same month he also executed two sheets of ground plans of the tower and later on 15 October he represented a view of the Cathedral tower and the old town hall from the Old Canal. The drawing in Paris, also showing the tower, is thought by P. T. A. Swillens to have been made in September as well.

In most instances, Saenredam eventually utilized his drawings for his paintings, sometimes many years later, but no painting of St. Martin's is known. The present drawing originates from the four-volume Atlas consisting of topographical drawings of the province of Utrecht. This Atlas known as the Atlas Munnicks van Cleef first entered the Royal Family when Prince Hendrik the Seafarer, Commander-in-Chief of the Dutch Royal Navy, acquired it in 1870.

LIT: C. Hofstede de Groot, *Utrechtsche Kerken, Teekeningen en schilderijen van Pieter Saenredam*, Haarlem, 1899, no. 2; P. T. A. Swillens, *Pieter Jansz. Saenredam*, Amsterdam, 1935, 47, no. 126, pl. 156; H. Brugmans and C. H. Peters, *De Nederlandsche Stedenbouw*, II, Leiden, s.d., 84, pl. 229; *Catalogue raisonné of the Works by Pieter Jansz. Saenredam*, published on the occasion of the exhibition *Pieter Jansz. Saenredam*, 15 September – 3 December 1961 (introduction by Dr. Maria Elisabeth Houtzager, essays by P. T. A. Swillens and J. Q. van Regteren Altena), Centraal Museum, Utrecht, 1961, 173, no. 118, fig. 119; Annelies Becker-Jordens, *Een Kabinet van Utrechtse Gezichten*, Bussum, 1973, no. 7 (the author has since reported that her statement that Saenredam received a commission to draw the churches of Utrecht in 1636 is incorrect).
EXHIBITED: Utrecht, Centraal Museum, *Nederlandse Architectuurschilders 1600–1900*, 1953, no. 140; Utrecht, Centraal Museum, *Pieter Jansz. Saenredam*, 1961, 173, no. 118, fig. 119 (see LIT); Paris, Institut Néerlandais, *Saenredam, 1597–1665: Peintre des églises*, 1970, no. 37, repr.; Laren N.H., Singer Museum, and Utrecht, Rijksarchief, *Zicht rond gooi en sticht*, 1973, no. 47
PROV: Hendrik Busserus (1701–1781); his sale, Amsterdam, 12 August 1782, 452; Hendrik Gartman (d. 1816); his sale, Amsterdam, 24 April 1843; Dr. Gerard Munnicks van Cleef (1796–1860; see L. J. van der Klooster in the catalogue *Zicht rond gooi en sticht*, Singer Museum, Laren and Rijksarchief, Utrecht, 1973); J. L. Beyers (to Prince Hendrik for 4,500 guilders); Prince Willem Frederik Hendrik, younger brother of King Willem III; his widow, Maria of Prussia (1855–1888); King Willem III; his widow, Emma von Waldeck Pyrmont; Queen Wilhelmina
H. M. THE QUEEN

132 BLACK LACE FAN WITH THE SIGNATURE OF QUEEN EMMA IN DIAMONDS

France or Belgium, 1901
INSCRIBED (in diamonds): Emma 1901
Black Chantilly, mother-of-pearl guards set with diamonds: radius ca. 30 cm

Queen Emma was an avid collector of lace and used lace for clothing and accessories.

She generally wore a folded, pinned lace frill in her hair. The Dutch people remember her as the old lady with the lace cap.

H. M. THE QUEEN

133 DESK SEAL OF QUEEN EMMA

Dutch(?), 4th quarter of the 19th century
Two white and one red carnelian matrixes, gold and enamel handle with pearls: height 8.5 cm

Two matrixes are engraved with the monogram of the Queen, a crowned double E, and one with the coats of arms of the Netherlands and Waldeck Pyrmont.

H. M. THE QUEEN

134 DESK SEAL IN THE FORM OF A LION'S FOOT

Dutch(?), 4th quarter of the 19th century
Carnelian matrix, gold mounted jasper handle: height 9 cm

The matrix is engraved with the crowned monogram of Queen Emma.

H. M. THE QUEEN

135 QUEEN EMMA

By JAN THEODOOR TOOROP (Purworedjo, Java 1858 – 1928 The Hague)
SIGNED: J.Th.Toorop. 31 Aug. 1923
Pencil and pen: 89 x 71 cm

Queen Emma was deeply loved by the Dutch people, and portraits of her tend to suffer from sentimental idealization. In contrast, Toorop's drawing is almost abstract in character. The subtle stylization of the features which show Emma's strong personality is emphasized by the linear patterns of the black diaphanous cape, the pleated front, and the white head-dress. Enclosed in its triangular outline, the composition has a monumental effect.

Toorop was an important Dutch representative of neo-impressionism and symbolism in the last years of the nineteenth century and the first decade of the twentieth century. His later highly linear works are generally confined to religious subjects, with the exception of his portraits.

PROV: presented to Queen Wilhelmina in 1923 by Art Gallery Kleykamp, The Hague
STICHTING HISTORISCHE VERZAMELINGEN VAN HET HUIS VAN ORANJE NASSAU

136 CHRIST CRUCIFIED BETWEEN THE TWO THIEVES: THE THREE CROSSES

By REMBRANDT HARMENSZ VAN RIJN (Leiden 1606 – 1669 Amsterdam)
Etching, drypoint, and burin, state IV: 38.5 x 45 cm

Rembrandt depicts the instant before the actual death of Christ, when He cries out: "My God! My God! why hast thou forsaken me?" (Matthew 27:46). The rearing horse to the left and the despairing gesture of St. John accentuate the mood of hopelessness.

Considerable changes have been made in the plate in this fourth state. Figures were burnished out and replaced when the plate was reworked around 1660. The etching is built up with angular lines and areas of light and dark. Strong parallel strokes of the burin and drypoint make the print much darker. The plate is inked in an exceptionally heavy way; consequently the details in the dark are barely visible.

The high hat of the commander is derived from a medallion by Pisanello portraying Gian Francesco Gonzaga.

The present etching, as well as the following one, belongs to a group of about seventy of Rembrandt's etchings collected by Queen Emma.

LIT: A. Bartsch, *Catalogue raisonné de toutes les estampes qui forment l'oeuvre de Rembrandt*, Vienna, 1797, 78; A. M. Hind, *Rembrandt's Etchings*, London, 1912, 270; L. Münz, *Rembrandt's Etchings*, London, 1952, 223; K. G. Boon, *Rembrandt de etser*, Amsterdam, 1963, 245; C. White, *Rembrandt as an Etcher*, London, 1969, 99ff., figs. 86ff.; J. P. Filedt Kok, *Etchings and Drawings in the Rembrandt House*, Maarssen, 1972, 74, 75
PROV: Queen Emma
H. M. THE QUEEN

137   THE ENTOMBMENT

By REMBRANDT HARMENSZ VAN RIJN (Leiden 1606 – 1669 Amsterdam)
Etching, drypoint, and burin, state IV, printed on Japanese paper with surface tone:
21.1 x 16.1 cm

The composition is influenced by a drawing from the school of Raphael, generally attributed to Perino del Vaga. From a copy of this Italian drawing, now in Haarlem, Teyler's Museum, Rembrandt adopted certain details. He disrupted the symmetrical and frontal composition of his model by placing the Holy Women, Nicodemus, and the other women on the far left. Rembrandt made the etching darker by allowing surface tone to remain on all the light areas except Christ's body and the space around it. The Japanese paper gives this impression a soft, warm tint.

LIT: A. Bartsch, *Catalogue raisonné de toutes les estampes qui forment l'oeuvre de Rembrandt*, Vienna, 1797, 86; A. M. Hind, *Rembrandt's Etchings*, London, 1912, 281; L. Münz, *Rembrandt's Etchings*, London, 1952, 241; K. G. Boon, *Rembrandt de etser*, Amsterdam, 1963, 260; C. White, *Rembrandt as an Etcher*, London, 1969, 82ff., figs. 102ff.; C. Tümpel, *Rembrandt legt die Bibel aus*, Berlin, 1970, 113; J. P. Filedt Kok, *Etchings and Drawings in the Rembrandt House*, Maarssen, 1972, 79, 80
PROV: Queen Emma
H. M. THE QUEEN

138 A ROMAN BRITISH POTTERY

By Laurens Alma Tadema (Dronrijp 1836 – 1912 Wiesbaden)
SIGNED: L. Alma Tadema, Op[us] CCLXIa
Canvas: 76.2 x 119.4 cm

This later work of Alma Tadema originally formed part of a large painting (219.8 x 169 cm) representing the Emperor Hadrian visiting a Roman British pottery in England, made in 1883–1884 as Opus CCLXI. The painting proved unsalable and about 1886–1887 the painter cut the canvas into three parts which he, after reworking some minor details, presented as three independent paintings. The upper half with the figure of Hadrian in the pottery shop is now in Amsterdam (Amsterdams Historisch Museum, 159 x 171 cm, Opus CCLXIb). The right part of the lower half, representing the semi-nude figure of a man bringing pottery from the workroom downstairs to the shop upstairs, is today in Paris (Centre Georges Pompidou, 152.5 x 80 cm, Opus CCLXIc). The left part of the lower half with a view in the workroom itself, and another man carrying some vases on his head, forms the present painting. These vases are characteristic of Alma Tadema's veracious working method; they are exact copies of existing specimens of Roman British pottery made in Northamptonshire in the second century A.D. On the wall is shown an altar of the *penates*, under which the inscription SALVE LUCRUM, according to F. L. Bastet, is probably related to the inscription *Salve Lucrum* (*lucrum* = profit) found on a Pompeiian mosaic.

The Dutch painter Laurens Alma Tadema was born in a small Frisian village. After studying in Antwerp from 1852 to 1864 he settled down in London in 1870. He became a British citizen in 1873 and was knighted by Queen Victoria in 1899, after which he was known as Sir Lawrence Alma Tadema. As a painter of scenes of ancient life in Greece, Egypt, and Rome he was one of the best known artists of his time. After his death, however, he was generally forgotten. Only recently has Alma Tadema been re-discovered and re-appreciated.

LIT: cat. exh. Royal Academy, London, 1884, no. 245; cat. *Tentoonstelling van het beroemde historische schilderij door Alma Tadema R.A. voorstellende: de Romeinse Keizer Adriaan in Engeland, diens bezoek aan een Romeinsch-Britsche pottebakkerij*, Rotterdam (Kunstzaal Oldenzeel), 1886, with reviews by C. Vosmaer in: *De Nederlandsche Spectator*, 1886, 294–296, and by J. Veth in: *De Nieuwe Gids*, 1886–1887, 94–96 (reprinted in J. Veth, *Hollandsche Teekenaars van dezen Tijd*, Amsterdam, 1905, 4–5); G. H. Marius, "Een praatje over schilderijen," *De Nederlandsche Spectator*, 1893, 396–397; E. Gosse, "Laurens Alma-Tadema," *Century Magazine*, XLVII, 1893–1894, 490, fig. 485; Anonymous, "Keizer Hadrianus in Engeland," *Eigen Haard*, XV, 1894, 172–173; L. van Deyssel, *Gedenkschriften*, I, Zwolle, 1962, 421–422; P. Hoenderdos, *Ary Scheffer, Sir Lawrence Alma-Tadema, Charles Rochussen of De Vergankelijkheid van de Roem* (exh. cat.), Rotterdam (Rotterdamsche Kunstkring), 1974, 7; J. Romijn, *L. Alma-Tadema* (exh. cat.), Leeuwarden (Gemeentelijk Museum Het Princessehof), 1974, nos. 31, 32; V. G. Swanson, *Sir Lawrence Alma Tadema. The Painter of the Victorian Vision of the Ancient World*, London, 1977, 23
PROV: bought by Queen Emma in November-December 1893, probably for the schoolroom of the young Queen Wilhelmina in the palace Noordeinde; after 1975 in the palace Soestdijk
H. M. THE QUEEN

QUEEN WILHELMINA

ONLY DAUGHTER of King Willem III and his second wife, Queen Emma, she was born in 1880. In 1890 Wilhelmina succeeded her father since his three sons had predeceased him. Her mother acted as Regent for her until 1898 when she came of age. In 1901 she married Hendrik, Duke of Mecklenburg Schwerin (1876–1934).

Queen Wilhelmina's role in the Second World War, when she was head of the government in exile in London, led Churchill to say that she was the only man in the Dutch government. The Dutch people gave her the title "Moeder des Vaderlands" (Mother of the Fatherland), a conscious echo of Stadholder Willem I's honorific "Vader des Vaderlands." In 1948 Queen Wilhelmina resigned from the throne after a reign of fifty years and was succeeded by her only daughter, Queen Juliana. Queen Wilhelmina loved Het Loo and lived there after her abdication until 1962, when she died at the palace. She was very interested in the history of the building and the surrounding grounds and she restored some parts of the interior of the palace in the style of William III.

139 QUEEN WILHELMINA AS A CHILD

By THÉRÈSE VAN DUYL-SCHWARTZE (Amsterdam 1851 – 1918 Amsterdam)
SIGNED: Th. Schwartze
Pastel: 60 x 50 cm

Princess Wilhelmina is represented as a young girl. The portrait should be dated before the death of her father in 1890 and the period of mourning following that event.

Thérèse Schwartze, who specialized in children's portraits, produced several works for the Royal Family. In the collection of Het Loo alone we find paintings of Wilhelmina as a baby on the arm of Queen Emma (1881), the first state portrait of Wilhelmina as Queen (1898), a round pastel portraying Princess Juliana as a baby (1910), and an oval half-length portrait of Princess Juliana at age six (1915).

Artistically Schwartze fits into the internationally fashionable portrait style of the time, which owed much to the eighteenth-century English portrait painters such as Reynolds, Gainsborough, and Lawrence.

LIT: W. Martin, *Thérèse van Duyl-Schwartze 1851–1918: Gedenkboek*, Amsterdam, 1921
STICHTING HISTORISCHE VERZAMELINGEN VAN HET HUIS VAN ORANJE NASSAU

140 PRIZE MEDAL WITH A PORTRAIT OF QUEEN WILHELMINA, 1891

By BARTHOLOMEUS J. W. M. VAN HOVE (The Hague 1850 – 1914 Amsterdam),
JOHAN PHILIP MATTHIAS MENGER (1845–1912), and W. J. SCHAMMER (?–1893)
SIGNED: (obverse) Bart van Hove, J. P. M. Menger; (reverse) W.S. [W. J. Schammer]
INSCRIBED: WILHELMINA KONINGIN DER NEDERLANDEN
Gold: 4.5 cm

Queen Wilhelmina was only ten years old when she became Queen, although she was not invested until she was eighteen. The stamps, coins, and medals issued before her investiture in 1898 bear a portrait of her as a girl with long, flowing hair. The medal was cast in gold, silver, and bronze. The specimen here was never used. Bart van Hove was a Dutch sculptor who made busts and medals of several members of the Royal Family.

LIT: W. K. F. Zwierzina, *Nederlandse penningen 1864–1898*, Amsterdam, 1905, no. 978; P. K. van Dalen, *Nederlandse beeldhouwers in de 19e eeuw*, The Hague, 1957, 172, no. 37
H. M. THE QUEEN

141 LETTER OF QUEEN VICTORIA TO QUEEN WILHELMINA

Size: 21 x 13 cm
TEXT:

Aug: 29. 1898.

My dearest niece.

I cannot allow this very important day in your life, without sending you a few unofficial lines which are to express how truly & warmly I pray that God may bless & protect you & guide you. I was just your age, when I ascended to the Throne, & I know all the difficulties & trials which surround a young Queen.—But you have such a dear, wise friend in your beloved Mother, who has held the reins of Government for so many years, that you can always turn to her for advice.

Accept again, the assurance of my true affection & friendship & believe me always your very affectionate Aunt & Sister

Victoria RI.

Queen Victoria of England (1819–1901) sent this letter, dated 29 August 1898, from Osborne to Queen Wilhelmina on the occasion of her accession to the throne on 6 September 1898, shortly after her eighteenth birthday. Queen Emma, mother of the young Queen, was Regent in the preceding years, from 1890 until 1898.

H. M. THE QUEEN

142 MINIATURE OF QUEEN WILHELMINA

By MARGUÉRITE PNIÈS DE MERBITZ
SIGNED AND DATED: M. de Merbitz-1901
Ivory, bronze-gilt frame: miniature 9 x 7 cm; frame 14 x 8.7 cm

The miniature, made in the year of Queen Wilhelmina's marriage, is reminiscent of the portraits of the Queen wearing her investiture robes.

Work by Marguerite Pniès de Merbitz is mentioned in exhibitions in Paris between 1878 and 1900.

H. M. THE QUEEN

143 TEA SERVICE PRESENTED TO QUEEN WILHELMINA AND PRINCE HENDRIK

Rozenburg factory, The Hague, 1901
Painted by SAMUEL SCHELLINK (Utrecht 1876 – 1958 The Hague) and others
INSCRIBED (back of tray): Aan H.M. de Koningin en Z.K.H. Prins Hendrik der Nederlanden Eerbiedig aangeboden ter herinnering aan VII Februari MDCCCCI door de Koninklijke Porcelein en Aardewerkfabriek "Rozenburg" [To H. M. the Queen and H. R. H. Prince Hendrik of the Netherlands, respectfully offered to commemorate VII February 1901 by the Royal Porcelain and Earthenware Factory "Rozenburg"]
Eggshell porcelain: tray: 35.5 x 40 cm; teapot: 18 x 15.5 cm; milk jug: 8 x 8.5 cm; sugar bowl: 16 x 11 cm; cup: 5 x 8.7 cm; saucer: diameter 12.1 cm
The set consists of a tray, a teapot, a milk jug, a sugar bowl, and six cups and saucers

The tea service, decorated with the coats of arms of Queen Wilhelmina and Prince Hendrik, Duke of Mecklenburg Schwerin, and their cypher, was a wedding present from the Rozenburg factory. As the painters still worked on the tea service on 15 February, the tea set must have been presented to the Queen and the Prince after their wedding. In 1899 the Delftware factory of Rozenburg successfully, after years of research, developed a process of producing hard-paste porcelain reminiscent of oriental eggshell china. This new china was shown to the public for the first time during the world exhibition in Paris, 1900. The form and decoration of this porcelain, with stylized flowers, made by the factory until 1914, was a high point of art nouveau.

LIT: M. Penkela, *European Porcelain*, Rutland, 1968, 166, 169; J. Romijn, "Rozenburg en Sam Schellink," *Mededelingen vrienden van de Nederlandse Ceramiek*, June 1968, 31ff.; *Rozenburger Ceramik*, Bremen (Focke Museum), 1976; C. J. S. Ruiter, "De fabrieks- en jaarmerken van de Haagse Plateelbakkerij Rozenburg," *Mededelingen vrienden van de Nederlandse ceramiek*, 1976, no. 4; 1978, no. 4
RIJKSMUSEUM PALEIS HET LOO, APELDOORN, INV. NO. L2680
On loan from H. M. the Queen

144 FAN OF WHITE OSTRICH FEATHERS

Ostrich feathers, tortoise shell, gold, diamonds: radius 62 cm

This fan with a golden W, surmounted by a diamond crown, was a wedding present to Queen Wilhelmina in 1901.

H. M. THE QUEEN

145 MEDAL COMMEMORATING THE FORTY-YEAR JUBILEE OF QUEEN WILHELMINA

By M. P. J. Fleur (ca. 1883–1946)
SIGNED: M. Fleur.
INSCRIBED: (obverse) TER HERINNERING AAN HET 40-JARIG REGEERINGSJUBILEUM 1898–1938 [In commemoration of the 40-year jubilee, 1898–1938]; (reverse) H. M. DE KONINGIN AANGEBODEN DOOR DE HULDIGINGS-COMMISSIE 1938 AMSTERDAM [H. M. the Queen Presented by the Honoring Committee . . .]; ONDER DEEZ' BOOM RUST IK VEILIG
[Under this tree I repose safely]
Gold: diameter 6 cm

This golden specimen of the medal issued to commemorate the forty-year jubilee of Queen Wilhelmina was presented to the Queen by the Honoring Committee.

H. M. THE QUEEN

146 PORTRAIT OF QUEEN WILHELMINA DESIGNED FOR THE DUTCH CURRENCY NOTES PRINTED IN THE U.S.A. DURING THE SECOND WORLD WAR

Engraving on paper: medallion, 4.1 x 3.5 cm
Mark: © ABNCO [American Bank Note Company]

In 1943 the Dutch government had currency notes made in the United States in order to enable the immediate resumption of the circulation of money in Holland after the liberation. The notes were printed by the American Bank Note Company. The denominations were: 1, 2.50, 10, 25, 50, and 100 florins. The portrait was printed in reverse on the *f*1 and *f*2.50 notes, which were issued in the Netherlands immediately after the war and dated 18 May 1945, thirteen days after the liberation.

Dutch silver coins were also minted in the U.S.A.: in San Francisco, Philadelphia, and Denver, but these were returned to the U.S.A. after the war, with the exception of one bag of ten cent pieces, which was stolen.

H. M. THE QUEEN

147 ADDRESS OF H. M. THE QUEEN ON MONDAY, 1 SEPTEMBER 1941, FROM LONDON TO THE DUTCH PEOPLE

Stencilled typewriting: 33 x 20 cm
Begins:

Landgenooten in alle deelen des Rijks en Nederlanders daar buiten vertoevend.

Gij zult ongetwijfeld begrijpen, dat mijn 61ste verjaardag niet de eigenlijke aanleiding is dat ik het woord tot U wensch te richten. De werkelijke reden daarvoor moet gij zoeken in het nauwe verband dat door U zelf gelegd is tusschen de herdenking van dien dag en Uwen wensch en wil weer vrij te worden. . . .

Daarom wil ik heden spreken over onze worsteling en onze komende overwinning.

De aartsvijand van het menschdom Adolf Hitler heeft ons willen vernietigen! Hij heeft Nederland niet alleen overweldigd, en zijn vrijheid ontnomen; waarna zijne horden het hebben leeggeplunderd, ons volk aan den honger prijsgevend, maar hij heeft ook gepoogd het van zijn heiligste goederen te berooven en zijn ziel te verbrijzelen.

Dat is hem niet gelukt!
Hij heeft het omgekeerde bereikt!
Na meer dan een jaar van onderdrukking *is*
Nederland en *voelt* Nederland zich sterker en onoverwinnelijker dan ooit te voren.

Translation of this beginning and also of the close of the speech:

Compatriots in all parts of the Realm and those who are abroad:

Undoubtedly you will understand, my sixty-first birthday is not my real motive for addressing you. The actual reason is the close relation between the commemoration of this day and your wish and will to be free again. Therefore I will speak today about our struggle and our coming victory. The archenemy of humanity Adolf Hitler wished to destroy us! He not only usurped the Netherlands, depriving them of their freedom, his bands looting the country while our people starved, but he also tried to deprive you of your holiest goods and to smash your soul. He did not succeed! He achieved the opposite effect! After more than a year of oppression, the Netherlands feel stronger and more invincible than ever. . . .

Compatriots at home, it is not only that I sympathize with your sorrows and sufferings and everything that the oppressors impose on you, but I also feel the pulsation of your life. I have managed to talk with well-informed Dutchmen who have visited me by devious ways, with whom I have contact and am able to deliberate.

I understand you and I know what you are thinking and feeling at this moment. Therefore I will be able, when time is ripe, to act in your spirit. Still the circumstances prevent me from addressing you freely and unfolding my plans to you, but the day will come that this will be possible. When and how this will be, only He who has the fate of people in His hands knows. He will do us right. Finally I will address you all personally, inhabitants of the Kingdom and those who are abroad, to thank you for your full-hearted sympathy on occasion of the beginning of the sixty-second year of my life. I thank all of you who were unable to send me these congratulations, prevented as they were by the tyrant. Although separated by a long distance I feel a close communion with you.

Your attachment, wherever you stay, and your confidence are for me an indispensable support to the inspiring but responsible task which will rest on my shoulders on that great day, the day of the resurrection of the Netherlands. A task which I will accept praying and looking up to God.

The Lord be with us and bless our resurrected, proud, and great Country for many years to come.

H. M. THE QUEEN

148 ADDRESS OF QUEEN WILHELMINA IN WASHINGTON, 6 AUGUST 1942

Account of the visit of Her Majesty Queen Wilhelmina of the Netherlands to the Senate of the United States on 6 August 1942. Followed by the text of the address of Her Majesty The Queen to the members of the Senate and the members of the House of Representatives. Gold-tooled blue leather binding and slipcase: 30 x 25 cm
The Queen's address begins, after the salutation:

Seeing this great democratic assembly, renewing itself at regular intervals and meeting under self-made rules of law, seems to me a sure guaranty that liberty is forever young and strong and invincible, whereas the autocrat, incapable of rejuvenating himself, is every day nearer to his end, his regime doomed to die with him.

The Queen's address ended:

It is not the first time that the Netherlands has been associated with the United States in common warfare.

In the days of Washington we were at one time comrades in arms, and it gives me pleasure to recall that the first salute given to the American flag on behalf of a foreign government was rendered by guns of my country.

That ancient partnership we see revived today.

One of your great men who stood at the cradle of American liberty, Benjamin Franklin, once wrote to John Adams, your first Envoy at The Hague:

I believe neither Holland nor we could be prevailed on to abandon our friends.

That was in 1782, and I think it still holds good today. We cannot be prevailed on, either of us, to abandon our friends.

That is why we considered the first Japanese bomb on Pearl Harbor as a bomb on ourselves.

That is why we never wavered in our resolve to be with the United Nations until the end.

United we stand, and united we will achieve victory.

H. M. THE QUEEN

149 TWO LETTERS FROM WINSTON CHURCHILL TO QUEEN WILHELMINA

(a) DATED: 29 July 1943
Typewritten letter; salutation and signature, autograph: 25 x 20 cm

In this letter written 29 July 1943 Winston Churchill invited Her Majesty Queen

Wilhelmina to the official residence, 10 Downing Street, on 3 August 1943, the third year of the Second World War, in order to discuss matters of importance. From the beginning of the war in May 1940, Queen Wilhelmina lived in London, where the Dutch government had established itself provisionally.

(b) DATED: 2 November 1945
Typewritten letter, signed: 25 x 20 cm

In a letter written two years later Winston Churchill thanks Her Majesty Queen Wilhelmina of the Netherlands for the present offered to him as an expression of thanks for his services and hospitality towards the Dutch people during the Second World War. The present was a casket of letters written by John Churchill, first Duke of Marlborough (1650–1722), to Anthonie Heinsius, Grand Pensionary of the Netherlands (1641–1720). Marlborough had been made Lieutenant-General and Commander-in-Chief by King James II. In 1688 he transferred his alliance to the King and Stadholder William III and was rewarded with membership in the Privy Council and continuation of his military rank. Marlborough led the allied armies to important victories over Louis XIV of France. An extensive correspondence about military and diplomatic affairs exists between Marlborough and Heinsius, who played an important role in European politics. In the absence of William III in England, Heinsius governed the Netherlands, and he and Marlborough were the chief negotiators of the Grand Alliance of 1701 for the defense of Europe against French aggression.

LIT: (b) G. G. Vreede, *Correspondance diplomatique et militaire de Marlborough, Heinsius et J. Hop*, 1850; B. van't Hoff, *The Correspondence of Marlborough and Heinsius*, 1951
H. M. THE QUEEN

150 WOODLAND SCENE AT MEYENDEL

By QUEEN WILHELMINA (The Hague 1880 – 1962 Apeldoorn)
SIGNED: W 1932
Black chalk, pencil and brush: 31.8 x 42.2 cm

The woods of Meyendel are situated in the surroundings of the royal country house De Ruygenhoek in the dunes near The Hague.

Queen Wilhelmina was a devoted painter of landscapes from her earliest youth to the end of her life. She painted regularly in Scandinavia, Austria, and Switzerland, besides the Netherlands. She held exhibitions in the Netherlands in 1932, 1936, 1949, and 1950, and in the East and West Indies in 1933 and 1951.

LIT: M. F. Hennes, "H. M. de Koningin als Kunstenares," *Maandblad voor Beeldende Kunsten*, 1948, 133–136
H. M. THE QUEEN

HET LOO

151 A BIRD'S-EYE VIEW OF THE PALACE HET LOO

By ROMEYN DE HOOGHE (Amsterdam 1645 – 1708 Haarlem)
SIGNED (at the bottom): Getekent en geEtst door Mr. Romeyn de Hooghe Rechtgel: en Comm:
van Syne M:van Gr:Britannien etc.etc. [Designed and engraved by Mr. R. de Hooghe,
lawyer and commissioner of H. M. of Great Britain etc.etc.]
INSCRIBED (in a garland with the arms of the King at the top): 't KONINGS LOO tot
Amsterdam / bij I / Oosterwyk / op den Dam / Met Privilegie.
Etching, composed of four plates: each 37.7 x 36.6 cm

The etching was made about 1698 shortly after the completion of the palace, which
began in 1685; after the coronation of William and Mary it had been enlarged from
1691 onwards. The colonnades, originally the connection between the main building
and the two L-shaped wings, were replaced by four pavilions and moved to the end
of the upper garden which was laid out in 1692. On the left-hand side we can see a part
of the castle Het Oude Loo, bought by William III in 1684. In the courtyard there is
the dolphin fountain and, on either side of the house, the private gardens of the King
(left) and the Queen (right); at the back of the palace the lower garden with the fountain of Venus; at the west side the cascade of Narcissus; on the east side the cascade
of Galathea; reversely represented in the etching in the upper garden are the colonnades and the garden pavilions; on the west side the six-forked road and the pond
with the cypher fountain. Most of the oak trees in front of the palace are still alive
today.

Series of prints of Het Loo were published by Gerard Valk in 1695, Justus Danckerts
before 1697, Petrus Persoy about 1698, Carel Allard in 1699, and Petrus Schenck in
1702. Cornelis Danckerts copied the series by Justus Danckerts after 1698 and Jan
van Call also made copies of Cornelis Danckerts' and Schenck's in 1702–1703.
Joannes van Keulen re-published the series of Justus Danckerts and re-touched them.
Van Egmond re-published those of Persoy. Bird's-eye views have been made by
Bastiaen Stopendaal, published by Valck before 1697, and some years later by Daniel
Stopendaal, published by Schenck. Isaac de Moucheron made a drawing of a bird's-
eye view, etched by an unknown artist, published by Schenck.

LIT: Walter Harris, *A Description of the King's Royal Palace and Gardens at Loo*, London,
1699; A. G. Bienfait, *Oud Hollandsche Tuinen*, The Hague, 1943; S. de Jong-Schreuder,
De tuinen van Het Loo, 1968 (manuscript, Rijksuniversiteit, Leiden); cat. *Europäische Barockplastik am Niederrhein, Grupello und seine Zeit*, Düsseldorf (Kunstmuseum), 1971, no. 60;
John Landwehr, *Romeyn de Hooghe, the Etcher: Contemporary Portrayal of Europe,
1662–1707*, Leiden, 1973, 340, 341
ATLAS VAN STOLK, ROTTERDAM, INV. NO. 2719(IX)

152 FOUR DESIGNS OF STATUES, PROBABLY FOR THE WATERWORKS OF HET LOO

By ROMEYN DE HOOGHE (Amsterdam 1645 – 1708 Haarlem)
Ca. 1686
Red chalk: (a) 31 x 52 cm; (b) 30.5 x 52.5 cm; (c) 30.5 x 54 cm; (d) 31.5 x 54 cm

The complete series of eight designs is a glorification of William III and represents river gods and nymphs. In the top left-hand corner of each design De Hooghe has explained the significance of the statues.

SHOWN HERE:

(a) Hercules, Acheloüs
  De Vorst, en den Ysel [The Prince and the river Yssel] N1

De Vorst als Hercules met de Leeuwenhuyt, de machten van de Staet. en sijn knodse, of Veltheerlyke moet en beleyt Slaet Achelous van d'eene form, uyt de andre, en na dat hij hem sijn slangenhuyt heeft doen v(er)laeten: gesuyvert van de franse en bisschoplijke gedrochten, slaet hij hem af sijn eene hoorn, dat is neemt van den Ysel die kronkelenden arm van de grift.

The Prince, represented as Hercules with the club, takes off Achelous' snakeskin, disposing of the domination of France and the Church of Rome, and then he knocks the only horn off his head, that is, he takes the curving Grift away from the Yssel. [The Grift was a tributary of the Yssel and William III claimed its waters.]

(b) N:2
welken hoorn hij schenckt aen de bosch berg en veltgodinnekens van Loo, welke nimphen, dien Achelous hoorn, of kronkelende Grift, de beek van het Loo, als den boorn van overvloet opsieren, die opvullende met allerleij bloemen en vruchten, so datse daer na. in plaets van een v(er)looren hoorn van Achelous, een beruchte hoorn van allerley weelde. en vruchtbaerheyt wiert in overvloet
  dese beyde Nymphen sijn echter deelgenooten aen de Grift. de eene sitte de in de lage beemden stuyrt en stert haer wateren tussen. de brocken van de veluwlanden in. de andere, als een water Centaura. jaegende langs de heuvelen (laet) beeken van onder uytvloeyen. die de Grift eynd lyke samenstellen

The Prince as Hercules gives his horn to the forest, mountain, and field goddesses of Het Loo. The two nymphs decorate Achelous' horn, filling it with flowers and fruit and turning it into a horn of plenty. One of the nymphs, together with the Grift, pours out her water over the fields of the Veluwe, while the other one, as a water centaura, chases along the hills and draws bubbling springs from them, representing the many tributaries that flow into the Grift

(c)
De Zuyder zee met een scheepskroon om haer oneyndige scheepvaert op het hooft; waer tussen om datse met de noord zee in een loopt schelpen als een feston hangen,

wier en zeegras slingert tusschen de locken in, hij houdt in sijn eene hand een tweetan-
dige vork, sijnde wat minder als de oceaen, in de andere den ryken overvloets hoorn
van 't welvaren welk hij in brengt, sijn grooten en ruymen schelp kruyk stort sijn
wateren gulpende uyt.

een Triton rijdende op een zeeton, waer aen de zeetel van de zuyder zee vast is,
plant in sijn wateren de bakens.

The Zuyderzee with a crown, because of its extensive navigation, holds in one hand a
two-pronged fork . . . , since the Zuyderzee was smaller than the oceans. In the
other hand he holds the horn of plenty, symbolizing the prosperity he brings. He pours
the water out of an enormous shell pitcher. A triton, attached to the Zuyderzee,
places the beacons in its water.

(d) NI   De Vorst

vertoont in de gedaente van Appollo die als de Son. aen alles het welvaeren ende was-
dom geeft. en so het sieraed aen de bosch en watergodin, van Loo.

Als de god van de jacht komt hij bij haer sijn self ververschen, gedempt hebbende
het Pythisch ongediert, sijnde de onvruchtbaerheijt. en woestheyt van de heij.

de Nymph: schenckt hem de overvlo(et) die se van sijn K: Hoocheyt ontfangen
heeft, wederom, se is gedeckt met een kostelyke rok, op een heuvel of (bergjen?)
geseten, haer locken, swieren, ryklyk over haer boesem, en achter haere rug vallende
als haere watervlietjens tussen de heuvelen in waer van se de watermolens doet gaen,
de rest van hare wateren stuyrt se om laegh na den Ysel.

The Prince is represented as the figure of Apollo, the giver of prosperity and growth,
that is, giver of the jewel of Het Loo to the goddess of woods and water. He comes as
the god of hunting to the water goddess to take some refreshment after having destroyed the Pythian vermin—symbolizing William III who establishes himself on the
grounds of Het Loo and destroys the barren heath. The water goddess returns to
him the abundance which she originally received from him. She sits on a hill, richly
attired. Her hair falls down like many waterfalls with which she turns the waterwheel
sending the remaining waters down to the Yssel.

LIT: G. van Rijn, *Katalogus der Historie-, spot- en zinneprenten betrekkelijk de geschiedenis
van Nederland*, verzameld door A. van Stolk, Amsterdam, 1897, fol. 3
ATLAS VAN STOLK, ROTTERDAM, INV. NO. 2719 I, 2, VI, VII

153   A BIRD'S-EYE VIEW OF THE PALACE HET LOO

By ISAAC DE MOUCHERON (Amsterdam 1670 – 1744 Amsterdam)
SIGNED: I. Moucheron Fecit
First quarter of the 18th century
Pen and wash: 36.1 x 48.4 cm

The drawing was used by Petrus Schenck for his etching. A comparison with the print
by De Hooghe shows that the trees have matured, and that four garden vases have

been added in the middle of the parterres. At the height of the palace's glory there must have been 122 vases in the garden.

De Moucheron, painter, designer, and engraver, is famous for his landscapes.

RIJKSMUSEUM PALEIS HET LOO, APELDOORN, INV. NO. PL786
On loan from H. M. the Queen

154 PLAN FOR THE FORMAL GARDEN OF THE PALACE HET LOO

By CHRISTIAAN PIETER VAN STADEN (active ca. 1730)
SIGNED (at the bottom): Door mij Christiaan van Staden [By me, Christiaan van Staden]
INSCRIBED (with pencil): Het Loo van Agtere [Het Loo from the back]
Pen and watercolor: 65 x 55 cm

The plan gives us a good impression of the garden with the parterres, in which elegant patterns were formed by box hedges, plants, grass, and colored stone chips. It shows the basement of the palace under the main building and the two inner pavilions, part of the King's and the Queen's gardens, the lower garden with the main fountains and sculptures, the drive, and the upper garden.

As Van Staden, a member of a gardener's family, is mentioned only from 1728–1735 in the archives of the Nassause Domeinraad (747–749), it is plausible that the plan, as Ozinga suggests, dates from this period. The elaborately drawn patterns of the "parterres de broderies" lead us to believe that the plan was a design for re-planting the parterres. For no apparent reason Van der Wijck dates it about 1690.

LIT: M. C. Ozinga, *Daniel Marot, de schepper van den Hollandschen Lodewijk XIV–stijl*, Amsterdam, 1938, 53; Jhr. H. W. M. van der Wijck, "Het Loo, Opmerkingen over Marot's en Desgots's plannen voor het Park van Het Loo," *Bulletin van de K.N.O.B.*, March 1974, 33–35
ALGEMEEN RIJKSARCHIEF, THE HAGUE, INV. NO. V T HINGMAN 1868

155 TWO VIEWS OF THE PALACE HET LOO

By JAN DE BEYER (Aarau 1703/5 – 1768 Kleef)
(a) *Southern Façade of the Palace Het Loo*
SIGNED (on the back): J. de Beyer ad viv. delin: 't Huijs 't Loo. [The House Het Loo.]
DATED: 1744 (in another hand)
Pen and wash and black ink: 17.1 x 21.2 cm
(b) *Garden Front of the Palace Het Loo*
SIGNED (on the back): J. de Beyer ad viv. delin: 't Huijs 't Loo, uit den tuijn, te sien.
[The House Het Loo, seen from the garden.]
DATED: 1744 (in another hand)
Pen and wash and black ink: 16.9 x 21.1 cm

· 161 ·

Jan de Beyer made these drawings of the palace in the days of Stadholder Willem IV (1711–1751), who with his wife, Princess Anne (1709–1759), daughter of King George II, spent many summers at Het Loo. They refurnished part of the palace.

In (b) the palace is viewed through the colonnades. The four pavilions symmetrically placed on either side are slightly hidden by the trees of the drive.

RIJKSMUSEUM PALEIS HET LOO, APELDOORN
On loan from H. M. the Queen

Plates

1. St. Thomas Aquinas, *Informacion des princes*, 1453

2. Knife and sheath of Stadholder Willem I, 1574

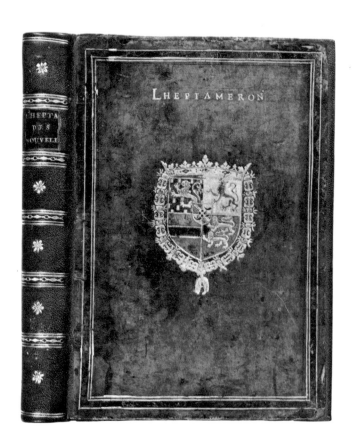

3. Binding with colored coat of arms
    of Stadholder Willem I,
    second half of the 16th century

4. Binding on hymnal dedicated
    to Stadholder Willem I
    and Charlotte of Bourbon, 1579

5. Letter from Stadholder Willem I to Juliana of Stolberg, 8 June 1580

8. Mother-of-pearl portrait medallion of Stadholder Willem I.
By Jean de Montfort, 1611

9. Bust of Stadholder Willem I.
By or after Hendrick de Keyser,
first quarter of the 17th century

10. The sons of Stadholder Willem I, Prince of Orange, and their cousins the Counts of Nassau, on horseback. Studio of Adriaen Pietersz van de Venne, ca. 1620

11. Philips Willem, Prince of Orange, Count of Nassau.
Studio of Michiel Jansz van Miereveld, ca. 1600

12. Binding for
Stadholder Maurits, ca. 1600

14. Stadholder Maurits.
By Michiel Jansz van
Miereveld, ca. 1617

13. Beaker with the coat of arms
of Stadholder Maurits, 1594

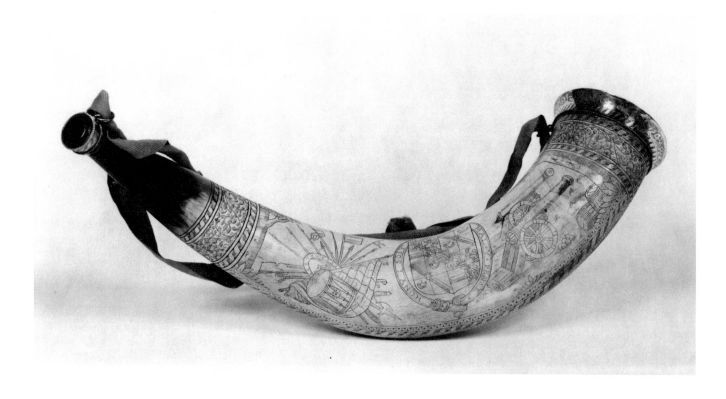

15. Hunting horn presented
to Stadholder Maurits, 1618

16. Silver portrait plaque
of Stadholder Maurits.
By Simon de Passe, ca. 1618–1620

17. Stadholder Maurits lying in state.
By Adriaen Pietersz van de Venne, 1625

18.   Binding with written chronogram, 1629

19. Portrait of Stadholder Frederik Hendrik
     engraved on mother-of-pearl, ca. 1630

20. Stadholder Frederik Hendrik.
     By Gerard van Honthorst, 1631

21. Stadholder Frederik Hendrik leading the siege of 's Hertogenbosch in 1629.
By Paulus van Hillegaert, 1631

22. Medal commemorating the
capture of Breda in 1637.
By Johannes Looff, 1637

23. Miniature of Stadholder Frederik Hendrik.
Attributed to Henri Toutin, ca. 1637

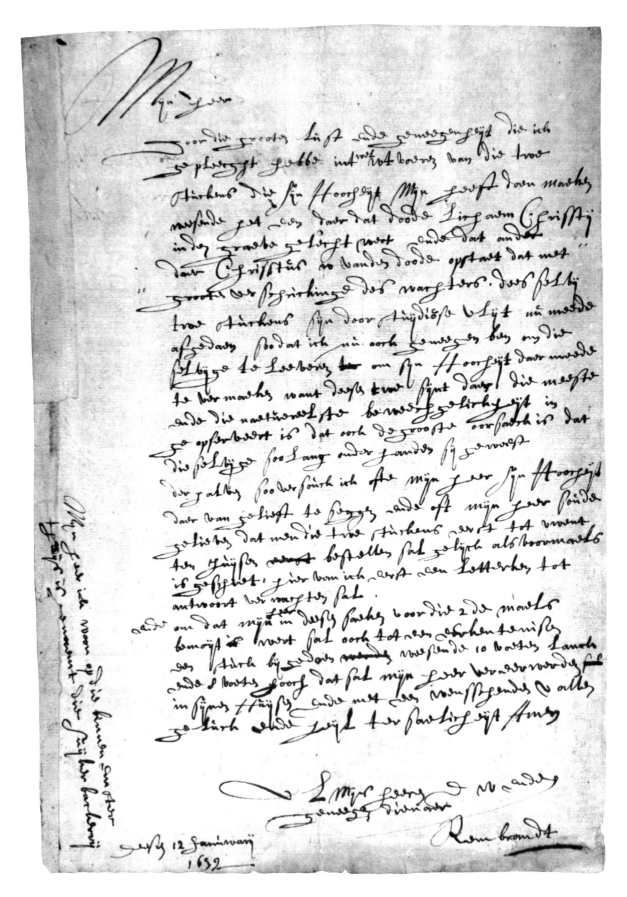

24.   Letter from Rembrandt to Sir Constantijn Huygens, 12 January 1639

25. Medal in honor of
Stadholder Frederik Hendrik
and the marriage of the
future Stadholder Willem II and
Princess Mary Stuart, ca. 1642

27. Marriage lottery of Louise Henriette, Princess of Orange.
By Adriaen Pietersz van de Venne, ca. 1646

26.   Binding with
      the coat of arms
      of Amalia van Solms,
      ca. 1660

28. Miniature of Albertine Agnes,
Princess of Orange, Countess of Nassau.
Attributed to David des Granges, ca. 1650

29. Miniature of Willem Frederik,
Count (later Prince) of Nassau Dietz.
After Adriaen Hanneman, ca. 1664

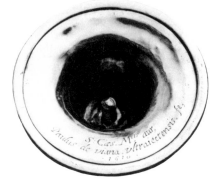

30. Cup and cover, showing outside of cover, inside of cover, and the interior of the base where it is signed and dated

30.   Cup and cover. By Paulus van Vianen, 1610

31. Sophia Hedwig, Countess of Nassau Dietz, portrayed as Caritas,
with her three sons. By Paulus Moreelse, 1621

32. Cabinet on stand,
with panels painted by
Frans Francken II, ca. 1630

Drop-front of cabinet
with stumpwork panels

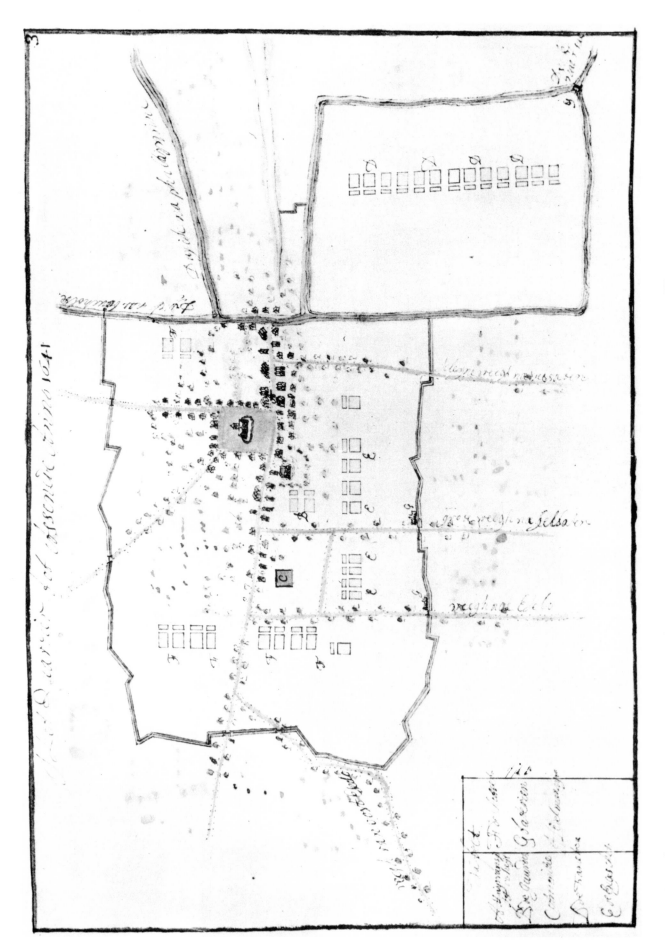

33. Plan of the quarters at Assenede, 1641, from a sketchbook of the future Stadholder Willem II

34. The future Stadholder Willem II and his bride, Princess Mary Stuart.
Studio of Anthony van Dyck, ca. 1641

35.   Miniature of Stadholder Willem II. By Jean Petitot, ca. 1650

36.   Miniature of Mary Stuart,
wife of Stadholder Willem II.
Attributed to
David des Granges, ca. 1650

37. Baby-linen basket. By Hans Coenraadt Brechtel, 1652

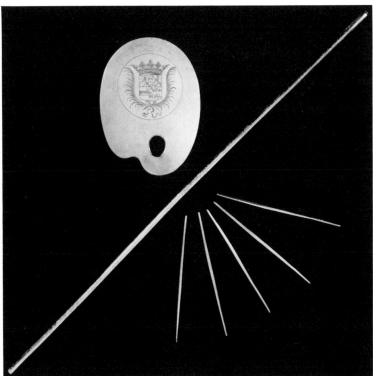

39. Gold palette, brush-sticks, and maulstick
given to Daniel Seghers.
By Hans Coenraadt Brechtel, 1649–1652

38. Armchair, Northern Netherlands,
third quarter of the 17th century

43. Silver beaker with portraits of the Stadholders Willem I,
Maurits, Frederik Hendrik, Willem II, and William III, 1658

40. William III as a child.
Studio of Gerard van Honthorst, ca. 1653

41. Medal with a portrait of
the four-year-old William III.
By Pieter van Abeele, 1654

42. Blue-and-white Delftware dish, ca. 1655

44. Emblematic drawing
made by William III, ca. 1660

45. Embroidered purse given
by William III to his professor,
Henricus Bornius, ca. 1665

47. Miniature of Queen Mary II.
     By Johan van Haensbergen, after 1685

46. Queen Mary II. By Caspar Netscher, ca. 1677

48. Silver snuffbox set with a
mother-of-pearl medallion
of William III, ca. 1690

50. Medal for the coronation of William III and Mary, 168
By George Bower, 1689

49. Binding from the Library of William III, ca. 1678

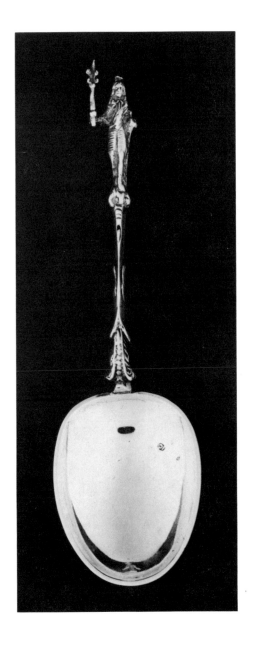

51. Spoon,
a shooting trophy
of matches held on
the coronation day
of William III and Mary,
1689

52. Marble medallion portraits
of William III and Mary, ca. 1690

53. Medal commemorating the celebration in Amsterdam of the coronation of William III and Mary in London, 1689

54. Medal commemorating the battle of the Boyne, after 1690

55.   Delftware bust of William III, ca. 1690

56.   Tulip vase with cypher and
      bust of William III, ca. 1690

57. Two hexagonal Delftware flower pyramids, ca. 1700

58.   Armorial tapestries of William III and Mary Stuart. Workshop of Jerôme LeClerc, ca. 1700

The landing of William III in 1691 on his return from England to the Netherlands. By Ludolf Backhuysen, 1691

The return to the Netherlands in 1691 of Stadholder William III as King of England. By Ludolf Backhuysen, 1692

61.   Exotic animals. By Melchior d'Hondecoeter, ca. 1692

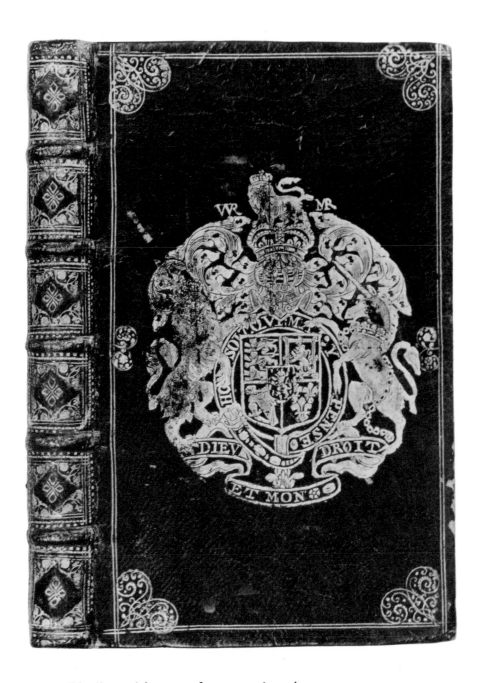

62. Binding with coat of arms and cyphers
of William III and Mary Stuart, ca. 1693–1695

63.   Long case clock made for William III. By Thomas Tompion, ca. 1699

64. Brass-bound travelling
coffer-on-chest, ca. 1690

65. Chair in the manner of Daniel Marot,
last decade of the 17th century

66. Chandelier made for William III. By Daniel Garnier, 1691–1697

68. One of two silver sconces with the engraved monogram of William III. By Philip Rollos, 1700/1701

67. One of four silver sconces with the cypher of William and Mary, ca. 1670

69. Design for a set of furniture for Het Loo.
By Daniel Marot, 1701

70. Engraved silver table top

70.   Silver furniture. By Johann I Bartermann, ca. 1700

72.   William III. By Jean Henri Brandon, ca. 1699

71.   Marble bust of William III. By Jan Blommendael, 1699

73. Miniature of William III, ca. 1700

74. William III stag-hunting. By Dirck Maas, ca. 1700

75. Robert Cheseman, courtier of King Henry VIII of England.
By Hans Holbein the Younger, 1533

76. Ivory carved handle
with the figures of
William and Mary,
ca. 1700

77. Spoon and fork
with William III and Mary
in coronation robes.
Spoon by Johannes Ennema.
Fork by Bernardus
Rienks Jelgerhuis

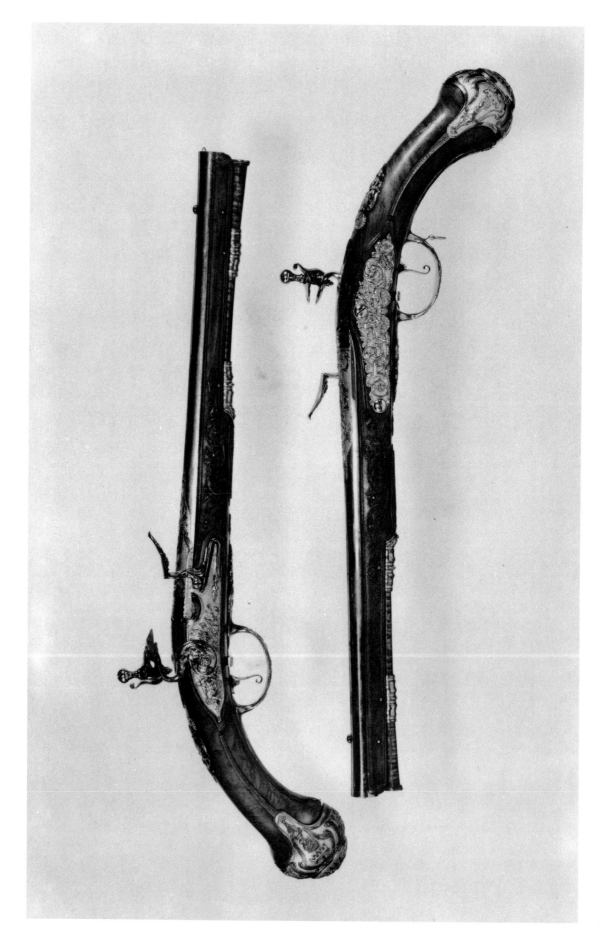

78. Pair of flintlock pistols for Stadholder Johan Willem Friso. By Gerrit Penterman the Elder, ca. 1700–1710

79. Two snuffboxes of amethyst quartz, ca. 1750

80. Part of a porcelain and vermeil solitaire, ca. 1723

81.   Part of a Chinese armorial tea service with the arms of Stadholder Willem IV, ca. 1747

82.   Commemorative plate with
the portrait of Stadholder Willem IV,
3 May 1747

83. Gold and silver miniatures
of Stadholder Willem IV and Princess Anne.
By Jeremias Stagman, 1748

84. Binding with
painted coats of arms
of Stadholder Willem IV
and Princess Anne, 1748

85. Fob seal with the portrait of Princess Anne, second quarter of the 18th century

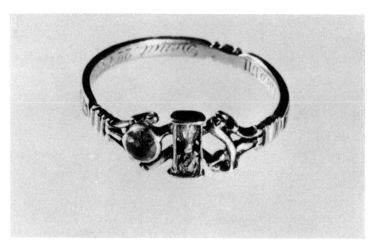

86. Mourning ring (shown enlarged) of Stadholder Willem IV, 1751

87. Toilet mirror with the coat of arms of Stadholder Willem IV, 1734/1735

89. Miniature of Stadholder Willem V.
By Robert Mussard, ca. 1751

88. Goblet engraved with
the coat of arms of
Stadholder Willem V,
third quarter of the 18th century

90. Pendant
of the Order of
the Garter, ca. 175

91.   Velvet binding with coat of arms of Stadholder Willem V, ca. 1756

92. Binding with the coat of arms
of Stadholder Willem V, 1760

92. Tool with coat of arms
of Stadholder Willem V

93. Two painted glass allegories
on the marriage of Princess
Wilhelmina of Prussia
to Willem V, Stadholder
of the Netherlands.
By C. F. Haegelin, 1767

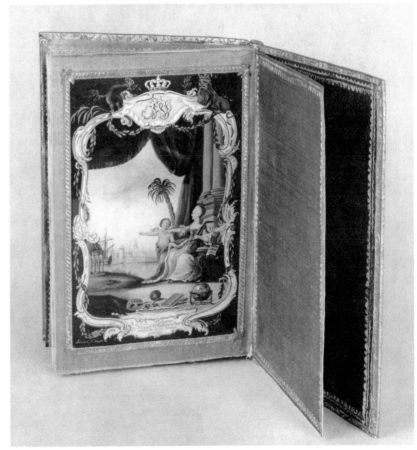

94. Hymnal presented to Stadholder Willem V and Princess Wilhelmina of Prussia by the Jewish parish in Amsterdam, 1768

95. A young lady composing music. By Gabriel Metsu

96. A boy blowing bubbles. By Frans van Mieris the Elder, 1663

97.   Self-portrait as a young man. By Rembrandt Harmensz van Rijn, ca. 1629

98.   View of the New Church in Delft with the mausoleum of Prince
Willem I of Orange at right. By Hendrick Cornelisz van Vliet

99. Part of the Meissen dinner service presented to Stadholder Willem V, ca. 1772

100. Tortoise-shell snuffbox decorated with gold piqué posé and mother-of-pearl, ca. 1750

101. Silver snuffbox
with equestrian portrait
of Stadholder Willem V.
By Petrus Stagman, ca. 1770

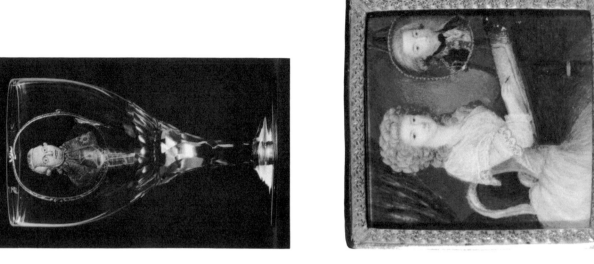

102. Stippled glass with the portrait of Stadholder Willem V. By David Wolff, 1784

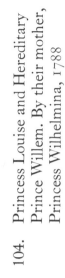

104. Princess Louise and Hereditary Prince Willem. By their mother, Princess Wilhelmina, 1788

103. Five silhouettes representing Stadholder Willem V, his wife, Princess Wilhelmina of Prussia, Princess Louise, Hereditary Prince Willem, and Prince Frederik, ca. 1785

105. The children of Stadholder Willem V. By Johann Friedrich August Tischbein, 1789

106. King Willem I
when Hereditary Prince.
By John Hoppner,
ca. 1799

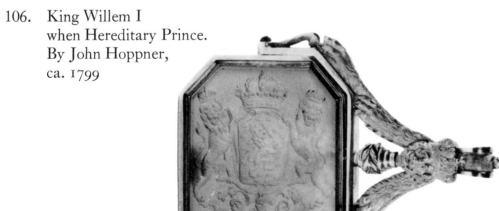

107. Swivel seal with the coat of arms
of King Willem I. By Ernst Simon

108. Armchair.
By François Honoré Georges
Jacob-Desmalter, ca. 1805–1808

109. Commode. By François Honoré Georges
Jacob-Desmalter, ca. 1806

110. The future King Willem II.
      By John Singleton Copley, 1813

112. Saber borne by King Willem II, when Crown Prince,
      during the battle of Waterloo; Turkish, ca. 1810

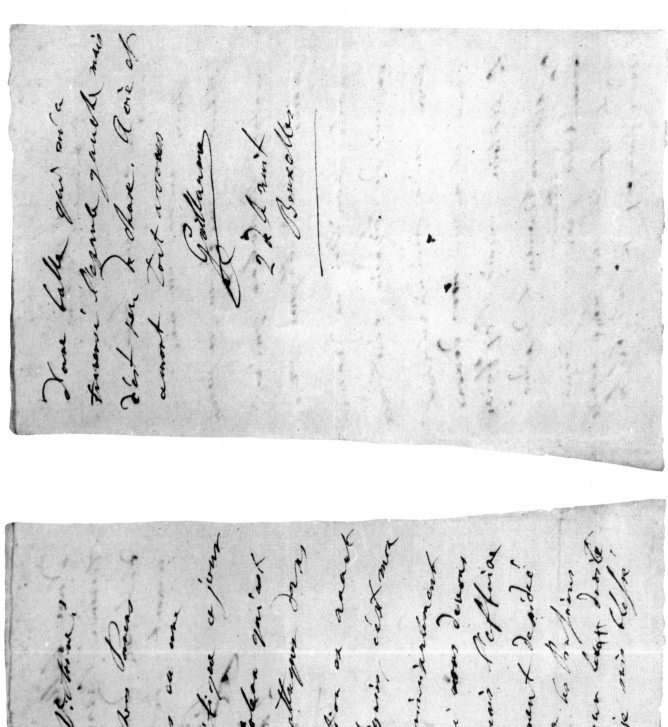

111. Letter written by King Willem II, when Crown Prince, immediately after the battle of Waterloo,
[19 June 1815]

113. Bracelet with the portrait of King Willem II, commemorating his martial exploits.
By Jean Baptiste Joseph Duchesne, 1822

114. Cameo with the portrait
of King Willem II.
By N. Julin, ca. 1840–1848

115. Crowned goblet with
the portrait of King Willem II.
By Dominik Bimann, ca. 1840

116. Queen Anna Pavlovna.
By Jean Chrétien Valois, 1845

117. Chalice of
Queen Anna Pavlovna.
By Alexej Ivanov Ratkov,
1816

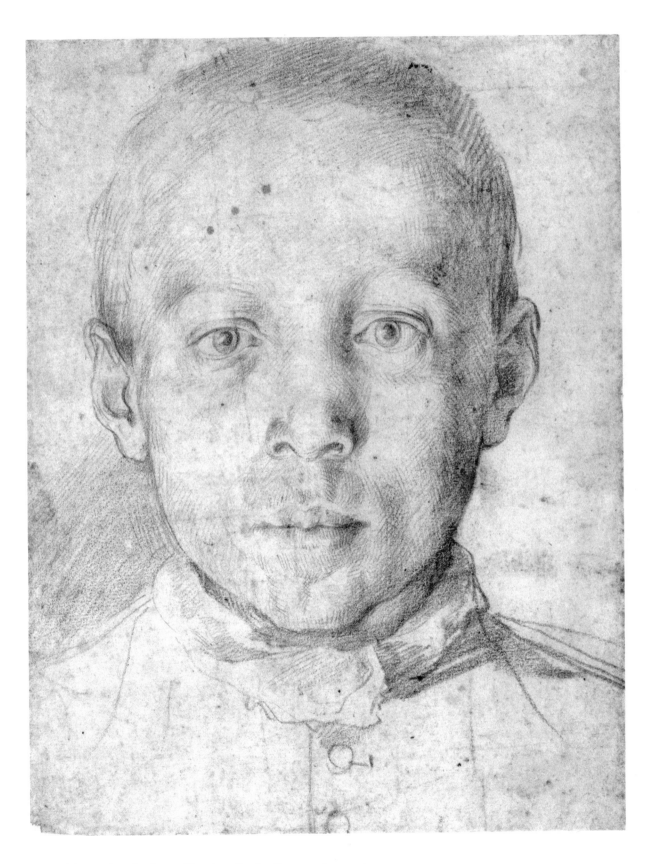

118.   Portrait of a boy. By Annibale Carracci

119.   St. Francis of Assisi. By Giovanni Francesco Barbieri, called Il Guercino

120.   Study of a male nude. By Peter Paul Rubens, ca. 1610

121. Garden front of the palace Het Loo. By Andreas Schelfhout, ca. 1837–1838

122. King Willem III.
By Jean Chrétien Valois, ca. 1849

123. Miniature of Queen Sophie.
After Nicaise de Keyser,
ca. 1845

124. Set of three golden bracelets of Queen Sophie with portraits of her sons
I, with portrait of Crown Prince Willem, miniature by Edouard de Latour, 1842
II, with portrait of Prince Maurits, ca. 1847
III, with portrait of Prince Alexander, miniature by Henri Philippe Heidemans, 1853

125. Seal of Willem,
 Prince of Orange,
 third quarter of the 19th century

126. Desk seal of Queen Sophie,
 third quarter of the 19th century

127. Desk seal with
 the coat of arms of Queen Sophie,
 third quarter of the 19th century

128. Souvenir album of Queen Sophie, ca. 1855

129. Riding whip
with a handle in the
form of a falcon
on a woman's hand

130. Franz Liszt at Het Loo.
By Charles Rochussen, 1875

St.ᵗᵉ Maertens Doms kerck, Binnen uytrecht.

131. St. Martin's Cathedral of Utrecht: interior of the Choir to the west. By Pieter Jansz Saenredam, 1636

132. Black lace fan with the
signature of Queen Emma in diamonds, 1901

133. Desk seal of Queen Emma,
fourth quarter of the 19th century

134. Desk seal in the form of
a lion's foot, fourth quarter of
the 19th century

135.   Queen Emma. By Jan Theodoor Toorop, 1923

136. Christ crucified between the two thieves: The three crosses.
By Rembrandt Harmensz van Rijn

137. The Entombment. By Rembrandt Harmensz van Rijn

138.   A Roman British pottery. By Laurens Alma Tadema, 1883–1884

139.   Queen Wilhelmina as a child. By Thérèse van Duyl-Schwartze, before 1890

140. Prize medal with a portrait
of Queen Wilhelmina.
By Bartholomeus J. W. M. van Hove, 1891

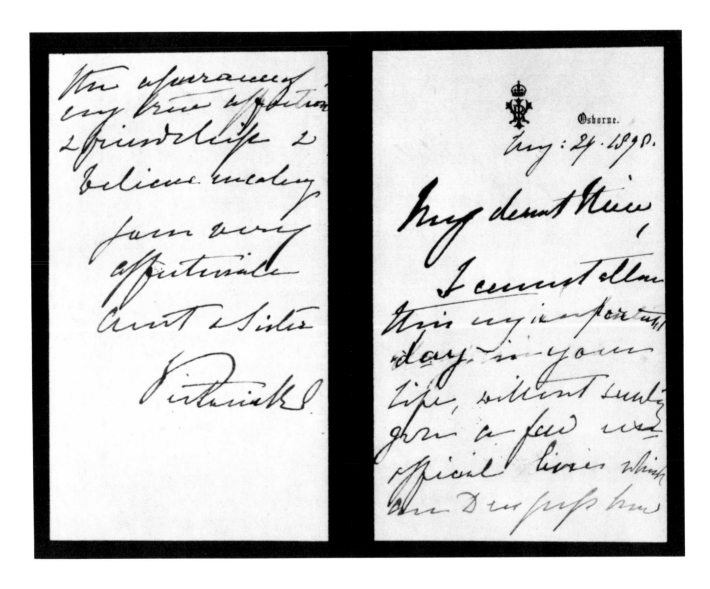

141. Letter of Queen Victoria to Queen Wilhelmina, 29 August 1898

142.   Miniature of Queen Wilhelmina.
By Marguérite Pniès de Merbitz, 1901

143.   Tea service presented to
Queen Wilhelmina and Prince Hendrik, 1901

144.   Fan of white ostrich feathers, 1901

145.   Medal commemorating the forty-year jubilee of Queen Wilhelmina, 1938

146. Portrait of Queen Wilhelmina designed for the Dutch currency notes
printed in the U.S.A. during the Second World War, 1943

150.   Woodland scene at Meyendel. By Queen Wilhelmina, 1932

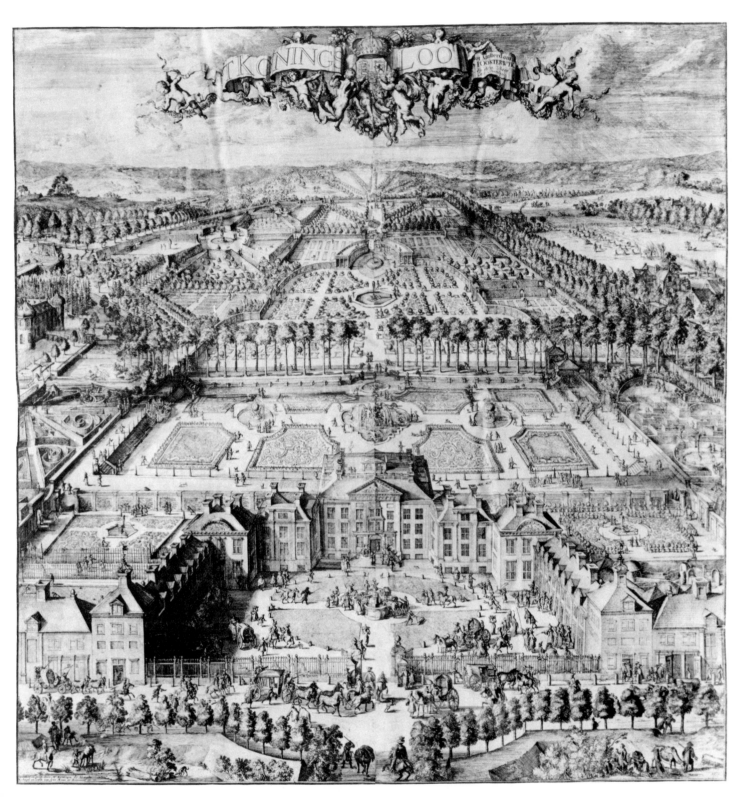

151.   A bird's-eye view of the palace Het Loo. By Romeyn de Hooghe, ca. 1698

Hercules, Achelous
De Vorst den Yssel

152. Four designs of statues, probably for the waterworks of Het Loo.
By Romeyn de Hooghe, ca. 1686

153.   A bird's-eye view of the palace Het Loo. By Isaac de Moucheron, first quarter of the 18th century

154. Plan for the formal garden of the palace Het Loo.
By Christiaan Pieter van Staden, ca. 1728–1735

155. Two views of the palace Het Loo. By Jan de Beyer, 1744

Index of Artists and Craftsmen

All numbers refer to items in the catalogue

Typesetting for this book was done at The Stinehour Press using Janson for display lines and Caslon Old Style for text. Both types have Dutch antecedents. The text pages have been printed directly from the types by letterpress. The illustrations have been printed by The Meriden Gravure Company, using their special fine-screen method of photolithographic reproduction. The paper has been especially made for The Pierpont Morgan Library by the Curtis Paper Company. Binding has been done at The Stinehour Press. The book has been designed by Roderick Stinehour.

HAEC OLIM MEMINISSE JUVABIT

December 1979